Faith First

CREED and PRAYER
JUNIOR HIGH

Faith First Junior High Development Team

RCL

RESOURCES FOR CHRISTIAN LIVING®

"The Ad Hoc Committee to Oversee
the Use of the Catechism,
National Conference of Catholic Bishops,
has found this catechetical series, copyright 2001,
to be in conformity with
the *Catechism of the Catholic Church*."

NIHIL OBSTAT
Rev. Msgr. Glenn D. Gardner, J.C.D.
Censor Librorum
IMPRIMATUR
† Most Rev. Charles V. Grahmann
Bishop of Dallas

January 17, 2000

The Nihil Obstat and Imprimatur are official declarations that the material reviewed is free of doctrinal or moral error. No implication is contained therein that those granting the Nihil Obstat and Imprimatur agree with the contents, opinions, or statements expressed.

Send all inquiries to:
RCL • Resources for Christian Living
200 East Bethany Drive
Allen, Texas 75002-3804

Toll Free   877-275-4725
Fax   800-688-8356

Visit us at **www.RCLweb.com**
         www.FaithFirst.com

Printed in the United States of America

20307   ISBN 0-7829-0931-0 (Student Book)

20317   ISBN 0-7829-0933-7 (Teacher/Catechist Guide)

  5 6 7 8 9 10

     04 05

ACKNOWLEDGMENTS

Scripture excerpts are taken or adapted from the *New American Bible with Revised New Testament and Psalms* Copyright © 1991, 1986, 1970 Confraternity of Christian Doctrine, Washington, DC. Used with permission. All rights reserved. No part of the *New American Bible* may be reproduced by any means without the permission of the copyright owner.

Excerpts from the English translation of the *Catechism of the Catholic Church* for use in the United States of America Copyright © 1994, United States Catholic Conference, Inc.— Libreria Editrice Vaticana. Used with Permission.

Excerpts from the English translation of *The Roman Missal* © 1973, International Committee on English in the Liturgy, Inc. (ICEL); excerpts from the English translation of the Psalm Responses, the Alleluia and Gospel Verses, and the Lenten Gospel Acclamations from the *Lectionary for Mass* © 1997, 1981, 1969, ICEL; excerpts from the *Rite of Christian Initiation of Adults*, © 1985 ICEL; excerpts from the *Book of Prayers* © 1982, ICEL; excerpts from the *Rite of Baptism for Children* © 1969, ICEL; excerpts from *Liturgy of the Hours*, ICEL; All rights reserved.

Excerpts from "Dogmatic Constitution on the Church," "Decree on the Bishop's Pastoral Office in the Church," "Dogmatic Constitution on the Church," "Constitution on the Sacred Liturgy," and "Pastoral Constitution on the Church in the Modern World" from *Vatican Council II; The Conciliar and Post Conciliar Documents*, New Revised Edition, Austin Flannery, O.P., Gen. Ed. Copyright © 1975, 1986, 1992, 1996 by Costello Publishing Company, Inc. Northport, New York. Used with Permission.

Excerpt from "Opening Address of Pope John XXIII to the Second Vatican Council" from *The Documents of Vatican II*, Walter M. Abbott, S.J., Gen. Ed. by Herder and Herder Association Press, Copyright © 1966 by The American Press, Inc. Published by arrangement with American Press, Inc. All rights reserved.

Excerpts from "Morning Prayer" and "Evening Prayer" from *Christian Prayer: The Liturgy of the Hours* by Catholic Book Publishing Company, New York, 1976.

Lyrics of hymn "The Glory of these Forty Days" by St. Gregory the Great copyright © by Oxford University Press. *Ritual Song* by GIA Publications, Inc. Chicago, Illinois, copyright © 1996.

Lyrics of twelfth-century Latin hymn, "Regina Caeli/O Queen of Heaven," tr. by Winfred Douglas © 1986 GIA Publications, Inc. *Ritual Song* by GIA Publications, Inc. Chicago, Illinois, copyright © 1996.

Photography and Art Credits appear on page 368.

Developing a religious education program requires the talents of many gifted people working together as a team. RCL • *Resources for Christian Living*® is proud to acknowledge these dedicated people who contributed to the development of the Faith First Junior High program.

Program Advisors
Rev. Louis J. Cameli
Rev. Robert D. Duggan

National Catechetical Advisor
Kim Duty

General Editor
Ed DeStefano

Advisory Board
Judith Deckers
Jacquie Jambor
Maureen A. Kelly
Elaine McCarron, SCN
Rev. Frank McNulty
Rev. Ronald J. Nuzzi
Kate Sweeney Ristow

Creed and Prayer Student Book
Authors
Rev. Robert D. Duggan
Rev. Steven M. Lanza

Contributing Writers
Eileen A. McGrath
Nancy DeStefano

Liturgy and Morality Student Book
Authors
Rev. Robert D. Duggan
Rev. Steven M. Lanza

Contributing Writers
Eileen A. McGrath
Nancy DeStefano

Creed and Prayer Guide Book
Author
Kathleen Holtsnider

Contributing Writers
Eileen A. McGrath
Barbara Gargiulo
Jack Gargiulo

Liturgy and Morality Guide Book
Contributing Writers
Kathleen Holtsnider
Ronald C. Lamping
Eileen A. McGrath
Jack Gargiulo
Keith E. Ksobiech

Editorial
Ed DeStefano
Executive Director, Editorial

Ronald C. Lamping
Keith E. Ksobiech
Jack Gargiulo
Joseph Crisalli
Barbara Bindhammer
Joan Lathen

Art and Design
Pat Bracken
Director, Art and Design

Kristy Howard
Ed Leach
Demere Henson
Sheila Lehnert
Lisa Brent
Carol-Anne Wilson

Photo Research
Margaret Matus
Patricia A. Classick
Susan Gibas

Production
Jenna Nelson
Laura Fremder
Mark Burgdorff
Kevin Fremder

Richard C. Leach
Chairman

Maryann Nead
President

3

CONTENTS

Unit 5—Church History

The Church Celebrates

Welcome to faith first Creed and prayer

As you begin this year you are continuing on an incredible journey of faith. At times it may seem like you are traveling on a fast-paced super highway with no time to think or relax. Other times it may seem as if you are walking a peaceful country road with opportunities to reflect upon the journey and appreciate all that life is offering. Yes, sometimes the journey may seem easy—other times challenging and, at times, even downright scary.

As you begin this next phase of your faith journey we hope that the Faith First religious education program will support and help you this year to

- ❑ grow in your relationship with God your Father as you come to know him better

- ❑ accept Jesus' invitation to follow him as a disciple and member of the Church

- ❑ listen and respond to the Holy Spirit who is your constant guide and support on your journey.

Reflecting on the Journey

As you begin Faith First take a few minutes to reflect on where you have been and where you are going. Reflecting on the past can help you to recognize God's presence in your life and in the life of others. Planning for the future can help you become the person God calls you to be and to accept the gifts God so generously wants to share with you. Take some time to reflect on your faith journey—past, present and future. Then write your thoughts in the boxes.

Important events in my faith journey . . .

People who have helped me to put faith first in my life . . .

An important life lesson I have learned . . .

Qualities or characteristics I would like to develop . . .

Something I would like to accomplish on my faith journey . . .

THE REVELATION OF GOD
UNIT 1

Parent Page—Unit 1

FAITH

The **Faith First Junior High** series consists of two student books. They are *Creed and Prayer* and *Liturgy and Morality*. Together both student books share with your child the teachings of the Catholic Church as presented in the *Catechism of the Catholic Church*. The Catechism, as first published in 1992, is divided into four major parts. **Faith First** *Creed and Prayer* opens up for you and your child the meaning of the Catholic faith outlined in the articles of the Creed and the tradition of Christian prayer.

Unit 1 of *Creed and Prayer*, "The Revelation of God," focuses on the mystery of God. Your child will learn that the human search for happiness is the search for God. God created us out of love to live in friendship with him now and forever. He did not leave us on our own to discover his identity and loving plan of creation and salvation. Throughout history God gradually revealed himself. God is one in three Persons. The one God is Father, Son, and Holy Spirit.

Faith gives us the vision and power to believe this truth about the mystery of God and all that God has revealed to us. God's revelation has been passed down to us through Sacred Scripture and Tradition. The Church helps us grow in understanding all that God has revealed to us.

WHAT DIFFERENCE
DOES IT MAKE?

Faith makes a difference in our lives. The truths about God, ourselves, and creation that God has revealed are truths that inspire our hearts to bring life to the world. Each lesson of **Faith First Junior High** contains two sections that guide you and your child to live your faith. These sections are "What Difference Does This Make in Our Church?" and "What Difference Does It Make in My Life?"

"What Difference Does This Make in Our Church?" is designed to help you and your child see and appreciate the difference faith has made and continues to make in the life of the Church since the days of the apostles. Unit 1 of *Creed and Prayer* connects the ministry of Catholic educators, the praying and reading of Sacred Scripture, the Church's rites of welcoming new members into the Church, the efforts of teens to live as images of God in their school and local civic community, and the life of the Christian family with the doctrine, or truths of our faith, presented in the unit.

"What Difference Does It Make in My Life?" looks at many of the issues your child and other junior high students deal with as they strive to grow as people of faith.

In Unit 1 your child has learned that each of us is called to have a personal relationship with God. As with human relationships, our relationship with God must be nurtured through thoughtful reflection and communication. Just as we think about, talk with, and spend time with our friends and family in order to build strong bonds of love, we must also spend time with God through prayer, worship, and reading of Scripture.

As a parent you can reflect on your own relationships—with God and with family and friends. Talk with your child about how you help nurture these bonds, particularly the relationship between you and your child and between your family and God. As a young adolescent, your child will be moving more and more toward peer relationships that will become extremely important. At the same time, the family continues to be a critical source of strength and guidance. Be sure to continue to spend time with your child so that you are in touch with the issues and concerns that he or she faces each day. A way to get started might be to review the "What Difference Does It Make in My Life?" pages in each unit. All relationships take time and care. As a family you can help your child learn how to form and nurture meaningful relationships with family and friends, as well as a strong faith relationship with God, that can be a great source of strength throughout your child's life.

We Believe

1

WE PRAY

My God, I believe in you,
I trust you, I love you above all
    things,
with all my heart and mind and
    strength.
I love you because you are
    supremely good and worth
    loving.

An Act of Faith, Hope and Love

People are always searching
for happiness. How would
you describe happiness?
Where do you think you will
find that happiness?

*"Come," says my heart,
    "seek God's face";
your face, Lord, do I seek!*
PSALM 27:8

9

Our Search for Happiness

Still, with all the discoveries that fill our hearts with adventure and excitement, we know there will be more—our discovery of the wonder of the world has really just begun! Just compare the accomplishments of Orville and Wilbur Wright on December 17, 1903, at Kitty Hawk, North Carolina, with a flight of D*iscovery*. With Orville at the controls, the first flight went only 127 feet and lasted only twelve seconds. Following a 4-million mile mission, the shuttle D*iscovery* landed on June 6, 1999, after a 9-day, 19-hour, and 13-minute flight. There is truly more and more to come.

What does our use of technology tell us about our discovery of the world?

FAITH FOCUS

Why do we say we are religious by nature?

Every person has an unquenchable thirst for happiness. Some search to satisfy that thirst by acquiring power or prestige or popularity or possessions. Getting a little power leads to seeking more power; becoming popular creates the need to be more popular. And so it goes. More . . . more . . . and more . . . It seems that "more" is never quite enough. The more we get, the more we seem to need—or want.

FAITH VOCABULARY

philosophers

theologians

revelation

faith

The Universal Thirst for More . . .

We live in a world and at a time when whatever we need or want seems to be waiting for us just around the corner. We watch the growth of technology in amazement. We can't even imagine what the newest technology will be or bring us a mere five years from now. Our discovery of the universe and its inner workings seems to be moving at the speed of light.

The Quest for God

Another search has filled the lives of all people since our beginnings. It is the search for God. Drawings and etchings on the walls of caves of the earliest humans document this search. The great temples of the Egyptians and Babylonians and Assyrians as well as the Pantheon of the Romans and the Parthenon of the Greeks tell yet another part of the story of humankind's search to live in friendship with and under the protection of some god.

The religions of people who have lived or who are living in Oceania, Asia, Europe, Africa, and the Americas remind us that human history itself can be told as the story of the search of the human heart and mind for God. We are religious by our very nature. God puts into the very core of every person something much deeper than our DNA that identifies us as humans. Being human means to have a longing for God. God made us with a desire for him.

Describe the human quest for God.

One of the most famous quotes in all of the world's religious writings appears in the *Confessions*, an autobiography by Saint Augustine of Hippo (A.D. 354–430). Augustine was born in Tagaste, a city that is near what is Souk-Ahras in Algeria, North Africa, today. His search for happiness first led him to seek "worldly" success. Augustine was a teacher of rhetoric in Carthage, North Africa, and then in Rome and Milan, Italy.

In 386 Ambrose, the bishop of Milan, helped Augustine place his trust and faith in Jesus. A year later Augustine was baptized. In 391 he was ordained a priest, and in 395 Augustine became bishop of Hippo, which was near Tagaste. In *Confessions* Augustine wrote about his search for God. Speaking to God, Augustine says:

> You have made us for yourself, and our heart is restless until it rests in you.

When we listen to the voice of our conscience, we can come to know with certainty that God exists and is the "more" we are always searching for. He is the cause and the end of everything. He is our creator and Lord.

Describe what Saint Augustine discovered about the human search for happiness.

We have been created to live in friendship with God. We become fully human only when we recognize that God made us and we find our happiness in him. When we believe this and have made this the most important value in our life, we will discover there is no "more" to search for.

WHAT DIFFERENCE DOES FAITH MAKE?

What are some of the ways you show that your relationship with God brings you happiness?

_____

_____

_____

Recall what you have learned about religion in social studies. What do these names mean to you: Anu and Enlil and Ea? Asshur and Marduk? Re, Osiris, and Isis? Zeus, Athena, and Apollo? Jupiter, Ceres, and Janus? They are the names of the gods people of the ancient world—Sumerians, Assyrians, Babylonians, Egyptians, Greeks, and Romans—believed they owed respect and allegiance.

Coming to Know God

People in every culture and in every age have been and are convinced that God exists and that it is worth believing and trusting in him. By nature we can come to know God through his creation. The beauty, greatness, and symmetry of the universe point to a God who made all things and keeps them in existence. The magnificence of the universe is a reflection of the awesome goodness and power of God. The more science enables us to discover the symmetry, or order, in nature, the more our belief in the existence of God is strengthened.

Saint Albert the Great

The Church is a community of believers. We are a people of faith. We are a community of people who stand in awe and wonder at the ability of the human mind to discover God in the secrets of creation and in the order of the universe.

Throughout our history Christians have taken their place among the great scientists of the world. Saint Albert the Great (ca.1206–1280) was one of the world's great scientists, **philosophers**, and **theologians.** A philosopher uses logical reasoning to study and discover truths about nature, life, morals, and God. Theologians study and deepen their understanding of the truths known by faith. Albert was so respected that he has come to be known as Albertus Magnus, or Albert the Great.

Albert was born about 1206 in what is today Germany. In 1223 he joined the Order of Preachers, who today are known as the Dominicans, or followers of Saint Dominic (1170–1221). Albert spent much of his time studying the writings of the great Greek thinker Aristotle (384–322 B.C.), especially Aristotle's teachings on physics. Because of this interest Albert studied the

The Parthenon, Athens, Greece. This ancient Greek temple was built between 497 and 432 B.C. Saint Paul gave a famous speech here. It stands on the Acropolis, a hill overlooking the city.

natural sciences and wrote about astronomy, chemistry, geography, and physiology.

Albert was also a person of faith who was convinced that our human minds were limited in what they could know on their own. He taught that we come to know things in different ways. Each type of knowledge has its own way of investigating or researching the truth. When other scientists and philosophers argued against the teachings of faith, Albert argued back. What we accept, or believe, in faith comes to us in a different way. We can never "prove" or "disprove" the truths of our faith by our human minds. Otherwise they would be proven, not believed!

The Church today celebrates the feast day of Albert the Great on November 15. We also honor him as the patron of students and of the natural sciences.

Explain what Albert the Great taught us about the different ways of knowing God.

The Search for Truth

Christians believe there can be no "real" contradiction between the "truths" that we believe in faith and the "truths" that we learn through science and other forms of human learning. This is another way of saying that faith and reason can never really contradict one another. Why do we make such a statement? We believe that God is the source of all truth.

Sometimes there may seem to be differences between what we know by faith and what we learn through science and human reason. We may

not be able to explain these differences—at the moment. This happens because our knowledge and understanding of the truth has its limits.

Describe why science and faith both help us understand the truth.

Our faith and our human knowledge must always search for a deeper meaning of the truth. There will always be more to know and understand not only about God but also about ourselves and the wonders of the created universe.

WHAT DIFFERENCE DOES FAITH MAKE?

Choose something you really believe about God. How would you answer someone who questioned you about your belief, saying, "I can't believe that! You can't prove it to me"?

_____

_____

_____

Divine Revelation

In addition to these human ways of coming to know and love God, we come to know God in another way. Out of love God has revealed himself to us. The word *reveal* means "to unveil." God has "unveiled" things about himself that we could never come to know on our own. He has revealed these hidden mysteries of who he is so that we could get to know and love him better.

When you think about it, this is the best way we come to know one another too. We can stand at a distance and look at people, listen to them, and evaluate what we hear and see. We can ask other people what they know about someone. All of these means of investigation will tell us something about another person. When we really want to get to know another person, nothing beats sitting down with them, talking with them, and spending time with them.

The Gift of Faith

God's **revelation** of himself is God's free gift of making himself known to us and giving himself to us by gradually communicating his own mystery in deeds and words. It is God inviting us to know him and love and trust him and to accept in **faith** what he has revealed. That is why we describe faith as both a gift and a response.

First, faith is a supernatural gift of God. God invites us and gives us the power to open our mind, our will, our whole being to him. Faith is the virtue, or power, that enables us to respond to God and to believe the truths he has revealed because of his own authority.

Second, faith is a relationship of trust. Faith is our free, conscious human response to God, who is all-good and all-loving. Faith is our personal, deliberate commitment to God. It is the free assent of our intellect and will to God's self-revelation that he has made through his deeds and words. We accept the full truth of God's revelation because of who God is and because God has given us his word.

What is revelation? What is faith?

Faith Seeks Understanding

Sometimes people have questions and even doubts about their faith. They struggle to grasp the meaning of some passage in the Bible or some teaching of the Church. When they have these questions, they may confuse those questions with a failure to believe. They worry that their faith may be weak—or even absent.

What should we do when we have these questions and feelings? Remember that Saint Augustine

of Hippo had many of these questions and feelings. They moved him to want to know and love God even more. Augustine said, "I believe in order to understand; and I understand, the better to believe." In other words, Augustine is reminding us that we always seek to understand better what we have come to believe in faith.

It is part of our human nature to constantly seek a deeper understanding of the truth, especially God's revealed truth. This human process of seeking a deeper understanding of our faith is the reason why religion textbooks

are written. It is the reason why religion teachers, or catechists, help students work at understanding in addition to memorizing answers to questions about their faith. The better we understand our faith, the more deeply we can believe it.

Why is it "natural" and important to seek to understand our faith?

God Is Always Mystery

No matter how deep our faith, no matter how much we think we understand our faith and can explain it to others, God will always remain a mystery. He is a mystery whom human understanding can never fully understand and human words can never completely explain. Saint Augustine put it this way: "If you understood him, he would not be God."

Paul the Apostle wrote this about revelation and the gift of faith:

> At present we see indistinctly, as in a mirror, but then face to face.
> 1 CORINTHIANS 13:12

Explain why we use the word mystery to describe God.

In other words, faith gives us a glimpse of the goal of our journey on earth. It helps us see in advance the happiness for which we are searching, the good things of heaven. With faith, we are given the eyes to see a glimpse of eternal Truth!

Members of a community develop a common language so that they can communicate and understand one another and the things that they hold in common.

The Church is a community of faith. Since its earliest days the Church has created written summaries of the faith. These are called creeds.

To pray the Apostles' Creed and the Nicene Creed is to give our heart to God the Father, God the Son, and God the Holy Spirit.

WHAT DIFFERENCE DOES FAITH MAKE?

Describe what you are doing to deepen your understanding of God.

_____

_____

_____

_____

WHAT DIFFERENCE

Does This Make in Our Church?

God has created us to know, love, and serve him and to be happy with him now and for ever. Another way of saying the same thing is that God has created us as religious beings. Human history teaches us this truth about ourselves. When we listen to the voice of our conscience and think about creation, we can come to know this about ourselves and about God. More importantly, we know and believe this in faith because God has revealed himself to us.

The Learning Church and the Teaching Church

Christians have always devoted themselves to studying and sharing with others what they have come to understand about God and his revelation to us. Catholic educators from the first days of the Church have sought to teach as Jesus taught. Jesus himself was honored as Rabbi, or Teacher.

Parish Religious Education Programs, Catholic Elementary Schools and High Schools

Catholic education has a long history in the United States. Missionaries traveled with the explorers teaching the Gospel to the native inhabitants of the New World. In 1662 the Jesuits opened a school in New York City, but they were forced to close in 1689. In 1782 the first parochial school was founded at St. Mary's Church in Philadelphia, Pennsylvania. The growth of Catholic elementary education in the United States increased in the early 1800s under the leadership of Catholic educators like Mother Elizabeth Bayley Seton. Mother Seton was named a saint of the Church in 1975 and is honored as a patroness of Catholic schools.

Today our parish religious education programs, parish schools, and Catholic high schools continue to help us learn and live our faith. In the United States of America almost 19,600 parishes serve over 4,500,000 elementary and high school students. Over 6,750 Catholic elementary schools serve nearly 1,965,000 students, and over 750,000 students are enrolled in 1,308 Catholic high schools.

Catholic Colleges and Universities

The story of Catholic colleges and universities in the United States of America began with Georgetown College (Georgetown University), which opened for classes in 1791. Today about 700,000 students are enrolled in 238 Catholic colleges and universities.

Who helps you learn about God and God's wonderful creation? Who helps you understand and live your faith?

Georgetown University, Washington, D.C.

WHAT DIFFERENCE
Does It Make in My Life?

For many years you have been learning about the Catholic faith and its importance for your life. One thing your parents and teachers and catechists have been emphasizing is that your search for God is the same as your search for real happiness. Many people still do not believe this truth about themselves. For them searching for happiness means accumulating more and more things. The truth is that happiness is really not about "things" at all.

Take a moment and think about your own search for happiness. What do your words and actions tell you and others about what you believe happiness is?

_____

_____

_____

_____

Getting in Touch with God

Father John Powell, a Jesuit priest, is a teacher and a widely read writer. In his book *Happiness Is an Inside Job* Father Powell reminds you that the real happiness you are searching for is within you. Knowing and building a deeper relationship with God will lead you to real happiness—now and forever in eternal life.

How can you go about searching for and discovering this happiness? Just as you hang out with your friends and talk and listen and enjoy their friendship, you also need to spend time with God. Here are some skills you can work on to do just that.

Praying

The very first thing to do is just be still and be with God. Prayer is communicating with God. Focus on God's presence with you. Listen first, then begin to talk things over with God.

What are some things you would like to talk over with God? How does praying help you grow in your relationship with God?

_____

_____

_____

_____

_____

Reading God's Word in Scripture

Scripture is God's own word to us. Read the Bible with a listening ear. You will be surprised how much God tells you about happiness.

What is your favorite Scripture story? How does it help you grow in your relationship with God?

_____

_____

_____

_____

Seeing God in Others

God dwells in each of us. He speaks to you through others and your relationship with them. He speaks to you through the daily events of your life.

Who are the people who help you grow in your relationship with God?

_____

_____

Reflecting on the Goodness of Creation

Creation is a reflection of God, the creator. A beautiful sunset, a majestic ocean, even the playfulness of a pet can help you discover God's love for you. All are signs of God—the source of the happiness that creation brings us.

Think about creation. How does it help you discover God's love for you?

_____

_____

_____

faith decision

- In a small group discuss ways you get in touch with God.

- Talk about ways you think God gets in touch with you.

This week I will be more conscious of how God is calling me to know him better. To do this I will

_____

_____

_____

_____

_____ .

Faith Vocabulary

Define each of these terms:

1. philosophers
2. theologians
3. revelation
4. faith

People and Places and Events

Identify the following:

1. *Confessions*
2. Saint Augustine of Hippo
3. Saint Albert the Great

Main Ideas

Choose either (a) or (b) from each set of items. Write a brief paragraph
to answer each of your choices.

1. (a) How are our search for happiness and our search for God similar?
   (b) Describe what Augustine of Hippo wrote about our search for happiness.

2. (a) Describe how we can come to know God through creation.
   (b) Explain what Albert the Great had to say about the ways we come to know
   the truth.

3. (a) Describe faith as both a gift and a response.
   (b) Explain why God, even after he reveals himself, is always a mystery.

Critical Thinking

Using what you have learned in this chapter, explain this statement:
Catholics believe there can be no real contradiction between the
truths of our faith and the truths we learn from science.

Family Discussion

Our life as people of faith is the quest to better
understand that faith. Describe together the type
of quest your family is on to better understand
our faith.

Visit our
web site at
www.FaithFirst.com

The Word of God

2

WE PRAY

Your word is a lamp for my feet, a light for my path.

PSALM 119:105

Scripture is God's own word to us. In the Bible, God speaks to us in human words. The writers of the Bible used many types of writings to communicate God's word to us. What types can you name that are in the Bible? When we read the Bible, why is it important to know the type of writing we are reading?

"[We] shall devote ourselves to prayer and to the ministry of the word."

ACTS OF THE APOSTLES 6:4

FAITH FOCUS

How do the different types of writings in the Bible help communicate God's word to us?

FAITH VOCABULARY

Bible

Sacred Scripture

inspiration

canon of Sacred Scripture

oral tradition

literary genre

salvation

covenant

Sacred Tradition

deposit of faith

If you saw a friend riding a bike into the path of an oncoming truck, it would not help much if you were to say, "Look out for that truck!" in a language that your friend did not understand.

The Inspired Word of God

God first chose writers to write down his message to his people in words they knew and understood. They are words that we can trust as true because we know they come from God.

These words then could be translated into any and every human language. This is what has happened and continues to happen. Everyone, no matter what language they speak, could read or listen to God speak to them.

The **Bible**, or **Sacred Scripture**, is the collection of all the writings God has inspired authors to write in his name. Although we think of the Bible as a single book, it is actually more like what we call an anthology or even a library. It is a collection of writings by different writers.

We believe that the Bible is the inspired word of God written by human authors. That means that God is the author of the Bible. We use the phrase **inspiration** of the Bible to name this belief of God's people. This means that all the writings that make up the Bible have been written down by human authors with the help of the Holy Spirit.

What does it mean to say that the Bible is inspired?

Lindisfarne Gospels, ca. A.D. 752.
Decorated initial to the Gospel according to Saint Matthew.

The Canon of Sacred Scripture

The list of books that the Catholic Church teaches to be the inspired written word of God is called the **canon of Sacred Scripture.** The word *canon* means "standard." There are forty-six books in the Old Testament and twenty-seven in the New Testament. This is why we describe the Bible as a minilibrary of sacred writings.

The Old Testament and the New Testament are the two main parts of the Bible. The writings they contain have been gathered together over many years. Scripture scholars teach us that God's message, or revelation, was first passed on to us by storytellers. We call this **oral tradition.** Oral tradition is the passing on of God's revelation by word of mouth. Eventually this revelation was written down by God's people. The writing of the Old Testament began about a thousand years before the birth of Jesus, and the New Testament was completed about seventy years after the death-resurrection of Jesus.

We believe that the Bible is one book. There is an unbreakable connection between the Old and the New Testaments. For this reason we say that the New Testament lies hidden in the Old and the Old Testament was unveiled in the New Testament.

The Old Testament contains the writings of the Jewish people. It tells us about God's plan of saving love from creation up to the birth of Jesus. The New Testament contains the writings of followers of Jesus.

The heart, or center, of the Bible is the four accounts of the Gospel because Jesus is their center. The writings of the New Testament pass on to us the faith of the church community. They share the Church's faith in who Jesus Christ is and the meaning of his life, death, and resurrection.

Describe the Old Testament and the New Testament.

Literary Genre

The vast collection of books that make up the Bible include many different styles of writing, or **literary genres.** These include history (Kings, Chronicles, the Acts of the Apostles), letters (Paul's epistles), and collections of sayings (Proverbs). Also included are many other kinds of literature such as poetry, fiction, and short stories just as a modern-day library has.

Just as our parents and teachers speak to us in many different ways, so do the writers of the Bible. They explain, warn, reprimand, comfort, praise, and so on. Each type of writing helps us, in its own way, to understand what God is saying to us.

WHAT DIFFERENCE DOES FAITH MAKE?

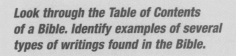

Look through the Table of Contents of a Bible. Identify examples of several types of writings found in the Bible.

_____

_____

_____

_____

How did God keep and continually renew his covenant with people?

Noah's Ark.
Leslie Xuereb, contemporary French artist.

Why would God inspire the people of God to write down his message to us? God wants everyone to know who he is and how much he wants us to be happy with him now and forever.

In the Bible God speaks to us about his loving plan of creation and **salvation**, or humanity's deliverance from the power of sin and death through Jesus Christ. God tells us about the wonderful **covenant** he made with humankind. A synonym for the word *covenant* is *testament*. The Old and New Testaments tell us about the story of that covenant and its fulfillment in Jesus Christ, the New Covenant who is the savior of the world.

The Covenant at Creation

The writings of the Old Testament pass on to us God's word about the beginnings of that covenant. In the creation story God enters an agreement with humankind through Adam and Eve. They have been created to live in happiness with God. God asks only one thing: Adam and Eve do not eat the fruit of the tree of good and evil. You know what happened. The temptation was too much and the first humans chose not to keep their part of the agreement.

What is the covenant God made with humankind at creation?

God's plan of creation would not be destroyed. God promises to send a descendant from Eve who would one day conquer the tempter, the devil. God's plan of loving and merciful salvation began.

The Covenant with Noah

Chapters three through eleven of the Book of Genesis tell us about the great evil of sin and its effects on people and God's creation. We read about Cain and Abel, Noah and the great flood, and the tower of Babel.

We learn that when sin so divided people, God renewed the covenant with Noah and all living things. In the Book of Genesis we read:

God said to Noah and to his sons with him: "See, I am now establishing my covenant with you and your descendants after you and with every living creature that was with you: all the birds, and the various tame and wild animals that were with you and came out of the ark. . . .This is the sign that I am giving for all ages to come, of the covenant between me and you and every living creature with you: I set my bow in the clouds to serve as a sign of the covenant between me and the earth. When I bring clouds over the earth, and the bow appears in the clouds, I will recall the covenant I have made between me and you and all living beings." GENESIS 9:8–10, 12–15

God's covenant with Noah and all living things remains in force as long as the world lasts.

Describe the covenant God made with humankind through Noah.

Abraham and Moses

God chose Abraham who lived in the land of "Ur of the Chaldeans." We know from the excavations of archeologists that at the time of Abraham (ca. 1800 B.C.) Ur was an important city of the Sumerians. God promised Abraham that he would become the father of a great nation. (See Genesis 12:1–12.)

As the story of God's promise, or the Covenant, unfolds, we learn that the Israelites are Abraham and Sarah's descendants. God would choose Moses to lead them out of slavery in Egypt. Through Moses God would reveal his Law to them and enter a covenant with them. He would be their God and they would be his people. (See Deuteronomy 7:6–9, Jeremiah 11:4.)

Explain the covenant God made with Abraham and with Moses.

The Promise of a New Covenant

God's people eventually became a great nation. Under the leadership of King David and King Solomon, they became respected by their neighbors. However, perhaps because of their power and wealth, future kings and the people soon forgot their promises to God. God sent prophets, like Ezekiel and Isaiah, Amos and Hosea, to remind them of their covenant and to promise a new covenant. (See Exodus 19–20.)

We believe that all these events point to Jesus Christ. Jesus did not abolish the Law and the Covenant of Sinai. He fulfilled and perfected them. In Jesus all of God's promises are fulfilled and we have the promise of salvation and eternal life. God has revealed himself fully by sending his own Son, in whom he has established his covenant with humanity forever. Christ saves all who believe in him and live his new law. He saves all those who seek to serve and love God with all their hearts.

Why do we say Jesus is the New Covenant?

WHAT DIFFERENCE DOES FAITH MAKE?

How should the covenant God made with us guide us in making choices each day?

_____

_____

_____

_____

25

Word and Eucharist.
Contemporary stained-glass window.

know something about the writings and their language, we can better grasp the meaning of God's word.

Discovering the Meaning of God's Word

The first thing we must know to understand the Bible is why God communicates his word to us. The real purpose of God's revelation to us is our salvation.

God does not speak to us in the Bible to give us a history lesson or a science lesson or to tell us details about the geography of the ancient world. In fact, the Bible has information about history and science and geography that we would consider outdated. This information comes from the human authors' lack of knowledge about these things. Even so, the truth that God wanted to communicate, which is a truth—not about science, history, or geography—but a truth about how we are saved, is clearly and unmistakenly in the Bible.

The second thing we must try to understand is the literary genre, or style of writing, a particular writer used to communicate God's message. If we do not understand what the human author was trying to do, it can be almost impossible to know what God is trying to say to us! Imagine a non-English speaking student in your school taking you literally when you say, "There must have been a million people at the game last night!" and all you really meant to say was there was a very large crowd at the game.

What is the purpose of God's revelation to us?

FAITH FOCUS

How do we discover the meaning of God's word to us?

Part of the reason for the difficulty of our understanding the Bible is the very fact that God chose human authors who used human words to tell us about himself. These writers lived in a time and culture far different from our own. They wrote in their own languages truths that we might otherwise never know. So, if we

Fortunately we belong to a community whose understanding of these inspired writings can be relied upon. We belong to the Church. That community—the Church—is guided today by the same Holy Spirit that inspired the original writers of the Old Testament and the New Testament. With the guidance of the Spirit the teaching office of the Church has the responsibility of authentically interpreting the word of God. The pope and the bishops in communion with him are the center of this teaching office.

Explain the role of the Church in helping us understand the word of God.

Sacred Tradition

The passing on of our faith in Christ by the Church through the power of the Holy Spirit is called **Sacred Tradition.** The Church passes on its living faith from generation to generation throughout all of history. The living faith is passed on by the Church, not just in the writings of the Bible but also in her prayer and in all of the many ways that the Church lives in faithfulness to the Lord.

We are part of the living Tradition of the Church. Through Scripture and Tradition God's revelation is passed on to us. Both Scripture and Tradition are connected to each other. They are not two separate ways of passing on God's revelation. Together they make up one source, or **deposit of faith.** From this source we continually draw our faith and are nourished at the banquet table of God's love.

Describe the role of Sacred Tradition in handing on God's revelation to us.

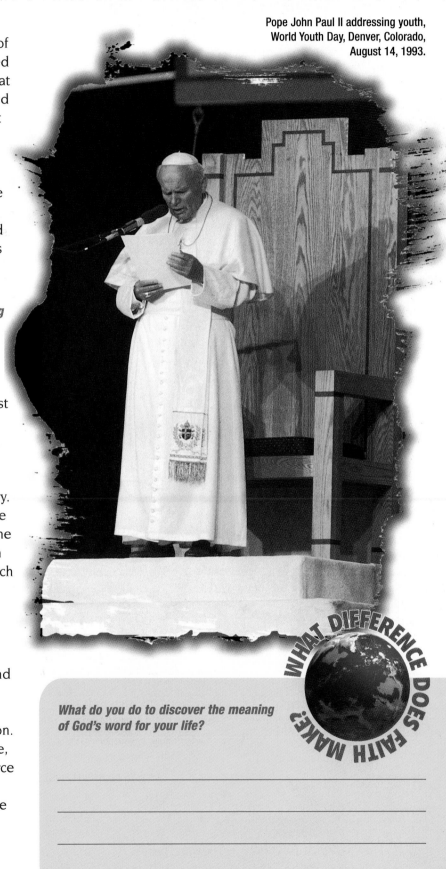

Pope John Paul II addressing youth, World Youth Day, Denver, Colorado, August 14, 1993.

What do you do to discover the meaning of God's word for your life?

WHAT DIFFERENCE DOES FAITH MAKE?

_____

_____

_____

_____

WHAT DIFFERENCE

Does This Make in Our Church?

Sacred Scripture is God's own word to us. God is the primary author of Scripture because he inspired its human writers. Through Scripture God reveals himself to us and shares his loving plan of creation and salvation with us. The Holy Spirit helps us understand God's word properly. Sacred Scripture must be read and interpreted with the guidance of the same Spirit who inspired its human writers. This is one of the reasons the Church authentically interprets God's word for us.

The Table of God's Word

Sacred Scripture has always had a central place in Christian life. This is one of the reasons that the Church always includes the proclamation of Scripture as part of the liturgy, the official prayer of the Church. When the Church gathers for prayer, the Holy Spirit is present within us in a very powerful way.

Saint Augustine of Hippo taught that there are two tables from which we are fed at every Mass—the Table of the Word and the Table of the Eucharist. We believe that the Church draws its life from these two tables.

That is why, at the end of the reading, we always say either "Thanks be to God" or "Praise to you, Lord Jesus Christ." We say this because we have just heard God speak to us. God's word has shared with us the deepest truth about life. God has spoken to us about how we can truly live in peace and happiness.

Praying the Scriptures

When we gather with the members of our community to worship or when we read the Bible alone, God is always there for us. Faith in this truth is the reason Christians set time aside each day for reading the Bible. The evidence for this is that the Bible continues to be the most widely read book in the world.

How does your parish community show reverence for the word of God proclaimed at Mass? How can you make Scripture a more important part of your life?

WHAT DIFFERENCE

Does It Make in My Life?

God wants to communicate with you. The Bible is the inspired word of God. When you read or listen to the Bible read to you, you need to remember it is God's own word you are hearing.

Communication Skills

You may believe that it is easy to communicate. You may think that if you just speak words clearly, you will be heard and understood. But to really communicate you need to develop certain skills.

Listening

Listening is crucial to communication. You may believe that communication is mostly talking, but talking is only half of it. Listening is the other half. If you do not listen to what is being said, there is no communication. Sometimes when someone speaks to you, your mind will begin to think its own thoughts—to think about what you want to say. You may not even hear the other person speaking.

This can happen when you pray. While you are trying to listen to God's message in your mind and heart, you may begin to think about something else. We call this a distraction. Distractions are thoughts that keep us from concentrating on the task at hand. You may have to say to yourself, "Wow, I'm thinking about that soccer game again. Okay, God, I want to think about you." When you are distracted while praying, take a deep breath, relax, and listen. You may have to do this several times.

Clarification

Clarification helps you know what the other person is really saying so there will be no misunderstanding of the message. This skill is needed to understand what is really being said. In the Old and the New Testaments, the writers used letters, poems, histories, and other different ways to make God's message very clear to us. Clarifying the type of writing you are reading is very important. Poetry is filled with images and symbols. A poet communicates truth to us very differently than an historian does.

Actions

Would it surprise you to know that experts say that only about 7 percent of communication has to do with words? Most of your communication, 93 percent, has to do with your actions—your facial expression and tone of voice. For example, your friend comes into the room and slams the door. You ask, "What's the matter?" Your friend answers with an angry look on his face and a mean tone of voice, "Nothing, I'm fine!" What is the real message your friend is communicating?

You might tell someone, "I like you, you're my friend," but your mean and hurtful actions might be communicating different messages. Remember that you show your love for God and others in both words and actions.

faith decision

- Form a group of three that includes a speaker, a listener, and an observer. The speaker begins a conversation. The listener listens attentively and responds. The observer sits or stands behind the speaker and the listener and observes, saying nothing.

- When the conversation is finished, the observer shares what he or she perceived by answering these questions: How well did the one student really listen as the other one spoke? How clear was the exchange back and forth? How well did the two students really communicate? How well did they listen or ask for clarification? Did they use words and actions (tone, facial expression, and so on) to make their message understood?

- If time permits, have the members of the triad switch roles.

This week I will try to communicate better with God by

_____

_____

_____

_____

_____.

Faith Vocabulary

Write a sentence that uses each of these terms correctly.

1. Bible
2. Sacred Scripture
3. inspiration
4. canon of Sacred Scripture
5. oral tradition
6. literary genre
7. salvation
8. covenant
9. Sacred Tradition
10. deposit of faith

People and Places and Events

Identify the role of each of these persons in God's loving plan of creation and salvation.

1. Adam and Eve
2. Noah
3. Abraham
4. Moses
5. Ezekiel

Main Ideas

Choose either (a) or (b) from each set of items. Write a brief paragraph to answer each of your choices.

1. (a) Explain why we say the Bible is God's own word to us.
   (b) Describe the role of the human writers of the Bible.
2. (a) Describe the story of God's covenant with humankind.
   (b) What does it mean to say that Jesus did not abolish the Covenant of Sinai?
3. (a) How would you go about trying to understand the meaning of a Bible story?
   (b) Describe how we are part of the living Tradition of the Church.

Critical Thinking

Using what you have learned in this chapter, explain this statement:
"The Bible is no mere book, but a living creature, with a power that conquers all." (Napoleon Bonaparte)

Family Discussion

How is family life a covenant between family members?

Visit our
web site at
www.FaithFirst.com

The Man Born Blind

A Scripture Story

3

WE PRAY

Father of mercy,
you led the man born blind
to the kingdom of light
through the gift of faith in
  your Son.
Free these elect
from the false values that
  surround and blind them.
Set them firmly in your truth,
children of the light for ever.
We ask this through Christ our
  Lord. Amen.

SCRUTINY PRAYER,
FOURTH SUNDAY OF LENT

In the Gospel there are many stories about Jesus healing people. The story of Jesus restoring sight to the man who was blind from birth is one of these stories. What other stories about Jesus healing people can you remember?

"I do believe, Lord."
JOHN 9:38

What are your favorite stories? What makes them your favorites? The characters? The plot? The setting? The action? The details? All of these elements make up a story.

A story is also written for an audience. Some writers write for young people. Awards like the Newbery Award recognize how well these authors write. Stories written by other authors capture the hearts and imaginations of grown-up and young people, for example, William Shakespeare's *Romeo and Juliet*. When an author writes for a special audience, she or he will tell a story in a certain way, emphasizing different details that relate to the audience, or readers for whom the story has been written.

Twelfth-century illuminated manuscript, Gospel according to John.

The Four Accounts of the Gospel

The four New Testament accounts of the Gospel—Matthew, Mark, Luke, and John—are similar to many of the stories you have read. Each of the evangelists also wrote for a special audience. The word **evangelist** means "teller of the good news, or the Gospel." While each of the evangelists emphasized certain details of the life and teachings of Jesus, the main characters and central plot of each of the accounts of the Gospel are the same. Each gospel account focuses on the events of the life, passion, death, and resurrection of Jesus and their meaning for our lives. (See Luke 1:1–4.)

How are the four accounts of the Gospel alike?

The Gospel According to John

The Gospel according to John was probably written between A.D. 90 and 100. John selected events from the life of Jesus that would have special meaning to his readers. John tells his readers:

> Now Jesus did many other signs in the presence of [his] disciples that are not written in this book. But these are written that you may [come to] believe that Jesus is the Messiah, the Son of God, and that through this belief you may have life in his name.
>
> JOHN 20:30–31

The **Fourth Gospel,** as this account of the Gospel is also called, was first written for a community of Jewish Christians. For these believers much of their life remained focused around the local synagogue in their town or village. At first the Jewish leaders accepted the Jews who had become followers of the way preached by Jesus. For many reasons this acceptance faded away and around A.D. 85 the Jewish Christians were formally banned from all synagogues.

The author of the Gospel according to John wrote to the Jews who were being excluded from the worship life of the Jewish community because they had become believers in Jesus. The pain they felt was deep. They became torn between the Jewish community and their faith in Jesus. Some began to waver and were tempted to abandon their faith in Jesus. The Fourth Gospel encourages and strengthens this early Christian community to have hope and to keep their faith and belief in Jesus Christ.

Describe the audience for whom the Fourth Gospel was first written.

The Book of Signs

The first part of the Gospel according to John is also called the **Book of Signs** because it includes many stories of miracles, or signs, in the life of Jesus. Each story is intended to strengthen the faith of its readers and listeners.

John very carefully constructed these stories like a skilled playwright by following a pattern:
- The story is told.
- There is a narrative explaining the story.

- Finally the evangelist includes a soliloquy by Jesus giving further insight into the story. A soliloquy is "a literary discourse in which a character reveals his or her thoughts when alone or unaware of the presence of others."

The writer of the Fourth Gospel arranges the characters and crafts the dialogues between them with great precision. He makes brilliant use of literary techniques that draw the audience deeply into the unfolding action of the story.

Explain why the writer of the Gospel according to John is considered to be a skilled writer.

Reading this account of the Gospel helped many early Christians strengthen their faith in God and in Jesus. They came "to see," a phrase John uses to mean "to believe," that Jesus was the Messiah, the Son of God.

John

How can reading about the signs of Jesus in the Fourth Gospel strengthen your faith and belief in Jesus?

WHAT DIFFERENCE DOES FAITH MAKE?

_____

_____

_____

The Miracle of Christ Healing the Blind.
El Greco (1541–1614), Spanish artist.

How does the man born blind respond to Jesus' healing of him?

The story of the man born blind in the Fourth Gospel is an example of why Scripture scholars describe John as a skilled playwright. Read this story as a play.

Act 1: The Healing of the Man
(John 9:1–12)

Act 2: Dialogue and Interrogation
(John 9:13–41)

Act 3: A Soliloquy by Jesus
(John 10:1–18)

Notice how there are no more than two characters or groups of characters who speak on stage at the same time.

What are the three parts to the story of the man born blind?

The Man Born Blind

The story of the man born blind begins with a recounting of the miracle of healing (see John 9:1–12).

Act 1:
The Healing of the Man

Jesus and his disciples had been driven from the Temple area. As they were walking, they came upon a man who was born blind. He was sitting near the Pool of Siloam, which was a place many used to bathe themselves. Seeing the man the disciples asked Jesus:

"Rabbi, who sinned, this man or his parents, that he was born blind?" Jesus answered, "Neither he nor his parents sinned; it is so that the works of God might be made visible through him. We have to do the works of the one who sent me while it is day. Night is coming when no one can work. While I am in the world, I am the light of the world." When he had said this, he spat on the ground and made clay with the saliva, and smeared the clay on his eyes, and said to him, "Go wash in the Pool of Siloam" (which means Sent). So he went and washed, and came back able to see.   John 9:2–7

Act 2:
Dialogue and Interrogation

The second act of the play (John 9:13–41) begins when others who knew the man asked how he could see. After the man told them what Jesus had done, his neighbors and others brought the man to the Pharisees, who asked the man how it was that he could now see.

When the man told them what Jesus had done, they did not believe him. They called the man's parents to testify that the man had truly been born blind. The man's parents refused to change their story. The Pharisees called the man back a second time and interrogated him. Refusing to budge, the man stood up to the Pharisees, saying:

> "If this man were not from God, he would not be able to do anything." They answered and said to him, "You were born totally in sin, and are you trying to teach us?" Then they threw him out. JOHN 9:33–34

The action reached a climax as Jesus sought out the man and asked him about his faith and belief.

> When Jesus heard that they had thrown him out, he found him and said, "Do you believe in the Son of Man?" He answered and said, "Who is he, sir, that I may believe in him?" Jesus said to him, "You have seen him and the one speaking with you is he." He said, "I do believe, Lord," and he worshiped him. JOHN 9:35–38

The man expressed his faith in Jesus by using the divine title, saying, "I do believe, Lord" (John 9:38) and he worshiped him.

Describe the climax of the story of the man born blind.

Blind Man Washes in the Pool of Siloam.
James J. Tissot (1836–1902), French artist.

In the interrogation of the man, the authorities tried to intimidate him. He remained steadfast. As a result, "they threw him out" (John 9:34). This is surely a deliberate allusion to the fate suffered by Jewish Christians for whom the evangelist is writing.

Read Act 3, the soliloquy by Jesus, in John 10:1–18. How does it help you understand the story of the man born blind?

WHAT DIFFERENCE DOES FAITH MAKE?

Describe a situation in life when people have been asked to stand up for their faith in Jesus. Explain what happened.

_____

_____

_____

How does the gospel story of Jesus healing the man born blind help us live our faith in Jesus?

The early Christians believed there was more to this story than just a **miracle** of a man gaining his sight. The effects of a miracle—for example, the restoring of sight to the man born blind—cannot be explained by any natural causes. In the Gospel a miracle is a wonderful sign of God working among people, inviting us to believe and trust in him. Recall what the writer of the Fourth Gospel wrote:

> Now Jesus did many other signs in the presence of [his] disciples that are not written in this book. But these are written that you may [come to] believe that Jesus is the Messiah, the Son of God, and that through this belief you may have life in his name.
>
> JOHN 20:30–31

Faith in Jesus

Faith in Jesus is the focus of this story. John's deepest concern was to help his readers explore the meaning of that faith. In the story of the man's journey from physical blindness to spiritual sight, the reader recognizes someone who receives physical sight, sees with the eyes of faith, and comes to new life in Christ.

The Fourth Gospel contrasts day and night, light and darkness, blindness and sight. The evangelist uses these symbols and other metaphors to talk about the choice that is involved in faith. For a Christian, faith is all about how one relates to God and his Son, Jesus. Those who scorn the light and do not come to believe in Jesus will perish. Those who come to the

light and believe in Jesus will not perish but will enjoy eternal life. Earlier the evangelist wrote:

> For God so loved the world that he gave his only Son, so that everyone who believes in him might not perish but might have eternal life. . . . Whoever believes in him will not be condemned, but whoever does not believe has already been condemned, because he has not believed in the name of the only Son of God.
>
> JOHN 3:16, 18

What does the story of the man born blind teach us about faith?

Baptism: New Life in Christ

The story of Jesus healing the man born blind has been used by Christians to help us understand Baptism. The evidence for this is found in a fresco (painting with watercolors on fresh, moist plaster) on a wall in one of the **catacombs.** A catacomb is an underground cemetery consisting of chambers or tunnels with recesses used as graves. This fresco portrays the story found in John 9 as a symbol of Baptism.

The early Christians saw a deeper meaning in the healing of the man of physical blindness and receiving sight. It symbolized for them the spiritual journey of a person who moved from lack of faith to knowing and professing their faith in Christ in Baptism. That is why Baptism is sometimes called the sacrament of enlightenment, a word that means "insight into something spiritual." Clearly those early believers in Christ recognized in this story deeper meanings that had to do with their own experiences of being initiated into the Christian community.

Describe how the story of the healing of the man born blind teaches us about Baptism.

Easter Vigil. Assembly standing during The Service of Light as the Easter proclamation is sung.

Children of the Light

We can see ourselves as actors in John's drama about the man born blind and the unseeing Pharisees. The story helps us recognize that we face the same choices as the man born blind and the Pharisees did. God acts in our lives. We too are called to express our belief in Jesus.

The Spirit invites us to choose the light over the dark. The Spirit invites us to profess our faith in God acting in our lives—even when it means facing opposition, even when it means being "excluded" from the "in" crowd.

At Baptism we are joined to Christ. We become one with him and one another. We publicly profess our faith in Jesus. We choose to follow the light and not live in darkness. When we profess our faith in Christ at Baptism and throughout our lives, we are showing that we have heard what the evangelist hoped for:

[T]hat you may [come to] believe that Jesus is the Messiah, the Son of God, and that through this belief you may have life in his name. JOHN 20:31

How can you choose Jesus in your life today?

_____

_____

_____

_____

WHAT DIFFERENCE DOES FAITH MAKE?

39

WHAT DIFFERENCE

Does This Make in Our Church?

The Gospel according to John was the last of the accounts of the Gospel in the New Testament to be written. Written for members of the Jewish community who became followers of Jesus, it is filled with symbols, or signs, that have a deeper meaning than their dictionary meaning. The story of Jesus healing the man born blind and restoring his sight is a miracle story in its truest sense. It is a story of faith inviting its readers to deepen their faith and trust in Jesus. *Water, sight, touch,* and other words point to spiritual things we may not at first think about when we hear these words.

Christian Initiation

The Church has always used symbols and symbolic actions to invite us to faith. In our celebration of the rites of Christian Initiation, the Church, as Jesus touched the eyes of the man born blind, signs the forehead and senses of the candidate, or person wishing to become a member of the Church.

CELEBRANT: [Names], Christ has called you to be his friends. Always remember him and be faithful to him.

Therefore, I mark your forehead with the sign of the cross. It is the sign of Christians; let it remind you always of Christ and how much he loves you.

The senses of the candidates are now also signed either by the celebrant, parents, sponsors, or catechists as the celebrant prays:

CELEBRANT: I [we] mark your ears with the sign of the cross: hear the words of Christ.

I [we] mark your eyes with the sign of the cross: see the works of Christ.

I [we] mark your lips with the sign of the cross: speak as Christ would speak.

I [we] mark the sign of the cross over your heart: make your heart the home of Christ.

I [we] mark your shoulders with the sign of the cross: be strong with the strength of Christ.

I [we] mark your hands with the sign of the cross, touch others with the gentleness of Christ.

I [we] mark your feet with the sign of the cross, walk in the way of Christ.

The sign of the cross is now traced above the whole person as the celebrant prays aloud:

CELEBRANT: I [we] place you entirely under the sign of Christ's cross in the name of the Father, and of the Son, and of the Holy Spirit: live with Jesus now and for ever.

CANDIDATES: Amen.

Each day we are called to live our faith in Jesus. Describe how you might use your eyes, ears, lips, hands, and heart to show you are a follower of Jesus.

WHAT DIFFERENCE

Does It Make in My Life?

Not only did the man born blind receive his sight but his eyes were opened to see things differently. He began to see people and situations through the eyes of faith. His eyes were opened because Jesus healed him. As a believer, your eyes have also been opened through the sacrament of Baptism.

But sometimes your eyes are clouded and there are things that blind you and keep you from seeing clearly.

Obstacles to Seeing with Eyes of Faith

Here are some common obstacles that can prevent you from seeing with eyes of faith. The first step to overcoming obstacles is to be aware of them.

Closed-Minded

Have you ever met someone who believes that they are always right? Someone who thinks everybody else's opinions are unimportant. Do you know someone who is prejudiced or someone who thinks that they have all the answers all the time?

Open–minded means to be able to consider other possibilities.

It means to try and be open to other people's opinions and to think about other suggestions. If your parents, a teacher, or a friend asks you to look at something differently, you can choose to open your eyes and your mind to the possibility that there could be wisdom and value in the suggestion. Try not to be blinded to new insights that could help you be a better person or live a better life.

How does this gospel story help you understand the special gift of sight Jesus has given you? How does this gift help you look at things and people in a new way?

Substance Abuse

Alcohol: It may seem cool to sneak a drink, but it's not. Alcohol is a drug that can be extremely dangerous, especially for young people. It can have harmful effects on your growth and development as well as your relationships and your decision-making skills. It can be very addictive. It can damage your brain cells.

Other Drugs: Illegal drugs can keep you from seeing reality. They stop you from dealing with whatever feelings you are feeling. Drugs not only blind you to the wonderful possibilities that lie ahead of you but also mess up your mind. Drugs destroy your relationships with your parents, brothers and sisters, family and friends. You may believe that drugs will not affect you, that they will not be able to hook you, but

"Came to See"

John wrote in his account of the Gospel that the blind man "came to see." John meant that the man began to see with the eyes of faith. He began to see all the wonderful things in his life and in his world. Jesus wants you to see. By overcoming these obstacles, by choosing to be open-minded rather than closed-minded, by making choices for your better health, and by striving to be in good relationships with God, others, and all of creation you will be able to see with eyes of faith. Keep your eyes open to the wonderful things that God wants to share with you.

they can and they will. Drugs are so powerful they can blind you from living a healthy life. They do not solve anything. Drugs can destroy you forever.

How does the gift of faith help you make choices to say no to anything that will harm you or your relationship with your family, with your friends, or with God?

Self-Centered

If you are totally absorbed with yourself, your clothes, your possessions, then you are blind to people and the world around you. God asks you to love your neighbor as yourself. You are not meant to live in isolation. You need to take care of yourself and your things, but you still need to reach out and be in relationship with others. We are all interrelated beings with God, our families, friends, and all creation.

faith decision

You are a person of faith. You have been given eyes of faith. In a small group of three or four students, discuss the following questions.

- How would a closed-minded person see a homeless person?
- How would an open-minded person see a homeless person?
- When you hear about a friend using tobacco, alcohol, or illegal drugs, what do you see?
- When you see a classmate disconnected from others, what do you see?

Each day I will ask the Holy Spirit to sharpen my vision so I can see things more clearly with the eyes of faith. This week I will try to evaluate situations with the eyes of faith by

_____

_____

_____

_____

Faith Vocabulary

Use each of these terms correctly in a sentence.

1. evangelist
2. Fourth Gospel
3. Book of Signs
4. miracle
5. catacombs

People and Places and Events

Identify the following:

1. Pool of Siloam
2. Pharisees
3. Son of Man

Main Ideas

Choose either (a) or (b) from each set of items. Write a brief paragraph to answer each of your choices.

1. (a) Describe the main focus of the Gospel.
   (b) Why was the Gospel according to John originally written for a community of Jewish Christians?
2. (a) Why was the Gospel according to John written?
   (b) Why is the first part of the Gospel according to John called the Book of Signs?
3. (a) Describe the response of the man born blind to Jesus.
   (b) Explain Jesus' response to the Pharisees.
4. (a) Why do we call the story of Jesus' curing the man born blind a story about faith?
   (b) How does this story help us understand Baptism?

Critical Thinking

Using what you have learned in this chapter, briefly explain this statement:
When we look at the world and ourselves with the eyes of faith, we see things in a unique way.

Family Discussion

How can seeing with eyes of faith guide us in responding to one another?

Visit our
web site at
www.FaithFirst.com

The Mystery of Creation

4

WE PRAY

God and Father of all gifts,
we praise you, the source
of all we have and are.
Teach us to acknowledge
    always
the many good things
your infinite love has given us.
Help us to love you
with all our heart
and all our strength.

OPENING PRAYER,
MASSES, IN THANKSGIVING B

In the Apostles' Creed we
pray, "I believe in God, the
Father almighty, creator of
heaven and earth." Explain
in your own words what it
means to say God is the
creator of heaven and earth.

In the beginning, when
God created the heavens
and the earth, the earth was
a formless wasteland, and
darkness covered the abyss,
when a mighty wind swept
over the waters. Then God
said, "Let there be light."

GENESIS 1:1–3

God the Creator

FAITH FOCUS

What is the difference between the way God creates and the way humans create?

FAITH VOCABULARY

analogy

create

attribute

divine nature

eternal

omnipresence

Divine Providence

soul

Think of the many ways some brothers or sisters look so much alike. Think about children who so resemble one or the other of their parents that there is no doubt they are all members of the same family.

It is not only our "looks" that reveal our connection with our parents. The expression "You're just like your father" applies to our behaviors too. Our looks and behaviors can so connect us with our parents that there is no doubt whose children we are.

A Reflection of the Creator

We can apply the same connections to God and creation. Taking a close look at creation, we can get a glimpse of the One who is the source of *all* creation. When we learn about God this way, we are learning by **analogy**. When we learn by analogy, we explain or understand something by comparing two things that are similar in some respects but are otherwise unlike.

What is an analogy?

The beauty of creation reflects the infinite beauty of God its creator:

> Ever since the creation of the world, his invisible attributes of eternal power and divinity have been able to be understood and perceived in what he has made.
>
> ROMANS 1:20

From examining and reflecting on the simplicity of a subatomic particle to the incomprehensible complexity of galaxies expanding through the void of space at the speed of light, we learn something about who God is by analogy. When we open our eyes and minds to ponder the majesty and the mystery of creation, we cannot help but be led to a sense of awe before the Creator whose image is traced in such vastness and diversity.

Describe how we use analogy to come to know God.

God the Creator

In the Apostles' Creed we profess:
    I believe in God,
        the Father almighty,
            creator of heaven and earth.

God is our creator and the creator of all things. When we say that God is the creator of heaven and earth, we use the word *creator* analogously. When humans **create** something, we take or use things that already exist to come up with something new. We explore and discover the world of God's creation and put it together in a new way. The something new we create, in a sense, already existed in a different way.

God does not create in the same way that we create. God freely, directly, and without any help created "heaven and earth" (Apostles' Creed), "all that is, seen and unseen" (Nicene Creed) out of nothing. This

to divert a flowing stream. Majestic redwoods did not reach up to the sky and wheat fields did not blow in the wind.

There was nothing and no one until God, out of love, freely chose to create. Now creatures share in his goodness and beauty and tell of the glory that belongs to God alone.

Describe what the Church means when we profess our faith in God, the creator of heaven and earth.

Did you Know...

The Babylonians who were neighbors of the Israelites also told a creation story, which is called Enuma Elish. Their creation story is unlike the two creation stories in the Book of Genesis. Creation according to Enuma Elish results from the fighting of the gods.

is what is different about the way God creates: Before God created the world, only God existed—no one else, nothing else.

There were no angels, no humans. No eagles soared over mountaintops nor did dolphins playfully splash in the oceans alongside whales. There were no sheep grazing on hillside pastures nor otters building dams

Explain one or two things in creation that help you come to know God.

WHAT DIFFERENCE DOES FAITH MAKE?

_____

_____

_____

_____

Why does reflecting in faith on the diversity within creation help us come to know more and more about who God is?

How many species of living creatures do you think have existed or exist today? Thousands? Millions? How many? The magnificence and beauty of creation is found in its diversity. The wonder and awe of creation is that each and every part has a special purpose in God's plan. Each part in its own unique way gives glory to God and points to God the Creator.

One God

Who is this creator who has given us all this? We use the word **attributes** to classify some of the things we have come to know about God. An attribute is a quality or characteristic that belongs to a person or thing. At the heart of God's revelation of himself, or his **divine nature,** is the attribute that he is one. The term *divine nature* means "that which makes God God."

Define the term attribute of God.

In the Old Testament we read:

"Hear, O Israel! The LORD is our God, the LORD alone!"

DEUTERONOMY 6:4

The Israelites came to know God as one. They believed, unlike their neighbors, that there is only one, true God who is the creator of everything. The belief in one God is called monotheism. It was far different from what the neighbors of the Israelites and the majority of the people who lived in Old Testament times believed about God. Most believed there were many gods. We call this belief polytheism.

Describe monotheism.

God Is Eternal

The Israelites also came to know that God alone has no beginning and no end. We use the attributes **eternal,** or everlasting, to describe this characteristic of God. God alone always was and always will be. Nothing and no one existed other than God until God freely chose to directly create "all that is, seen and unseen" out of nothing and without any help. The attribute everlasting belongs only to God.

What does it mean to call God eternal or everlasting?

The LORD is our God, the LORD alone. Deuteronomy 6:4

God Is Truth

In reflecting on creation and God's word to his people, the inspired writers of the Bible share with us their belief that God alone is the source of all truth and knowledge. One sacred writer puts it this way:

> For he gave me sound knowledge
> of existing things,
> that I might know the
> organization of the universe
> and the force of its
> elements. . . .
> Such things as are hidden I
> learned, and such as are plain;
> for Wisdom . . . taught me.
> WISDOM 7:17, 21–22

The sacred writer is not suggesting that God gave him detailed answers to every question about science. No, we must use our intelligence to learn about the workings of the world. What the sacred writer is telling us is this: Because God is the source of all creation, all truth ultimately comes from him. There can be no deception in God. Under the guidance of the Holy Spirit, the Church guides us in understanding the meaning of the truth that God reveals.

We believe and trust everything the living God reveals to us. He gives us his word, and his word is always true. God always keeps his word.

Explain why we believe God is Truth.

God Is Always Present

God's people in the Old Testament also use the term *presence* to describe God. This expresses their belief that God does not create and abandon his people. He is always present to all of his creation.

Without God's presence, creation would cease to exist. We call this attribute of God his **omnipresence.** We believe the almighty power and loving care of God, or **Divine Providence**, is always with us.

Explain the two attributes of God, omnipresence and Divine Providence.

God Is Love

By sending his Son, who would freely choose to die for us, God revealed the innermost mystery, or secret, about himself: "God is love" (1 John 4:8). God created us and saved us and chose us to be his people because of who he is: love. We exist to share in the beauty and goodness and love of God. This is the glory for which God has created us. This plan and promise will be fulfilled in the new creation in Christ when Christ comes again in glory at the end of time.

Why do we say the innermost secret about God is that "God is love" (1 John 4:8)?

No matter how much we come to understand about God, God will always remain a mystery. Our knowledge and love of God can always grow.

What can you do to grow in your knowledge and love of God?

_____

_____

_____

_____

WHAT DIFFERENCE DOES FAITH MAKE?

Made from the clay of the earth, we have received the breath of life from God. God created us with a body and a **soul.** Our soul is the spiritual part of who we are that is immortal, or never dies. God has given us an intelligence and a free will. These powers are gifts from God that give us the power to know and love God, other people, and ourselves. This unique privilege is ours alone among all the creatures of earth.

Describe what it means to believe that we have been created with a body and a soul.

Male and Female

When we read or listen to the first creation story, God also tells us that he did not create us to be alone. There is another side to us. We have been created to live with others in community. We read:

> God created man in his image;
>   in the divine image he
>   created him;
>   male and female he created
>   them.   GENESIS 1:27

Men and women share equally the honor and dignity of being made in God's image and likeness. Men and women have been created to live as partners. It is part of the divine plan that a man and a woman join together in marriage. This partnership of man and woman, the family, is the first and basic form of community. Created in the image and likeness of God, a married couple is a sign of God's life-giving love for us.

Describe the relationship between a man and a woman in God's plan of creation.

Created in God's Image

The first story of creation in the Book of Genesis (see Genesis 1:1–2:4a) makes it clear that people are the summit of God's creation. After God finished creating the universe and saw how good it was, he said, "Let us make man in our image, after our likeness" (Genesis 1:26).

The writer of the second story of creation in Genesis (see Genesis 2:4b–25) describes the creation of the first human this way:

> The LORD God formed man out of the clay of the ground and blew into his nostrils the breath of life, and so man became a living being.   GENESIS 2:7

Original Justice

God created us not only to share the gift of life with us. He created us to share in his happiness—in his very own goodness and love both now on earth and forever in heaven. This is our destiny, the reason God created us: to freely cooperate with God's plan and share in his glory in heaven.

God created the first humans in the state of original justice. The word *justice* means "being in the right order." God created us in a life-giving relationship with him, with one another, and with all creation. When

we freely cooperate with God's plan, we live in right order with God, with other people, and with all creation.

The writer of the story of the Fall in the Book of Genesis (see Genesis 3:1–24) tells us that the first humans, Adam and Eve, lost that state of original justice. They committed the original, or first, sin. They knowingly and freely rejected God's plan of creation. They knew God's plan and chose to replace it with their own.

Describe the meaning of the term original justice.

New Creation

We know the consequence of that choice. The rest of the Bible is the story of God's commitment to restore his original plan. It is the story of God's plan of salvation, the deliverance of creation from the power of sin and death. The plan of God's loving goodness will be fulfilled in the new creation in Jesus Christ, the Son of God made man. He is the new Adam. (See 1 Corinthians 15:20–28.)

Explain the connection between the terms salvation *and* new creation.

Visible World

God himself created the visible world with all its richness, diversity, and order. Each of his creatures possesses a ray of God's goodness. And while we are interdependent with all creatures, God destined all creatures for the good of the human race. This means we have a big responsibility. We are to respect God's creatures and care for God's creation. If we fail to do so, we are not fulfilling our role as stewards of God's gift of creation.

Did you Know...

God also created angels. Angels do not have bodies as humans do. Angels are spiritual beings who are servants and messengers of God. Their work is to glorify God and cooperate with God in his saving plan for other creatures. Read these Scripture passages to discover the role of angels in God's plan:

- Genesis 21:17
- Genesis 22:11
- 1 Kings 19:5
- Isaiah 6:6
- Mark 1:13
- Luke 1:11, 26
- Luke 2:13
- John 20:12
- Hebrews 1:6

WHAT DIFFERENCE DOES FAITH MAKE?

How are you fulfilling your responsibility to cooperate with God's plan of creation?

_____

_____

_____

WHAT DIFFERENCE

Does This Make in Our Church?

Out of love God freely and directly created us to share in his goodness. Created in the image and likeness of God, who is truth and love, human beings are the summit of all God's creatures. Created male and female we have been created to live in community. Together we are to live as images of God, reminding others of God's caring presence with us.

Recreating All Things in Christ

The students, faculty, and families of Bishop Lynch High School in Dallas, Texas work diligently to put into practice the faith they talk about and study while at school. They strive to be living images of God to one another and to others. One way they do this is by building live-giving relationships within their school community and with the larger civic and church community of which their school is a part. These life-giving relationships are strengthened through a peer ministry program called "Peer Helpers."

Peer Ministry

At the beginning of the school year, Peer Helpers serve as ambassadors. They welcome new students, answer questions, guide the lost, and make everyone feel comfortable.

The Peer Helpers also sponsor a one-day camp for new students to help them become familiar with their school, one another, and the entire school community. This day covers helpful information that is not normally included in an orientation process. They answer questions that are best discussed student-to-student.

Other peer ministry programs include a one-on-one tutoring program and the Student Symposium, where students can openly discuss school issues, seek advice, and discover solutions to problems they identify.

Hearts & Hammers

Members of the Bishop Lynch community are also involved in the civic community. They clean area parks, paint over graffiti, work with area food banks, and join with the Hearts & Hammers project. Founded in the Dallas area, Hearts & Hammers unites volunteers who work together to renovate the homes of the elderly, of the disabled, and of families living immediately above or below the poverty level. Some of the homeowners are in danger of losing their homes because they are physically or financially unable to keep the property in compliance with county code requirements.

Nearly two hundred students, parents, faculty members, and alumni recently took part in their annual Hearts & Hammers project. On the first weekend of the project, Bishop Lynch volunteers took part in powerwashing, scraping, and priming the exterior of a house in Dallas, Texas. Volunteers also kept busy clearing the front and back yards of brush and trash, and making flower beds ready for planting. Returning a second weekend, they finished painting the house and planting flowers and new shrubbery.

In what ways can you be a living image of God the Creator for others?

WHAT DIFFERENCE

Does It Make in My Life?

You have been created in the image and likeness of God, who is one God in three Persons. What does it mean for you to be created in the image and likeness of God?

Building Relationships

Relationship is a word we think about when we reflect on the meaning of the Trinity for our own lives. You have been created to live in a relationship with God and others. Jesus taught us that everything we say and do can be summed up this way: We are to love God with our whole mind, heart, soul, and strength. We are to love our neighbor as ourselves. (See Matthew 22:34–40.)

You now live in many relationships. What are some of those relationships?

_____

_____

_____

Some of your present relationships will continue throughout your lifetime. You will also develop new relationships. In the midst of all your relationships with people, God is always calling you to deepen your relationship with him.

Healthy Relationships

As you grow you continually need to develop skills that help you live in healthy relationships with others. Respectful and life-giving are two of the most important qualities of healthy relationships.

- Respectful relationships honor the dignity of yourself and others. Developing respect in our relationships works toward eliminating prejudice, violence,

Signs of a Healthy Relationship

Respect for
Each other
Loving, loyal,
  listening
Attentiveness, attitude
  of caring
Trust of each other
Interest in each other's
  well-being
Openness to each other, freely
  sharing and expressing opinions
Nurturing and supporting each
  other to be one's "best"
Sharing hopes, dreams, fears,
  beliefs, spirituality
Humor
Integrity, honor and loyalty, treat
  others as you wish to be treated
Positive attitude, play fair, disagree
  peacefully
Skills that you need to practice.

and all other forms of verbal and physical and spiritual harm from our relationships.

- In life-giving relationships we support one another. We develop one another's gifts and talents. People in life-giving relationships grow in the image and likeness of God.

Describe some of the ways that respect is part of your relationships with others.

_____

_____

_____

_____

faith decision

- Think about your own relationship with God and your relationships with others.

- Work with a partner. Brainstorm ways you can develop the signs of healthy relationships in your life.

I will try to improve my relationship with God by

_____

_____.

I will try to improve my relationship with a friend or family member by

_____

_____.

Faith Vocabulary

Define each of these terms:

1. analogy
2. create
3. attribute
4. divine nature
5. eternal
6. omnipresence
7. Divine Providence
8. soul

Main Ideas

Choose either (a) or (b) from each set of items. Write a brief paragraph to answer each of your choices.

1. (a) How can the use of an analogy help us come to know God?

   (b) Explain what the Church means when it teaches that God is the creator of all, seen and unseen.

2. (a) Explain the meaning of the divine attribute *everlasting*.

   (b) How does the divine attribute *love* help us understand why God created everything?

3. (a) Explain what it means to say that people are created in the image and likeness of God.

   (b) Describe the term *original justice*. How does it help us understand God's plan of creation?

Critical Thinking

Using what you have learned in this chapter, briefly explain the first section of the Nicene Creed:
"We believe in one God, the Father, the Almighty, maker of heaven and earth, of all that is, seen and unseen."

Family Discussion

What are some things we can do to help one another grow in our knowledge and love of God?

Visit our
web site at
www.FaithFirst.com

God: Father, Son, and Holy Spirit

5

WE PRAY

God, we praise you:
Father all-powerful, Christ Lord
    and Savior, Spirit of love.
You reveal yourself in the
    depths of our being,
drawing us to share in your life
    and your love.
One God, three Persons,
be near to the people
    formed in your image,
close to the world your love
    brings to life.

FROM *ALTERNATIVE OPENING PRAYER,
TRINITY SUNDAY*

God has revealed to us a glimpse of who God is—one God in three Persons. We call this the mystery of the Holy Trinity. Share what you have come to know about the Trinity.

"The Advocate, the holy Spirit that the Father will send in my name—he will teach you everything." JOHN 14:26

The Mystery of the Holy Trinity

FAITH FOCUS

Why do Christians believe in the mystery of the Holy Trinity?

FAITH VOCABULARY

mystery

Holy Trinity

blasphemy

dogma

divine missions

People of faith often wonder and ask questions such as: How did the universe begin? Is there life somewhere in the universe other than on earth? If so, what is that life? How did it get there? Have you ever asked these questions? What answers have you come up with?

The Mystery of God

Scientists and philosophers struggle to come up with solutions to these and other mysteries that fill the universe. As they gather more data and weigh the evidence, researchers make breakthroughs in their knowledge and understanding of these mysteries.

The deepest **mystery** of all is the mystery of God. The word *mystery* has a special meaning when we speak of God as mystery. It means more than the solvable problems posed and solved by the great mystery writers. When we speak of God as mystery,

we mean that we can never fully comprehend or fully grasp God or feel that we have God "figured out." We depend on God's loving willingness to share himself or reveal himself so that we can come to know the truth of God's inner life and his plan for our salvation.

Explain the word mystery *in the phrase* mystery of God.

One God in Three Persons

When you bless yourself, saying, "In the name of the Father and of the Son and of the Holy Spirit," you are professing your belief in the central mystery of the Christian life. You are professing your faith and trust in one God who is Father, Son, and Holy Spirit. We call the mystery of one God in three Persons the mystery of the **Holy Trinity.** The word *trinity* comes from the Latin words *tri* and *unus*, meaning "three" and "one."

Explain what it means to describe God as the mystery of the Holy Trinity.

Father   Son   Holy Spirit

The New Testament

Our Christian belief in the Blessed Trinity is based on God's revelation of himself to us. Through listening to the Scriptures we come to clearly see and believe that God, who created and saves us and shares his life and love with us, is one God who is Father, Son, and Holy Spirit.

Jesus Calls God His Father

The writers of the Gospel identify God as the Father of Jesus Christ 170 times—42 times in Matthew, 4 times in Mark, 15 times in Luke, and 109 times in John. Without doubt the early Christians came to believe that there is a unique relationship between Jesus and God. In the face of his disciples' struggle to understand who he was, Jesus asked:

> "Do you not believe that I am in the Father and the Father is in me?"   JOHN 14:10

Christians understood that Jesus was putting himself on a par with God the Father. Jesus is the Son of God who is equally God as the Father is God. Such a statement shocked and outraged and offended many pious leaders of the Jewish community of Jesus' times. Why? Because for Jews who did not come to believe in Jesus, this assertion by Jesus contradicted the heart of what they believed about God's revelation of himself: There is one God. They expressed this faith each and every day in prayer:

> "Hear, O Israel! The LORD is our God, the LORD alone."
>   DEUTERONOMY 6:4

So clearly did the Jewish leaders understand Jesus' assertion that they accused him of **blasphemy**, which is "the act of claiming to be God."

Jesus and the Father Will Send the Spirit

In his final words to his disciples at the Last Supper, Jesus did not speak only about himself and the Father. He also taught his disciples about the Holy Spirit:

> "And I will ask the Father, and he will give you another Advocate to be with you always, the Spirit of truth."   JOHN 14:16–17

Briefly explain why Christians came to believe that there is one God in three Persons.

The first Christians gradually came to understand and express their belief in one God who is mysteriously Father, Son, and Holy Spirit. Professing belief in the Holy Trinity became the norm or standard by which someone became a follower of Jesus Christ.

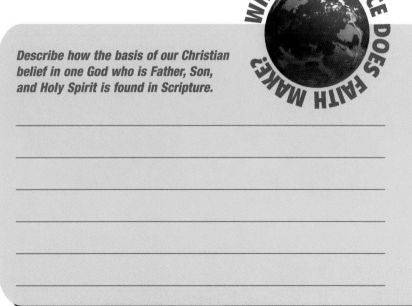

WHAT DIFFERENCE DOES FAITH MAKE?

Describe how the basis of our Christian belief in one God who is Father, Son, and Holy Spirit is found in Scripture.

_____

_____

_____

_____

_____

_____

Christians have always sought to explain their faith in the mystery of God, who is Father, Son, and Holy Spirit. This is as true today as it has been throughout the history of our Church.

The Early Councils

Beginning in the fourth century the bishops of the Church began meeting in a series of councils at Nicaea (325), Constantinople (381), Ephesus (431), and Chalcedon (451). One of the main purposes of these councils was to discuss and explain the authentic beliefs of the Church about Jesus Christ and his relationship to the Father and the Holy Spirit. At the center of this debate was Arius, who asked, "How can Jesus be God and the Father also be God?" Because he could not solve his dilemma, Arius taught that Jesus was not truly God. He believed that Jesus was created by God the Father superior in dignity to any other creature, but that Jesus was not equal to God the Father.

What was the work of the early councils of the Church?

At the Council of Nicaea, Athanasius (d. 373), the bishop of Alexandria, was one of the strongest defenders of the Church's teachings against Arius. Angered by Athanasius's unwavering stand against Arius, Emperor Constantine, a friend of Arius, took the side of Athanasius's enemies and sent him into exile. When Constantine died, Athanasius returned from exile only to find the anger of his enemies stronger than it had ever been. This forced Athanasius to flee to Rome for protection. His safety did not last very long, and four more times Athanasius was sent into exile.

Athanasius is called the Father of Orthodoxy, a word meaning "true teaching." He is honored as a saint and a Doctor of the Church.

Describe the work of Athanasius.

View of modern-day Istanbul, Turkey, site of ancient city of Constantinople.

Nature and Person

At these early councils of the Church the terms *substance* (or *nature* or *essence*) and *person* were given special meanings to explain the Christian belief in one God, who is Father, Son, and Holy Spirit. How did they use these terms to help us understand the meaning of the Trinity?

First, the *substance* (nature or essence) of God is that which makes God to be God and belongs only to God. There is only one divine nature equally and totally shared by the Father, Son, and Holy Spirit. There is only one God.

Second, they used the term *person* to explain that Father, Son, and Holy Spirit are not simply ways of looking at God. There are three divine Persons—Father, Son, and Holy Spirit—who are really distinct from one another. The Father is not the Son nor the Spirit; the Son is not the Father nor the Spirit; and the Spirit is not the Father nor the Son.

Third, the three divine Persons are "related" to one another. That relationship is like but unlike any relationship we have with someone. The relationship of the divine Persons—Father, Son, and Holy Spirit—is so close, it unites them as one God.

Explain what the Church teaches about the Holy Trinity.

The mystery of the Trinity is a **dogma** of our faith. A dogma is a truth taught by the Church as revealed by God. While this great mystery of our faith is difficult to explain in words, we believe this about God because God has revealed this truth about himself to us.

The Baptism of Jesus. Contemporary stained-glass window.

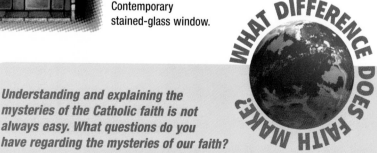

WHAT DIFFERENCE DOES FAITH MAKE?

Understanding and explaining the mysteries of the Catholic faith is not always easy. What questions do you have regarding the mysteries of our faith?

_____

_____

_____

Why do we say that everything God does all three divine Persons do?

When you read the first words of the Bible, "In the beginning, when God created the heavens and the earth" (Genesis 1:1), who do you think of when you read the word *God*? Do you think of God the Father? God the Son? God the Holy Spirit? Do you think of all three divine Persons?

The Work of the Trinity

Our language seems to limit specific works of God to a particular Person of the Holy Trinity. In the Nicene Creed we credit the work of creation to God the Father. We profess:

> We believe in one God,
> the Father, the Almighty,
> maker of heaven and earth,
> of all that is, seen and unseen.
> NICENE CREED

In talking about God's work among us, we identify each divine Person with a particular work. We call these works of God the **divine missions** of the three Persons of the Holy Trinity. We attribute the work of creation to the Father, who sent us his Son; the work of salvation to the Son, who came and lived among us and was raised from the dead; the work of sanctification, or our holiness, to the Holy Spirit, who is the love of God sent to us by the Father and the Son.

The truth is that just as God is one, God's work is also one. God's whole plan of loving-kindness is the work of God—Father, Son, and Holy Spirit. The Father is never separated from the Son and the Spirit; the Son is never separated from the Father and the Spirit; the Spirit is never separated from the Father and the Son.

How do we describe the works of the Trinity?

The Work of Creation. Contemporary stained-glass window.

The Work of Creation

Let us now take a look at the work of creation as the work of the Trinity.

God the Father

While we attribute the work of creation to God the Father, creation is truly the work of the Trinity. A closer reading of Scripture helps us see that the Son and the Holy Spirit are just as much involved in creation as the Father.

God the Son

The Gospel according to John opens:

> In the beginning was the Word, . . . and the Word was God. . . . All things came to be through him, and without him nothing came to be." JOHN 1:1, 3

The Word of God is the Son of God. Echoing the Genesis story, John the Evangelist passes on the Church's belief that the work of the Father is the work of the Son. "All things came to be through him."

God the Holy Spirit

In the Genesis account of creation, we read:

> [T]he earth was a formless wasteland, and darkness covered the abyss, while a mighty wind swept over the waters.
>
> GENESIS 1:2

We use the English word *wind* to translate the Hebrew word *ruah*. It is important to point out that the deeper meaning of the Hebrew word *ruah* cannot be captured by any one English word. What then is the meaning of this image "a mighty wind"?

At first, we might only imagine a natural phenomenon such as a hurricane or a gust of wind that sweeps us off our feet. When we read the account of creation in Genesis in light of the whole Bible, we come to understand that the phrase "a mighty wind" means much more.

Throughout the Bible, the word *spirit* is used most often to translate *ruah*. Because of this Christians have come to see this image as indicating the work of the Spirit in creation. Remember the Pentecost story? The sign of the Holy Spirit's coming upon the disciples is "a strong driving wind" (Acts of the Apostles 2:2).

Describe creation as the work of the Holy Trinity.

The work of God—Father, Son, and Spirit—among us is always the work of the Trinity. God the Father, God the Son, and God the Holy Spirit are inseparable. God has created us to share in the life of the Blessed Trinity here on earth in faith and after death in the eternal life of heaven. This is God's loving plan of creation, salvation, and sanctification.

WHAT DIFFERENCE DOES FAITH MAKE?

How is the work you do an image of the work of God in the world?

_____

_____

_____

_____

_____

WHAT
DIFFERENCE
Does This Make in Our Church?

We believe that God has revealed himself to be one God in three Persons—Father, Son, and Holy Spirit. We call this dogma of our faith the mystery of the Holy Trinity. Inseparable as one God, the divine Persons are inseparable in what they do. The Trinity creates us in the image and likeness of God and invites us to share in God's life and love here on earth in faith and after death in the eternal life of heaven. This is God's loving plan of creation, salvation, and sanctification.

The Christian Family

The Christian family is a community of persons created by God in the image of God. The family is an image of the communion of love that unites the Father and the Son in the Holy Spirit. It is a community of faith, hope, and love that is a sign of God's work among us.

A Community of Faith

It is in the family that we first learn about God and grow in our trust in his love for us. As we grow, our family teaches us many ways to live our faith. They do this in many ways—perhaps through bedtime prayers, meal prayers, reading Bible stories, celebrating Christmas and Easter, and through special family faith traditions. In our families we witness the faith of our parents, grandparents, and other family members who live the faith in their normal everyday lives.

A Community of Love

The family is where we come to know and experience what love is. The love we experience in a family is a reflection of God's great love for us. Through the experience of family love we begin to get our first glimpse of God's love for us.

Through the sacrifices our parents make for us we come to know there is no limit to God's love for us. The hugs, the smiles, the kind words lead us to see that God is Love.

A Community of Hope

It is with our family that we make our journey on earth. We discover our talents and gifts and take up our responsibilities after building a community of justice and peace, compassion and forgiveness. We become people of hope, trusting in God's promises that his kingdom will triumph. Pope John Paul II described the work of the family as "building up of the kingdom of God in history by participating in the life and mission of the Church."

The Church and the Christian family are so linked together that it creates a bond making a family a "church in miniature" or "domestic church" (*Dogmatic Constitution on the Church*, 11). The family is a living image of the mystery of the Church.

How can families show that they are communities of faith, hope, and love?

WHAT DIFFERENCE

Does It Make in My Life?

In this chapter you learned that there is one God who is Father, Son, and Holy Spirit. The Trinity is a relationship of love. You too live in a series of relationships. At the center of these relationships is God. Relationships with your family and friends are also very important. You might discover that time with your friends can sometimes get in the way of family time. When this happens, balancing friends and family isn't always easy. But it can be done.

Balancing Relationships

As teenagers you are experiencing rapid changes in your life. Your body is growing and changing. You are seeking more independence, and this may at times seem to cause a power struggle between you and your parents. Learning how to handle the increased personal responsibility that comes with more independence may sometimes seem exciting and other times it may be downright scary.

What Can You Do?

All of this is part of normal growing up. What is not part of the normal process is deliberately upsetting or destroying the harmony of your family life. How can you balance getting your needs met as a growing teenager with meeting your responsibilities as a member of your family? Learning family-living skills can help.

Skills to Help Maintain Balance in the Family

- **MUTUAL RESPECT** is honoring each family member's gifts and talents. It includes working together to find a way to meet each family member's needs in the best way possible. It is the give and take, the back and forth, and the blending of the ME and WE that makes a healthy family work.

- **COMMUNICATION** is another way to keep balance in the family. Each member of your family has his or her own views about things. A very good way to express your opinion is to use "I feel" statements. For example, "I feel angry when Johnny monopolizes the TV. I feel we should take a vote on what program we could all watch." By using "I feel" statements you can express your feelings and views calmly without forcing them on other family members. This approach can lead to respectful family discussions.

- **INDIVIDUAL RESPONSIBILITIES** are essential to family life. You belong to your family, and your family belongs to you. A family is not simply a place where we stop by to eat and sleep and refuel. The other members of your family depend on you as much as you depend on them. Taking ownership and fulfilling your responsibilities within your family goes hand-in-hand with handling your growing need for independence.

- **COOPERATION** is the wonderful thing that happens when family members look out for one another. Family is a together thing. There are no perfect families and no perfect family members, but you are very special and a very important part of your family. Remember that God loves each of you and is with you to give you help and support in your efforts to love one another.

faith decision

- Choose a partner. Have one student role-play the parent and the other role-play a teenage family member. Discuss one of the following topics: music, a curfew, an allowance, or another topic of your choosing.

- Practice using "I feel" statements as you role-play your parts. Then reverse the roles.

This week I will try to balance my need for independence with my family responsibilities by

_____

_____

_____

_____

_____ .

Faith Vocabulary

Define each of these terms:

1. mystery
2. Holy Trinity
3. blasphemy
4. dogma
5. divine missions

People and Places and Events

Identify these people, places, and events:

1. Council of Nicaea
2. Saint Athanasius
3. Constantinople, Ephesus, and Chalcedon
4. Arius
5. Emperor Constantine

Main Ideas

Choose either (a) or (b) from each set of items. Write a brief paragraph to answer each of your choices.

1. (a) What is the mystery of the Holy Trinity?

   (b) What do we learn about the Trinity from the New Testament?

2. (a) Describe the work of Athanasius and the early councils of the Church.

   (b) How do the terms *substance* and *person* help us understand the meaning of the Trinity?

3. (a) Describe the work of creation as a work of the Trinity.

   (b) Describe God's loving plan of creation, salvation, and sanctification.

Critical Thinking

Using what you have learned in this chapter, briefly explain this part of the Athanasian Creed:
"We worship one God in the Trinity and the Trinity in unity."

Family Discussion

How do we as a family continue the work of God's creation in the world?

Visit our web site at www.FaithFirst.com

JESUS CHRIST, THE ONLY SON OF GOD
UNIT 2

Parent Page—Unit 2

FAITH

In the second part of the Apostles' Creed, Christians profess their faith in Jesus Christ and his work among us while he lived on earth. Who is Jesus Christ? What is the meaning of his work among us? Unit 2 of *Creed and Prayer*, "Jesus Christ, the Only Son of God," presents the Church's teachings about Jesus.

This unit begins with the Scripture story of the Transfiguration of Jesus. By reflecting on this story, your child will be reminded that Christians believe that Jesus is the Son of God only *because* he himself has revealed his identity to us. In faith Christians believe in the unexplainable mystery of the Incarnation.

Jesus "was conceived by the Holy Spirit and born of the Virgin Mary" (Apostles' Creed). The Son of God took on flesh and became man. Jesus is truly God and truly man.

The heart of Christ's work among us is called the Paschal mystery—Christ's passion, death, resurrection, and ascension. Why did the Son of God choose to suffer so deeply, so painfully? This unit helps your child grow in his or her understanding of this mystery of God's love. By meeting Christians such as Mother Teresa of Calcutta and Archbishop Helder Camara, your child will learn how the Paschal mystery of Christ is the source of hope for all people.

WHAT DIFFERENCE DOES IT MAKE?

In this unit your child will reflect upon the birth, life, death, and resurrection of Jesus Christ. These events and their meaning are, of course, the central focus of the Christian life. When we are born into a Christian family and baptized as an infant, we grow up hearing these beautiful and powerful stories over and over. So often have we heard these gospel stories that we can easily retell them. That familiarity can, at times, disguise the deep, profound, and life-changing effect that their message should bring. Take a fresh look at these stories and your own faith in Christ. Share the "What Difference Does It Make in My Life?" pages with your child. Working through these pages together helps you breathe new meaning into the stories you know so well.

The Christian life calls each believer to see the world and all creation in a new way, through the heart and mind and eyes of Jesus Christ. This call invites each of us to examine our relationships, our attitudes, and our behaviors to see whether they have been transfigured to reflect our faith in Jesus. Do you see the face of Christ in others? How can you live in such a way that other people, especially your child, can see the face of Christ in you? As a parent you are called to respond to and reflect Jesus in your daily interactions with other people, especially with the members of your family.

This unit invites you to spend time, both alone and with your child, to reflect on the opportunities you have to see the face of Christ in others. Who in your neighborhood, in your child's school, in your workplace or faith community can Christ reach out to through you? To whom can you and your child bring Christ's message of hope in their suffering? In what concrete ways can you and your child share your faith and hope in Jesus with others?

Faith in Jesus Christ makes a difference not only in how we view life on earth but also in our hope for life with God in heaven. Loss, suffering, and death are part of every family's experience. Such times can mysteriously bring families closer together or, sadly, tear them apart. As you share this unit with your child, you might talk with him or her about times of loss in which your faith and hope in Jesus have been a source of strength and consolation for you. Perhaps there are experiences in your child's life right now that you can help her or him deal with by sharing your faith in Jesus and how it gives you strength in dealing with similar situations. These are not always easy talks to have, but they can be most meaningful for both of you. Faith in Jesus and in the meaning of his life, death, and resurrection can truly be transfiguring for those who believe!

The Transfiguration of Jesus

A Scripture Story

6

WE PRAY

God our Father,
in the transfigured glory
    of Christ your Son,
you strengthened our faith
by confirming the witness
    of your prophets,
and show us the splendor of
    your beloved sons and
    daughters.
As we listen to the voice
    of your Son,
help us to become heirs to
    eternal life with him
who lives and reigns with you
    and the Holy Spirit,
one God, for ever and ever.

FROM *ROMAN MISSAL, OPENING PRAYER,
FEAST OF THE TRANSFIGURATION*

Events that take place on mountains play an important role in the history of God's people. What stories in the Gospel do you know that contain events that take place on a mountain or a mountainside?

*LORD, God of hosts, who is
    like you? . . .
Tabor and Hermon rejoice
    in your name.*

PSALM 89:9, 13

71

Bible Background

FAITH FOCUS

Why are the events in the Bible that take place on mountains so important?

FAITH VOCABULARY

Transfiguration

tabernacle

Messiah

theophany

Mount Sinai.

Mountains just seem to attract people. Climbers are always ready to accept the challenge of climbing Mount Kilimanjaro and other majestic peaks that disappear into the clouds. For other reasons, year after year, millions of Americans and visitors from other countries vacation in the grandeur and peace of the Grand Canyon and Yosemite National Park. Why do you think people stand in wonder and awe at the base of mountains?

Mountains in the Scriptures

Mountains played a very important role in the life of God's people. Throughout the Bible the sacred writers describe key events that took place on mountains. We read about the bluffs of Moab, Gilead, and Bashan, as well as the heights of Sinai, Horeb, Hermon, Ebal, Geresim, Nebo, Tabor, and Carmel. What do these all have in common? Some of the key events of salvation and God's revelation of himself took place on mountains.

Mount Carmel.

Old Testament

Two events at the center of the history of God's people occurred near or on Mount Horeb. First, it is near Mount Horeb that God revealed his name, Yahweh, to Moses and sent Moses back to Pharaoh to free the Hebrews from slavery. Second, during the Exodus, the journey of the liberated Hebrews to the land God promised them, God entered a covenant with the Israelites on Mount Horeb and revealed the Law of the Covenant, the Decalogue. On this same mountain God appeared to Elijah.

Gospel

In the Sermon on the Mount Matthew collects a summary of Jesus' teachings. The Ascension of

72

Mount Hermon.

Did you Know...

The exact location of the Mount of the Transfiguration is not known. Many believe it is one of these three mountains: **Mount Carmel** is one of the mountains to which Elijah fled during his ordeal with the priests of Baal. It ascends steeply to a height of 2,000 feet. Covered with thickets it is very difficult to ascend.

Isolated on a plain, **Mount Tabor** rises steeply to 1,850 feet.

Mount Hermon is the highest of the three mountains. Visible from the Sea of Galilee, its summit is always snow-covered. The highest of its three peaks rises to 9,232 feet.

Jesus occurred on the Mount of Olives. It was also on a mountain that the **Transfiguration** of Jesus took place.

What is the significance of mountains in Sacred Scripture?

The Feast of Tabernacles

Some biblical scholars think that the event of the Transfiguration took place during the celebration of the Jewish feast of Tabernacles, or Booths. The word **tabernacle** comes from the Latin word meaning "tent."

The name *feast of Tabernacles* has two meanings. First, it recalls the booths or tents that the workers constructed in the fields during the harvest. Second, it refers to the story of the Israelites dwelling in tents as they wandered forty years in the desert, journeying from slavery in Egypt to the land promised them by God. Thanking and blessing God for saving his people, the Jewish people would offer an individual basket of harvest fruits and recall the saving acts of God during the Exodus.

The Prophet Elijah

Moses and the prophet Elijah both play an important role in the gospel story of the Transfiguration of Jesus. The meaning of the Hebrew name *Elijah*, "my God is Yahweh," identifies this prophet's work: Elijah championed that only the God of the Israelites, Yahweh, is the one true God.

Elijah lived in the Northern Kingdom of Israel in the ninth century B.C. This was a time that many Israelites were abandoning their faith in Yahweh as the one true God and joining their neighbors in worshiping Baal, a god of the Canaanites.

The inclusion of Moses and Elijah in the story of the Transfiguration highlights that Jesus is the final prophet in God's plan of salvation. Jesus is the final word of God.

Describe the role of Elijah in the gospel story of the Transfiguration of Jesus.

WHAT DIFFERENCE DOES FAITH MAKE?

Where do you listen for God? How do you prepare yourself to listen to God?

_____

_____

Reading the Word of God

At the conclusion of his work as a prophet, Elijah was carried to heaven in a fiery chariot with the expectation that he would one day return (see 2 Kings 2:11). Some people of Jesus' time thought Jesus was Elijah (see Matthew 16:14; Mark 6:15, 8:28; Luke 9:8).

The Transfiguration

The disciples had just told Jesus that some people thought he was Elijah, Jeremiah, or one of the other prophets. Jesus, turning to Peter, asks, "But who do you say that I am?" (Matthew 16:15). Peter enthusiastically responded, "You are the Messiah, the Son of the living God" (Matthew 16:16).

The Transfiguration.
James J. Tissot
(1836–1902), French artist.

Messiah is a Hebrew term for *Christ*, meaning "anointed one." Jesus continued, much to the objection of Peter and the certain confusion of the other disciples, saying that he, the Messiah, must go to Jerusalem to suffer, be killed, and on the third day be raised from the dead. The Messiah was the leader that Jews believed God would send to free them from oppression.

Who did Peter say that he believed Jesus to be?

Six days later, the last day of the feast of Tabernacles, Jesus took Peter, James, and John his brother up a high mountain by themselves. Matthew writes:

And he was transfigured before them; his face shone like the sun and his clothes became white as light. And behold, Moses and Elijah appeared to them, conversing with him. Then Peter said to Jesus in reply, "Lord, it is good that we are here. If you wish, I will make three tents here, one for you, one for Moses, and one for Elijah." While he was still speaking, behold, a bright cloud cast a shadow over them, then from the cloud came a voice that said, "This is my beloved Son, with whom I am well pleased; listen to him." When the disciples heard this, they fell prostrate and were very much afraid. But Jesus came and touched them, saying, "Rise, and do not be afraid." And when the disciples raised their eyes, they saw no one else but Jesus alone. MATTHEW 17:2–8

Describe the gospel story of the Transfiguration.

restore all things; but I tell you that Elijah has already come, and they did not recognize him but did to him whatever they pleased. So also will the Son of Man suffer at their hands." Then the disciples understood that he was speaking to them of John the Baptist.

MATTHEW 17:9–13

The story of the Transfiguration clarifies the identity of Jesus and his work, or ministry, on earth. Jesus is the Son of God. He came not to abolish the Law of Moses. He fulfills the Law.

Explain how Jesus clarified his work.

The greatest masterpiece of the German composer Felix Mendelssohn (1809–1847) was his oratorio *Elijah*, which he composed in 1846. An oratorio is a story told with music, using soloists, chorus, and orchestra without acting, costumes, or scenery. The drama of the story is suggested by the music, the singers, and the orchestra. Usually an oratorio is a religious story. In the first part of *Elijah* the priests of the pagan god of Baal march against Elijah and dramatically challenge God to prove he is the real God. Elijah prays to Yahweh, the God of Israel, who brings the quenching rain to the land after a long drought.

The Coming of Elijah

As they were coming down from the mountain, Jesus charged them, "Do not tell the vision to anyone until the Son of Man has been raised from the dead." Then the disciples asked him, "Why do the scribes say that Elijah must come first?" He said in reply, "Elijah will indeed come and

Church of the Transfiguration on Mount Tabor.

WHAT DIFFERENCE DOES FAITH MAKE?

How can you come to know Jesus better?

_____

_____

_____

_____

Understanding the Word of God

FAITH FOCUS

Why is it important for Christians today to read and retell the story of the Transfiguration?

Stained-glass window of Moses receiving the Ten Commandments on Mount Sinai (Deuteronomy 9:10–11).

Stained-glass window of Elijah riding to heaven. (2 Kings 2:11).

The word *transfiguration* means "marked change in appearance, especially a change that glorifies." Something so amazing occurred on the mountain that Matthew can barely describe it. Peter, James, and John were astounded. One moment Jesus was as they knew him; the next he appeared very different; then he was the same again. Jesus' appearance changed so incredibly that the evangelist has to compare Jesus' appearance to a powerful natural phenomenon: Jesus' face becomes bright "like the sun and his clothes became white as light" (Matthew 17:2).

What is the meaning of the word transfiguration?

A Theophany

Matthew wrote his account of the Gospel for Jewish Christians who were being pushed out of the Jewish community. These readers would quickly make a connection between the radiant change in Jesus' appearance and the place of that change, a mountain. Listening to the account of the Transfiguration, they would interpret the Transfiguration as a **theophany.** The word *theophany* means "an appearance of God."

Matthew's readers would do this for three reasons. First, the history of God's dealing with his people is filled with stories of God appearing and revealing himself to them on a mountain. Second, Moses and Elijah were included in the story. Third, a voice came from heaven.

Moses and Elijah

The inclusion of Moses, who spoke with God on Mount Sinai, and Elijah, who spoke with God on Mount Carmel, are symbols of the Law and the Prophets. In Jesus the Old Covenant is being fulfilled. The two pillars upon which Jewish tradition is based—the Law (delivered by Moses) and the Prophets (symbolized by Elijah)—are brought to fulfillment in Jesus.

A Voice from Heaven

A voice from heaven said, "This is my beloved Son, with whom I am well pleased; listen to him" (Matthew 17:5). The disciples cowered in fear—a reverential fear of God, who is all holy. From then on, the disciples were to listen to Jesus. Jesus is the Word of God.

Describe the meaning of Matthew's account of the Transfiguration.

Jesus' Passion and Death

Jesus soon traveled to Jerusalem where he was arrested, tried, and crucified upon the cross. At the Transfiguration Peter, James, and John were given a glimpse into the meaning of that suffering. After witnessing the Transfiguration, the disciples learned that suffering and death were the way to Jesus' future glory. This faith would sustain the disciples and the readers of Matthew in the dark days ahead.

How does the Transfiguration help us understand the future events in the life of Jesus?

We too need to hear and believe in the message of the Transfiguration. Jesus is God's beloved Son. To live as Jesus' disciples, we must listen with faith. When we do, the appearances of things change. We will see things in a new light.

When you see things with the eyes of faith, how does it transfigure, or change, what you see and what you hear?

WHAT DIFFERENCE DOES FAITH MAKE?

Describe a situation in your life that made all the difference when you looked at it with eyes of faith.

_____

_____

WHAT DIFFERENCE

Does This Make in Our Church?

Mother Teresa in Atlanta, Georgia.

In the gospel story of the Transfiguration, the body of Jesus was transfigured, or changed in appearance. The disciples saw Jesus in a new way. They came to see Jesus with the eyes of faith. They came to believe that Jesus is truly the Son of God and the fulfillment of the Law and the Prophets.

Her work made a difference in our world. Filled with the spirit of compassion, Mother Teresa saw beyond the pain and disease that disguised the human dignity of those who were destitute and suffering and dying on the streets of Calcutta, India. She was drawn to be a sign of God's love in action to the poorest of the poor.

Mother Teresa made such a difference in the world that in 1979 she was awarded the Nobel Prize for Peace. In 1996 she became the fourth person ever to be nominated as an honorary citizen of America.

Mother Teresa of Calcutta

Mother Teresa of Calcutta (1910–1997) saw everyone and everything through the eyes of faith. She dedicated the last forty years of her life to ministering with the poorest of the poor of the world.

The Difference a Life Makes

The entire world mourned Mother Teresa's death on September 5, 1997. This poem by Elsa Joy Bailey reflects on Mother Teresa's life and message.

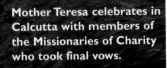

Mother Teresa celebrates in Calcutta with members of the Missionaries of Charity who took final vows.

MOTHER TERESA
1910–1997

Once
Mother Teresa was asked
how she could continue
day after day after day,
visiting the terminally ill:
feeding them, wiping their brows,
giving them comfort
as they lay dying.

And she said,
"It's not hard
because in each one,
I see the face of Christ
in one of His more
distressing disguises."

And that
is Mother's teaching:
To urge us to see
the face of Christ
in each one of His
numerous disguises
wherever we go.

And not just in those
who are ill or in pain
or in obvious hunger,
but in all the others, too.
I mean those
who are suffering
from spiritual poverty
and bleak, imprisoned mindsets
which block their freedom;
and wall them off
from personal growth
and self realization.

The Missionaries of
Charity distributing
food, clothing, and
medicine in Kosovo.

These beings too,
need our Silent Love
for their pain is just as deep.

That is Mother Teresa's message
about spiritual power.
There are thousands
of brothers and sisters
who need our blessing.

You don't have to go far
to find them.
They're right beside you
at work or in school.
They drive next to you
on the freeway.
They shop with you at
the grocery store.

In fact,
you can probably
find someone
you need to bless
right in your own mirror.

*Who has inspired you to see people and
events with the eyes of faith? When have
you seen someone suffering with the eyes
of faith? How did you respond?*

WHAT DIFFERENCE

Does It Make in My Life?

The events Peter, James, and John experienced at the Transfiguration changed the way they looked at things. At Baptism you receive a new gift of sight. You receive the power to see things in a new way. You are blessed with the grace to see people, places, and events with the eyes of faith. What some may see as a majestic mountain, you can now see as a sign of the presence of Almighty God in your life.

Seeing with Eyes of Faith

Here are some skills you can practice to help you see things differently. Using these skills will help you move beyond the first impressions you may have of people, places, and events. These skills will sharpen your vision. They will help you place your expectations aside; they will help you look for the deeper meaning of things. They will help you see God present in your life and the life of others.

1. **Take some time.**
   Look more closely and see beyond the surface. At first glance a person or a situation may be easily misinterpreted.

2. **Ask questions.**
   This helps clarify the situation. Sometimes things are not what they seem. People are not always who they appear to be. Some people put on masks and pretend to be tough or aloof or not friendly.

3. **Get to know the person.**
   Sometimes people are afraid to let you know who they really are because you may laugh at them or not like them or accept them. Reach out to someone new. Be willing to give someone a chance to share who they really are.

4. **Take off your masks.**
   Do not put on airs or pretend to be something or someone else. Let people really get to know you and you'll find out they can really like you. If possible, try always to be yourself. Remember an original is better than a copy. There is no one else quite like you. You truly are unique and special in all the world.

5. **Don't judge.**
   There is a saying, "Don't judge a book by its cover." Don't judge others because of the clothes they wear or the music they like or their appearance. The best skill to practice is not to judge anyone at all. Judging others before you have all the facts is the basis of prejudice. See the goodness within people. Try to treat others the way you would like them to treat you. Remember we are all God's children.

faith decision

- Form a small group. Discuss ways you can see things differently if you try to practice one of the above skills.

- Describe a situation where you learned more information and you gained new insight by getting to know someone better.

- Explain how Jesus showed us that you cannot "judge a book by its cover."

This week I will try to see with the eyes of faith by

_____
_____
_____
_____
_____
_____ .

Faith Vocabulary

Define each of these terms:
1. transfiguration
2. tabernacle
3. messiah
4. theophany

People and Places and Events

Identify these people, places, and events:
1. Elijah
2. Mount Sinai
3. feast of Tabernacles
4. Mount Tabor
5. Moses

Main Ideas

Choose either (a) or (b) from each set of items. Write a paragraph to answer each of your choices.

1. (a) Describe the importance of mountains in the events of God's people.

   (b) Describe what the presence of Moses and Elijah at the Transfiguration tells us about the meaning of this event.

2. (a) What does the voice from heaven at the Transfiguration tell Peter, James, and John?

   (b) What is the main message of the event of the Transfiguration?

3. (a) Why do we call the Transfiguration a theophany?

   (b) What is the connection between the Transfiguration and Jesus' passion and death?

Critical Thinking

Using what you have learned in this chapter, briefly explain this statement:
When we see people, places, and events in our lives through the eyes of faith, they are "transfigured" before our eyes.

Family Discussion

Why is the true meaning of things that happen in our family not always what it first appears to be?

Visit our
web site at
www.FaithFirst.com

Jesus Christ, the Son of God

7

WE PRAY

Father, all-powerful and
    ever-living God,
we do well always and
    everywhere
to give you thanks
through Jesus Christ
    our Lord.
His future coming was
    proclaimed by all the
    prophets.
The virgin mother
bore him in her womb
with love beyond all telling.

From *Preface, Advent II*

Would you agree or disagree
that the words *Christmas* and
gift are synonymous? In your
own words explain why we
celebrate Christmas.

*But when the fullness of time
had come, God sent his Son,
born of a woman, born under
the law.*   Galatians 4:4

The Word Became Flesh

FAITH FOCUS

What was Mary's role in God's plan of salvation?

FAITH VOCABULARY

Immaculate Conception

Lord

YHWH

Incarnation

kingdom of God

Excitement fills a family as it awaits the birth of a child. Family members carefully prepare for the newest member to be born. Friends bring gifts to make the baby's arrival special. Parents and siblings wonder, How much will the baby weigh? What color eyes will the baby have? Who will the baby look like? A name is chosen. The crib is carefully made up. What other things might family members do or talk about as they await the birth of a new baby?

Preparing the Way

God worked for centuries among his people, the Israelites, preparing the world for the birth of his Son. Through kings, like David and Solomon, and prophets, like Isaiah and Jeremiah, God promised to send his people a messiah, or an anointed one, who would save his people. The mighty, like David and Deborah, as well as the humble, like Ruth and Naomi, all had a role to play in setting the stage for the most important birth that the human family would ever experience. In ways that we still do not fully recognize, the Holy Spirit was at work in human history and in the hearts of individuals bringing about God's plan for the birth of the Savior, Jesus Christ.

Paul the Apostle wrote:

> But when the fullness of time had come, God sent his Son, born of a woman, born under the law.
>
> GALATIANS 4:4

In the fullness of time, the Holy Spirit brought that plan about in Mary. By the action of the Spirit in Mary, God the Father gave the world his Son, Emmanuel (a name meaning "God with us"), who is Jesus, the Savior. The name *Jesus* means "God saves." (See Isaiah 7:14 and Matthew 1:22–23.)

How did the Holy Spirit help prepare people for the birth of the Son of God?

Mary Visits Elizabeth. Stained-glass window.

84

Blessed Mary, Ever-Virgin

From among all the women who ever lived, God chose the Virgin Mary to be the mother of his Son. She is God's "favored one" (Luke 1:28), who was full of grace from the very beginning of her existence. Prepared by the grace of the Holy Spirit for the unique role that she would play in God's plan, Mary was

totally preserved from the stain of original sin. Neither did she commit any personal sin throughout her entire life. We call this her **Immaculate Conception.**

The Virgin Mary carried in her womb and gave birth to her only son, the only begotten Son of God, whom she and Joseph named Jesus. We honor Mary as Blessed Mary, Ever-Virgin.

Mary remained a virgin in conceiving her Son, a virgin in giving birth to him, and after giving birth to him Mary remained a virgin her whole and entire life. (See *Catechism of the Catholic Church,* 510.)

Mary is truly the Mother of God because she is the mother of Jesus, the eternal Son of God. Through Mary the Eternal Word was made visible in human flesh, revealing to the Gentiles, or non-Jews (see Matthew 2:11) and to the poor and lowly (see Luke 2:15–20) the good news of God's love for the world. Through her and in her son, Jesus, everything in the Old Testament converges and comes to fulfillment.

Describe the special role of Mary in God's plan to send us a savior.

Proclaiming the Good News

The Holy Spirit prepared the heart of Mary and countless others for the coming of the Lord. So too the Holy Spirit works in us and through us to bring Jesus to others. As we come to know and love Jesus ourselves, the Holy Spirit stirs within us the desire to share his good news with others. We, like Mary, do what God asks of us.

Did you Know...

The Holy Spirit also worked through John the Baptist to prepare for the coming of Jesus. During her pregnancy, Mary visited her relative Elizabeth, who was herself pregnant. The Holy Spirit stirred the infant in Elizabeth's womb, and he leapt for joy at the coming of the Messiah. (Read about the birth of John the Baptist and Mary's visitation of Elizabeth in Luke 1:5–80.)

In several places the Gospel also describes John the Baptist's work. You can learn more about John the Baptist by reading:
- Matthew 3:1–17
- Matthew 11:2–19
- Matthew 14:1–12
- Mark 1:2–11
- Luke 7:18–35

WHAT DIFFERENCE DOES FAITH MAKE?

What are some of the ways that you think the Holy Spirit may be asking you to tell others about Jesus?

_____

_____

_____

The story is told that in the early days of the Church, during the era of persecutions, Christians developed secret signs to identify themselves to fellow believers. One of these signs was the outline of a fish, which could be easily traced in the dirt.

Why, you might ask, did the early believers in Jesus choose the shape of a fish to identify themselves to one another? In Greek the letters ICHTHUS spell the Greek word for "fish." But the letters are also an acronym meaning "Jesus Christ, Son of God, Savior." An acronym is a word or phrase formed from the first letters or syllables of other words.

Truly God and Truly Human

In order to be a Christian, a person must believe that Jesus Christ is truly the Son of God. The willingness and readiness of Christians to make this profession of faith in Jesus Christ is what makes us Christians.

What are the letters of the Greek word for "fish"? What meaning did the early Christians give these letters?

The Word of God

The Gospel makes it clear that Jesus' relationship with God the Father is totally unique.

The Gospel according to John begins with this profession of faith in Jesus:

> In the beginning was the Word,
> and the Word was with God,
> and the Word was God. . . .
> And the Word became flesh
> and made his dwelling
> among us.   JOHN 1:1, 14

Jesus is the eternally existing Word, who has always existed with the Father. Christians have believed this from the earliest days of the Church.

Jesus Is Lord

Christians believe that Jesus is divine. He is truly God. This belief is proclaimed in many ways in the Gospel and other New Testament writings. For example, in the New Testament we read the expression "Jesus Christ is Lord" (Philippians 2:11). This was a clear profession of faith that Jesus is truly divine, or God.

The English word **Lord** translates the Greek word *kyrios*. It is important to know that *kyrios* is also the Greek word the writers of the New Testament used to translate **YHWH.** YHWH are the Hebrew letters for the name God revealed to Moses (see Exodus 3:14). It is the name that the writers of the Scriptures used only for God.

Describe the importance of using the word kyrios for Jesus in the New Testament.

Two Natures in One Person

For many centuries Christians searched for the words to express this great mystery of our faith. They knew Jesus was human—he lived and walked among us; he died and was raised from the dead and appeared to his disciples before he ascended to his Father. The evidence for this is unmistakable. It is found not only in the four accounts of the Gospel but also in other Christian and non-Christian writings.

But how can we express our faith that Jesus is both human and divine? What words could possibly help others understand this great mystery of our faith?

Drawing from the language of the philosophy of their day, the bishops at the first two ecumenical councils of Nicaea (A.D. 325) and Constantinople (A.D. 381) chose the words *nature* and *person*. Our nature makes us what we are. Our person makes us who we are. For example, our human nature is what makes us human or gives us our humanness. This is different from the nature of an animal, like a squirrel, which gives the squirrel its "squirrelness."

In Jesus there are two natures, one human and one divine, that are united in a single Person, the Son of God, the second Person of the Trinity. This teaching does not mean that Jesus is part God and part man. Jesus Christ is true God and true man. The Son of God truly became human while remaining truly God.

Describe how the Church explains our belief that Jesus is truly God and truly man.

We call this the mystery of the **Incarnation.** The Incarnation is the wonderful union of the divine and human natures in the one Person of God the Son. God the Son became truly and fully human, or "took on flesh," without ceasing to be God.

Today, in most countries around the world, Christians do not have to secretly identify themselves as Christians. We can publicly and openly profess our faith in Jesus Christ. Each Sunday at Mass Catholics proclaim this faith for all to hear:
> We believe in one Lord, Jesus Christ.

Nativity detail. Bronze doors, Church of the Annunciation, Nazareth.

Did you Know...

An ecumenical council is a meeting of the bishops with and under the leadership of the pope. An ecumenical council has supreme authority over the Church in matters of doctrine, morals, worship, and discipline. There have been twenty-one ecumenical councils of the Church. The last council, Vatican Council II, was held in four sessions in Saint Peter's Basilica in Rome, Italy.

Pope John XXIII convoked Vatican II and opened the first session on October 11, 1962. Pope John died on June 3, 1963. Pope Paul VI, the next pope, reconvened the council for three more sessions. The fourth and last session ended on December 8, 1965.

WHAT DIFFERENCE DOES FAITH MAKE?

How would you explain your faith that Jesus is truly God and truly man?

_____

_____

_____

Jesus told his disciples, "Whoever has seen me has seen the Father" (John 14:9). Imagine the questions that ran through the minds of Jesus' disciples. What might they have been thinking of when Jesus continued:

"How can you say, 'Show us the Father'? Do you not believe that I am in the Father and the Father is in me?"   JOHN 14:9–10

This gospel story reminds us that Jesus' entire life—his words and actions, his gestures and silences, everything about him—reveals the mystery of God—Father, Son, and Holy Spirit—at work among us. As one Christian put it: Jesus is, in a real sense, the human face of God among us.

The Infancy and Childhood of Jesus

The gospel accounts of Matthew and Luke share with us stories about Jesus' infancy and childhood. Each of these stories points to what the early Christians came to believe about Jesus.

- Jesus' birth in Bethlehem points to our belief that Jesus is the savior whom God promised would come from the house of David. (See Matthew 1:18–25, Luke 2:1–20.)

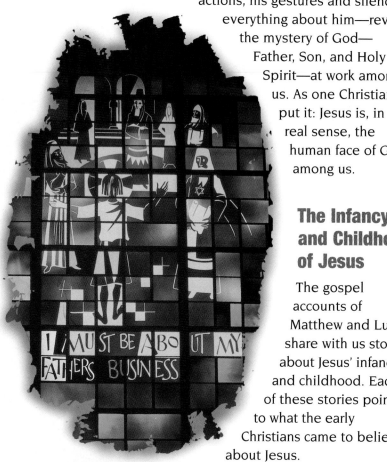

Jesus at Twelve in the Temple. Stained-glass window.

- The magi tell us that Jesus is the Savior of all people. (See Matthew 2:1–12.)
- The circumcision and naming of Jesus, the Savior, fulfills the Law of Moses and the covenant that God entered into with the Israelites. (See Luke 2:21.)
- The flight of the Holy Family to Egypt and their return to Nazareth remind us of the Exodus. In Jesus all people would be freed from the power of sin. (See Matthew 2:13–15, 19–23.)
- His presentation in the Temple shows that Jesus is dedicated to God and the service of God. (See Luke 2:22–40.)
- The story of finding the boy Jesus in the Temple in Jerusalem teaches us that doing his Father's will is the focus of Jesus' whole life on earth. (See Luke 2:41–51.)

What do the infancy stories in the gospel accounts of Matthew and Luke tell us about Jesus?

The Public Life of Jesus

Details of the public life of Jesus vary in each of the four accounts of the Gospel. But the major lines of the story in each account of the Gospel offer a basic shape to the life of Jesus on earth and its meaning for humankind.

Jesus' public ministry began with his baptism in the Jordan River by John the Baptist (see Luke 3:21–22). Then filled with the Holy Spirit, Jesus journeyed into the desert. There the devil tempted Jesus to betray his Father and the work given to him. After rejecting the devil's offers, Jesus returned to Galilee and his

Jesus Washing the Feet of Peter at the Last Supper. Stained-glass window.

hometown of Nazareth. There on the Sabbath he met in the synagogue with his neighbors as he had so often done before.

What happened this time was different—and unexpected. All eyes were riveted on Jesus. He stood, took the scroll of the prophet Isaiah, and deliberately unrolled it, obviously looking for a particular passage. Finding the passage, he read it aloud:

> "The Spirit of the Lord is upon me,
> because he has anointed me
>   to bring glad tidings to
>   the poor.
> He has sent me to proclaim liberty
>   to captives
>   and recovery of sight to the
>   blind,
>   to let the oppressed go free,
> and to proclaim a year acceptable
>   to the Lord."   LUKE 4:18–19

Jesus' entire ministry is marked by a tireless proclamation that the kingdom promised by God through the prophets "is at hand" (Mark 1:15). The invitation to be part of the kingdom is directed to everyone, but in a special way to the poor and lowly (see Luke 14:15–24) and those who acknowledge they are sinners (see Luke 15:1–32, 19:1–10). Teaching in parables, Jesus explains the true meaning of the **kingdom of God** (see Matthew 13:31–33; Luke 13:18–21, 14:15–24). The kingdom of God is the image used in the Bible to describe all people and creation living in communion with God. It will come about when Christ comes again at the end of time. There all his faithful followers will one day live with him and his Father in happiness forever (see Matthew 5:3–12, 25:31–46).

Describe the purpose of the public ministry of Jesus.

Since the beginning of his public ministry, Jesus has gathered disciples (see Matthew 4:18–22). Through his teachings Jesus makes it clear that at the heart of all that his disciples are to say and do in his name is the command: "[L]ove one another. As I have loved you, so you also should love one another. This is how all will know that you are my disciples, if you have love for one another" (John 13:34–35).

WHAT DIFFERENCE DOES FAITH MAKE?

How can you be a sign that helps others come to know God a little better?

_____

_____

_____

89

WHAT DIFFERENCE

Does This Make in Our Church?

God worked for centuries among the Israelites, preparing the world for the birth of the Savior. In the fullness of time the Holy Spirit brought that plan about in Mary. By the action of the Spirit in the Virgin Mary, God the Father gave the world his Son. We call the mystery of the Son of God taking on flesh, or becoming human, the mystery of the Incarnation.

Symbols for Jesus Christ

From its beginning the Church has created and used symbols to help us understand and profess our faith in Jesus. Christian symbols express in images the same gospel message that the Bible and the Church express in words.

Alpha and Omega

The alpha and the omega are the first and last letters of the Greek alphabet. In the New Testament Book of Revelation, Jesus calls himself the Alpha and the Omega. He existed before anything else and will always exist. He is the First and the Last. This symbol expresses our faith both in the eternity and infinity of God and in Christ, who is the Beginning and the End.

Chi-Rho

The Chi-Rho is an abbreviation of *Christ*. The chi and the rho are the first two Greek letters of the word *Christ*.

Lamb of God

The lamb has been a symbol of both innocence and sacrifice. The Lamb of God is an ancient symbol of the sinless Christ and his sacrifice.

Butterfly

The butterfly is a symbol of the Risen Christ. A butterfly metamorphoses from a caterpillar to a chrysalis and finally becomes a butterfly. Christ was born of Mary to become human, was crucified and buried in a tomb, and then was raised from the dead as the glorified Christ.

Loaves and Fishes

The Gospel tells many stories in which Jesus feeds the crowds with bread and fish. From the earliest days of the Church, loaves and fishes have been a symbol both of Jesus, the Bread of Life, and the Eucharist.

Dogwood

The dogwood is a symbol of the suffering Christ. When the dogwood tree blossoms in the springtime, the blossom resembles a cross. There is a marking on the rim of each blossom that looks like a nail print. The center circle resembles a crown of thorns.

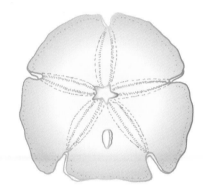

Sand Dollar

The sand dollar is a symbol of Christ, the Son of David, who is the Savior of the world. The sand dollar is an animal that lives slightly buried in the sand in shallow waters along the coastline. Its dried skeleton forms a shell that looks like a large coin. The top of the shell has openings for breathing that resemble the five-pointed star of Bethlehem. The five narrow slits also are symbolic of the five wounds of Christ.

Think about your faith in Jesus. Choose a belief that is very important to you. Create a symbol that you can use to share your faith with others.

WHAT DIFFERENCE

Does It Make in My Life?

As a disciple of Jesus, you are one of the greatest symbols of Christ. You are a follower, or disciple, of Christ. When members of your family, classmates, and neighbors see you and listen to you, you are a sign or symbol of God's saving love for them. Christ works through you to bring his love, healing, understanding, and compassion to others.

Respecting and Accepting Differences

Jesus treated everyone with love and respect. He accepted all people—Jewish people and Romans, children and adults, widows and newlyweds, soldiers and scribes and tax collectors. Respecting others and accepting others are the keys to loving one another as Jesus loves us. They are keys to being a living symbol of Christ.

Get Together. Diana Ong, Chinese/USA, 1940.

Living Symbols of Christ

Being a living symbol of Christ is not always easy. You, like everyone else, need to work at accepting all people—even those you do not like.

Most people find it easy to like people who seem to be somewhat like themselves. Think of how much you and your friends have in common. You probably share more likes than differences. You may share the same music, sports, and hobbies. You enjoy being together and just seem to get along well, at least most of the time.

Sometimes the differences we have keep us from accepting and respecting others. For example: They speak a language different from yours, or the color of their skin might be different from yours. They might not be as athletic or smart or popular as you would like them to be. Or you might not like someone because their personality clashes with yours.

Not liking something about a person is okay. What is not okay is ridiculing and making fun of someone because they are different from you. We all need to work at treating people with the respect they deserve because they are children of God, created by God as unique and special persons.

How does peer pressure affect your acceptance of others?

What Can You Do?

Here are some things you can do to work on accepting others and treating everyone with the respect they deserve.

❖ Remember that each person is a child of God.
❖ Take the time to get to know the other person.
❖ Look for the goodness within each person.
❖ Treat others as you would want them to treat you.
❖ Ask the Holy Spirit to be your helper and guide.

faith decision

- Form a small group. Identify ways that students in your school treat one another with respect.

- Describe a situation when students' differences are used to leave them out of things.

- How can you be a living symbol of Christ in that situation?

This week I will work at being a clearer sign of Christ in my school by

_____
_____
_____
_____
_____
_____ .

Faith Vocabulary

Define each of these terms:

1. Immaculate Conception
2. Lord
3. YHWH
4. Incarnation
5. kingdom of God

People and Places and Events

Identify these people, places, and events:

1. Mary
2. Council of Nicaea
3. Council of Constantinople

Main Ideas

Choose either (a) or (b) from each set of items. Write a brief paragraph to answer each of your choices.

1. (a) Describe the role God chose for Mary in his plan of salvation.

   (b) Explain how God prepared the way for the coming of his Son to live among us.

2. (a) Explain what the Church means when it teaches that Jesus Christ is truly God and truly man.

   (b) What did the early Christians mean when they said "Jesus Christ is Lord" (Philippians 2:11)?

3. (a) Describe what the infancy stories in Matthew's and Luke's accounts of the Gospel teach us about the Church's faith in Jesus.

   (b) What do we mean by the public life, or ministry, of Jesus?

Critical Thinking

Using what you have learned in this chapter, briefly explain this statement:
In order to be a Christian, a person must believe that Jesus Christ is the Son of God.

Family Discussion

Through his teachings Jesus made it clear that at the heart of what his disciples are to do and say in his name is the command: "[L]ove one another. As I have loved you, so you also should love one another" (John 13:34). What things do we say and do that are signs we are living this command of Jesus?

Visit our web site at www.FaithFirst.com

The Suffering Servant

8

A Scripture Story

WE PRAY

Lord,
by shedding his blood for us,
your Son, Jesus Christ,
established the paschal
    mystery.
In your goodness, make us holy
and watch over us always.

FROM *OPENING PRAYER,*
GOOD FRIDAY

In the Bible a prophet is someone God chooses to speak to God's people in his name. Who are some of the prophets you have learned about? Briefly describe their message to God's people.

Son though he was, he learned obedience from what he suffered; and when he was made perfect, he became the source of eternal salvation for all who obey him.

HEBREWS 5:8–9

Bible Background

FAITH FOCUS

What was the role of the servant songs in the prophecy of Isaiah?

People get messages all the time. Delivering messages and delivering them safely and on time is so important that today companies have been formed just for that purpose. When have you ever been asked to deliver a message to someone? How important was it for you to get the message there correctly and on time?

FAITH VOCABULARY

prophet

suffering Servant

Prophets in the Bible

The Bible is filled with people whom God chose to deliver his message to God's people. Among these messengers the **prophets** have an important place. The word *prophet* comes from a Greek word that means "one who speaks before others."

The biblical prophets from Israel were a unique group of individuals who were appointed and chosen by God to speak in his name. Sometimes the person welcomed God's call. At other times the prophet feared the consequences of accepting God's call and bringing the often unwelcome message of God to the people.

What is a biblical prophet?

The Messages of the Prophets

The prophets brought many varied messages to the people from God. Many prophets, like Jeremiah, often denounced God's people for abandoning the Covenant and placing their trust and faith in the false gods their neighbors worshiped and honored. Other prophets, like Amos, condemned injustice and reminded God's people of their obligation and responsibility to care for one another—especially the poor and widowed. Still other prophets,

Isaiah. Stained-glass window.

like Isaiah, delivered messages of hope to God's people during times of suffering and persecution. All the prophets encouraged God's people to place their trust in God. They reminded God's people that God was always with them and always faithful to them—even when they abandoned God.

What were some of the messages the prophets brought to the people?

Isaiah the Prophet

Of all the Old Testament prophets, Isaiah is named most often in the New Testament—thirteen times in the accounts of the Gospel, three times in the Acts of the Apostles, and six times in the Letter to the Romans. We know very little about the life of the prophet Isaiah. The only details about his life are found in the Book of Isaiah.

Isaiah lived and worked in the city of Jerusalem between 742 B.C. and 701 B.C. during the time of the Assyrian conquest of western Asia. He was married and had two sons, and probably came from an aristocratic family. The message of Isaiah to God's people is perhaps clearly summarized in the very meaning of the name I*saiah*, which is "Yahweh is salvation."

The Servant Songs

The Book of Isaiah has sixty-six chapters, which are divided into three parts: Chapters 1–39, Chapters 40–55, and Chapters 56–66. The second part of the book contains four poems, or songs, called servant songs. These passages focus on a figure called the "Servant of Yahweh." The best known of these images of the servant is that of the **suffering Servant.**

The suffering Servant was probably not a specific person but rather the idealization, or ideal or perfect image, of the faithful Jew suffering in exile. The suffering of the Jewish people in exile would serve as a light to the nations. Their lives were an offering for the sins of the nations. When the Jewish people were freed from exile, other nations would acknowledge Yahweh as the one true God.

Describe the servant songs.

The second part of the Book of Isaiah was also written to celebrate God's promise to free the Jews from exile. It encouraged the people in the huge task of rebuilding the nation of Israel.

WHAT DIFFERENCE DOES FAITH MAKE?

Write a message for a bumper sticker that tells its readers about God.

_____

_____

_____

_____

FAITH FOCUS

What is the message of the fourth servant song?

The last of the four servant songs gives an extraordinary description of a sinless servant who by his voluntary suffering atones for the sins of his people.

See, my servant shall prosper,
    he shall be raised high and
        greatly exalted.
Even as many were amazed
        at him—
so marred was his look beyond
    that of man,
and his appearance beyond
    that of mortals—

So shall he startle many nations,
    because of him kings shall
        stand speechless;
For those who have not been told
    shall see,
    those who have not heard shall
        ponder it.

Who would believe what we have
    heard?
To whom has the arm of the
    LORD been revealed?
He grew up like a sapling
    before him,
    like a shoot from the parched
        earth;
There was in him no stately
    bearing to make us look
        at him,
    nor appearance that would
        attract us to him.

Stations of the Cross.
Contemporary stained-glass windows.

Seventh Station.
Jesus Falls the Second Time.

Ninth Station.
Jesus Falls the Third Time.

Eighth Station.
Jesus Meets the Women.

He was spurned and avoided by
      men,
   a man of suffering, accustomed
      to infirmity,
One of those from whom men
      hide their faces,
   spurned, and we held him in
      no esteem.

Yet it was our infirmities that he
      bore,
   our sufferings that he endured,
While we thought of him as
      stricken,
   as one smitten by God and
      afflicted.
But he was pierced for our
      offenses,
   crushed for our sins,
Upon him was the chastisement
      that makes us whole,
   by his stripes we were healed.
We had all gone astray like
      sheep,
   each following his own way;
But the LORD laid upon him
   the guilt of us all.
Though he was harshly treated,
      he submitted
   and opened not his mouth;
Like a lamb led to the slaughter
   or a sheep before the shearers,
   he was silent and opened not
      his mouth.
Oppressed and condemned, he
      was taken away,
   and who would have thought
      any more of his destiny? . . .

If he gives his life as an offering
      for sin,
   he shall see his descendants in
      a long life,
   and the will of the LORD shall be
      accomplished through him.

Because of his affliction
   he shall see the light in
      fullness of days;
Through his suffering, my servant
   shall justify many,
   and their guilt he shall bear.
Therefore I will give him his
      portion among the great,
   and he shall divide the spoils
      with the mighty,
Because he surrendered himself
      to death
   and was counted among the
      wicked;
And he shall take away the sins
      of many,
   and win pardon for their
      offenses.

ISAIAH 52:13–15; 53:1–8, 10–12

**Why did the servant of God described in
this passage from Isaiah suffer?**

Jesus' first followers were Jews who
would have been very familiar with
the writings of the prophet Isaiah.
Reflecting on this passage, they
would come to believe that this
prophecy of Isaiah was fulfilled in
Jesus Christ, who suffered and shed
his blood "on behalf of many for the
forgiveness of sins" (Matthew 26:28).

*When have you suffered
for someone else?*

_____

_____

_____

The Suffering Church

Christians quickly came to realize that they, like Jesus, would suffer too. It didn't take many years for them to understand the meaning of Jesus' words:

> "Whoever wishes to come after me must deny himself, take up his cross, and follow me. For whoever wishes to save his life will lose it, but whoever loses his life for my sake will find it."
>
> MATTHEW 16:24–25

Still struggling with the suffering and crucifixion of Jesus, they were soon faced with the need to make sense of their own suffering. The fourth servant song not only helped the followers of Jesus understand why Jesus had to suffer and die but also gave meaning to their own suffering. Joined to Christ in Baptism, Christians now recognized that their pains and suffering were making a difference. They came to realize that their suffering has meaning and value for their own salvation and the salvation of the world.

How did the prophecy of Isaiah help the early Church understand Jesus?

FAITH FOCUS

Why did Christians come to identify Jesus as the suffering Servant described by Isaiah?

This fourth and last of the servant songs is an extraordinarily clear description of Jesus, the Son of God, who would freely choose to shed his blood for the forgiveness of sin. Jesus, the sinless Servant of God, suffered voluntarily to atone for the sins of all people. The agony of the suffering Servant, Jesus, saved all the people from just punishment from God.

In what way can Jesus be referred to as the suffering Servant?

Celebration of the Lord's Passion, Good Friday. Ministers reverence altar.

Good Friday

Today the Church remembers and celebrates Christ's passion and death at the Good Friday liturgy. The events of this holy day, the second day of the Easter Triduum, help focus on Jesus, the suffering Servant of God.

the prophecy of Isaiah. In his agony in the Garden of Gethsemane, in his scourging at the pillar, in his crucifixion on the cross, Jesus took on and shared in all human pain. Christ still suffers in his members, joined to him in Baptism. As Christians our own suffering and pain is a sign of Christ's suffering. We proclaim the great mystery of our faith—by the death of Jesus, we are freed from dying.

Celebration of the Lord's Passion, Good Friday. Veneration of the Cross.

The Good Friday liturgy helps open our eyes to see what Jesus did for us. Through hearing and reflecting on the Scripture readings, we see that Jesus was not the helpless victim. Jesus freely suffered and gave his life for us. The veneration of the cross, which is another part of the Good Friday liturgy, is a tangible sign of our deep gratitude and love for Jesus, the Son of God, who suffered, died, and gave his life for us.

Describe the liturgy for Good Friday.

The celebration of Good Friday helps us connect the suffering of Christ with our own life in Christ. Christ, who was without sin, fulfilled

WHAT DIFFERENCE DOES FAITH MAKE?

What prayers or thoughts help you deal with suffering?

_____

_____

_____

WHAT DIFFERENCE

Does This Make in Our Church?

The prophet Isaiah comforted and encouraged the Jewish people as they were suffering during and after the Babylonian Exile. As the early Christian community read the servant songs from the Book of Isaiah, they identified Christ with the suffering Servant of Isaiah. They also came to see a deeper value and meaning to their own suffering.

Archbishop Helder Camara

In our own time, people bring us comfort and hope when we are suffering. As the prophets of old did, they remind us of God's presence with us during our suffering. They also speak out against the injustices that cause suffering in our world and work to rebuild society according to the teachings of Jesus.

Archbishop Helder Camara of Brazil did just that. In Christ's name he was a champion for human rights and a defender of the poor. Most people knew Archbishop Camara by the simple title of "Dom Helder." He died on August 27, 1999, at the age of ninety-two.

When he was a young priest in Rio de Janeiro, Dom Helder ministered with many people who were living in substandard housing, were underfed, and went without medical care. This began a life dedicated to working with people who were living in poverty—a poverty often caused by the injustices of society.

When Dom Helder became Archbishop of Olinda and Recife in Brazil in 1964, he chose to live the remaining thirty-five years of his life in one room behind the Church of the Frontiers in Olinda. This simple room was furnished with only a sink, a stove, a table, and a hammock that he used as his bed.

Dom Helder constantly spoke out for the poor and against the many violations of the human rights of the poor—especially their torture—which the government security forces practiced. This so angered the Brazilian government that its officials pressured the news media never to mention his name.

In 1980 when Pope John Paul II visited Brazil, he embraced Archbishop Camara before a nationwide television audience. John Paul II called Dom Helder an energetic pastor and praised his work with the bishops of Brazil promoting human rights.

The Work of Brother Francis and Year 2000 without Misery are two international movements that promote the work of Dom Helder. The Work of Brother Francis is an international foundation that ministers with the poor and spreads the ideals of nonviolence. Launched in 1990, the Year 2000 without Misery was an international campaign to eradicate poverty among the world's poorest people before the end of the millennium.

Dom Helder once said, "When I feed the poor, I'm called a saint. When I ask why the poor have no food, I'm called a communist." Truly Archbishop Camara was a prophet for today.

Where do you see people suffering in your community? Who reaches out to share comfort and hope with them?

WHAT DIFFERENCE

Does It Make in My Life?

Suffering and death are part of the human condition. Jesus suffered and died for us so that we might live. During his life on earth Jesus showed us how to deal with all kinds of suffering, both physical and emotional.

Dealing with Loss

Have you ever had a friend turn against you? Have you ever lost a game in the last few seconds? We suffer from all kinds of losses during our life. Here are some common losses. Place a check (✓) next to the losses you have suffered:

____ Confidence
____ A friend
____ A parent through divorce
____ A parent or a loved one through death
____ Missing the honor roll by half a point

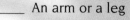

____ An arm or a leg
____ Health
____ A game
____ A test
____ Not making the team
____ Money or your bike
____ Your family pet
____ Your home due to fire, flood, hurricane or tornado.
____ Other: _____
_____

A loss of any kind stirs up feelings and emotions inside you. The deeper the loss, the deeper the pain and suffering may be. When you suffer a loss, you may feel sad, mad, hurt, shocked, disappointed, defeated, depressed, lonely, scared, guilty, or rejected. You may feel some of these feelings intensely.

What Can You Do?

How you choose to handle the losses and experiences that happen to you makes all the difference. You can choose a positive way to deal with your emotions or a negative way of staying trapped in these feelings. You can choose to avoid the feelings and pretend they don't bother you, but they will keep surfacing until you deal with what happened to you. Whatever emotions you may feel are real. Remember feelings are not bad or good; they just are. Choose to deal with what you feel and you can heal.

Christian Hope

As Christians we believe that good will triumph over evil. By Jesus' suffering and death on the cross and his resurrection to new life, he has saved us and has given us the gift of hope. Hope makes all the difference. Defeat cannot trap a Christian. Hope is the fuel of the Christian attitude. Hope helps us change and grow stronger as we work through our suffering and loss. Our Christian hope means we believe and trust that God will never abandon us. Jesus promised us eternal life with God.

HOPE means we live with an
   Honest,
   Optimistic,
   Persistent,
   Effort to **H**andle **O**ur **P**ainful
      Emotions and attain
Heaven, **O**ur **P**romise of **E**ternity.

faith decision

- Share one of the losses you checked on page 104 with a partner or in a small group.

- Discuss how your Christian hope has helped you deal with the situation.

- Name a person who is a role model for you or an example of how to deal with suffering and loss.

Christians are people of hope. We believe in the Resurrection. It is the pledge of our own resurrection. This week I can be a living sign of hope by

_____

_____

_____

_____

_____

_____ .

Faith Vocabulary

Define each of these terms:

1. prophet

2. suffering Servant

People and Places and Events

Identify these people, places, and events:

1. Isaiah

2. Babylonian Exile

Main Ideas

Choose either (a) or (b) from each set of items. Write a brief paragraph to answer each of your choices.

1. (a) Describe the role and message of a biblical prophet.

    (b) What are the servant songs found in the Book of Isaiah?

2. (a) What are some of the images found in the fourth servant song?

    (b) What are some of the burdens that the suffering Servant would bear?

3. (a) Describe the way the early Christian community explained the servant songs.

    (b) How does the Church use the servant songs in the Good Friday liturgy?

Critical Thinking

Using what you have learned in this chapter, briefly explain how the fourth servant song explains the Paschal mystery.

Family Discussion

In times of loss and suffering how can we support one another?

Visit our web site at www.FaithFirst.com

The Paschal Mystery: Jesus' Passion and Death

9

WE PRAY

Lord,
send down your abundant
    blessing
upon your people who have
    devoutly recalled the death
    of your Son
in the sure hope of the
    resurrection.
Grant them pardon; bring them
    comfort.
May their faith grow stronger
and their eternal salvation be
    assured.

FROM *PRAYER OVER THE PEOPLE,*
GOOD FRIDAY

Describe the details of the
story of Jesus' passion and
death that you can recount.

*"It is finished." And bowing
his head, he handed over
the spirit.*   JOHN 19:30

Jesus: The New Adam

FAITH
VOCABULARY

Satan

original sin

moral evil

redemption

expiation

The world's greatest writers could not have crafted a more compelling drama than the story of Jesus Christ. His whole life was a continual unfolding of God's loving plan for his people. Jesus was God's chosen instrument to make "all things work for good" (Romans 8:28). Everything about him—his silences, his miracles, his gestures, his approach to individuals, his prayer, his genuine affection for people, his special care for the vulnerable and the poor—teaches us about God's love for us.

Adam and Eve

Prior to the Incarnation the pages of Sacred Scripture paint a troubling picture of God's people. They are increasingly resistant to God's outstretched hand. The problems began with Adam and Eve, from whom the whole human race can trace their common origin. Adam and Eve are the names the sacred writer gave to the first man and first woman created by God.

This chosen couple had everything going for them. They had a perpetual lease on the garden of paradise in the midst of a creation that God had modestly called "good." In fact, it was great—in today's terms, even "awesome."

Garden of Eden.
Contemporary
stained-glass window.

It was filled with abundance, everything was in harmony with God, justice and order prevailed, tension was nonexistent, and death was unheard of. The term to describe this initial condition of human life, you will remember, is *original justice*, or original holiness.

Describe what you remember about paradise from reading the story of creation in the Bible.

Enter the Serpent-Tempter

God created Adam and Eve in his own image. He set them over the whole world to serve God and care for all creatures. God's abiding friendship gave our first parents a deep sense of happiness and total freedom. They were so free, in fact, that they could even turn their back on God and choose to go their own way. Sadly for the human race, they did just that.

Genesis describes how **Satan**, the serpent-tempter, lured Adam and Eve to test the limits of their freedom and see how much they could get away with. Satan enticed them to eat from "the tree of knowledge of good and bad" (Genesis 2:17), which symbolized the temptation to become like God.

Adam and Eve gave in to this temptation. They displayed disrespect, disobedience, and distrust toward God. They earned for themselves, and for all their descendants, discord, violence, an inclination to sin, and death.

Jesus: The New Adam

God did not stand by idly. He promised that his plan of creation would be repaired. Life would be victorious over death, and justice and holiness over sin. (See Genesis 3:15.) The Old Testament is a testimony to God's efforts to have humanity turn its life over to his care.

The time finally came for God to send forth the One who would repair the damage, his Son. This Promised One would undo what Adam had done and redeem us from the tyranny of sin.

Jesus fulfilled God's promised plan of salvation and was seen by Christians as the new Adam (see 1 Corinthians 15:20–28). By freely choosing to give up his life in obedience to God's will, Jesus has given us even greater blessings than those that Adam's sin had taken from us. The cross of Christ demonstrates just how effectively God can transform evil into good and make "all things work for good."

Explain why Christians describe Jesus as the new Adam.

Did you Know...

Paradise. The word *paradise* comes from an old Persian word. It painted a vibrant visual picture for the people of biblical times of an extensive walled-in park on the grounds of a royal palace. The park was alive with flowers, trees, and lush green grasslands watered by natural streams. Pools were in abundance as was wild game.

Garden of Eden. Contemporary stained-glass window.

Original Sin

Adam and Eve's choice of evil over good, of doing their own thing over obedience to God, is called **original sin.** "Original sin is transmitted with human nature" (see *Catechism of the Catholic Church,* 419). That was not the destiny God had planned for those whom he had lovingly created in his own image. As a result of original sin, human nature is weakened. Instead of an inheritance of harmony and unity with God, this misguided couple left us a legacy of wars, destruction, injustice, murders, prejudice, anger, envy, greed, guilt, and the possibility of eternal separation from God after death.

What are some of the effects of original sin that you see in the world today?

WHAT DIFFERENCE DOES FAITH MAKE?

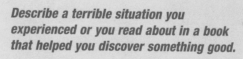

Describe a terrible situation you experienced or you read about in a book that helped you discover something good.

_____

_____

_____

_____

If God, whom we know as a just and loving Father, truly cares for his people, why does evil exist? If God, the creator of a well-ordered and wonderful world, is really in charge, why are so many of the world's poorest people made to work like slaves? Why have there been so many mass murders in recent history, even in schools and churches?

The Problem of Evil

If we want quick and easy answers to this very human phenomenon of **moral evil**, we will be disappointed. Moral evil is the harm we willingly inflict on one another and on God's good creation. It is linked to the mystery of human freedom, a great, and in many ways, incomprehensible gift that God gives to human creation.

From Sacred Scripture, we know that the only key to unlock the problem of evil is faith—faith in the goodness of creation, the patient love of God, the compassion of Christ; faith in the life-giving influence of the Holy Spirit over lives. By strengthening our faith, God gradually gives us the power to see with his eyes. While we will never have all the answers to the problem of evil, we will gain a deeper understanding of and the skills to live in a world where evil and goodness dwell side by side.

Explain why moral evil is a problem.

God is in no way, directly or even indirectly, the cause of moral evil. Because he has gifted us with the freedom to believe in him and the freedom to love him, he does not stop us from choosing evil. Moral evil is the result.

Never, however, underestimate God's power to bring good out of evil. The Paschal mystery of Christ's death spotlights this transforming power of God. From the greatest evil—the crucifixion of God's only Son—God brought about the greatest of

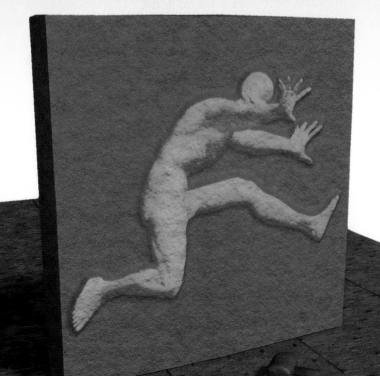

goods: Christ's resurrection and our **redemption** from sin. Redemption is the word we use to describe Christ delivering us from sin and death through his Paschal mystery (see Acts of the Apostles 4:12).

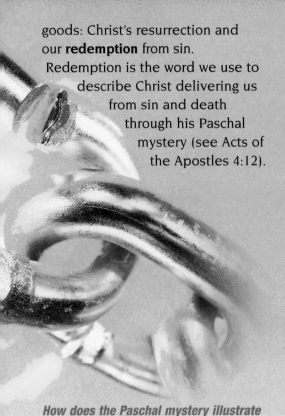

How does the Paschal mystery illustrate good coming out of evil?

Jesus' Cross/Our Crosses

Evil happens today in all of our lives. Evil—such as being ridiculed at school, violence, injustices, betrayal by friends, harassment, and gossip—catches up with us and hoistes us up on our own bitterly painful crosses. Jesus invited his disciples to take up their crosses and follow him (see Matthew 16:24). When we suffer, we join our sufferings with Christ's. In some way, known only to God, Jesus also suffers with us.

Name some of the crosses that people have to carry today.

The Son of God became a human being to save us from our sins. (The name *Jesus*, by the way, means "God saves.") The Father anointed Christ (that title, in fact, means "Anointed One") with the Holy Spirit to bring us out of the mess into which we had gotten ourselves.

Think of a once stately house that has become a dump. Its beauty is gone, the windows are boarded up allowing no light to enter, and dust and cobwebs choke the air. This was humanity's state when God took the initiative to restore our beauty and sent his Son's light into our musty world. The Son of God entered human history and converted darkness into daylight, decay into life, moral clutter into holy order, and perpetual exile into eternal salvation.

Why did the Son of God become a human?

Jesus' death on the cross was an **expiation** for our sins. The word *expiation* means "an act that takes away guilt or makes amends for a wrongdoing." Expiation heals a broken relationship. Jesus paid the price for all the evils men and women produce and made amends for all of the harm we willingly inflict on one another. God's suffering Servant cleaned house of sin and guilt.

How does understanding about Jesus' cross help you carry your cross?

WHAT DIFFERENCE DOES FAITH MAKE?

On May 28, 1888, an amateur photographer snapped a picture of a shroud, or burial cloth, that showed an image many believed was an image of the body of Jesus. This shroud, the Shroud of Turin, is believed by many to be the cloth that wrapped Jesus' body for burial. The Church has not officially declared the Shroud of Turin to be Jesus' burial cloth, but the shroud remains an image that awakens deep faith.

The Death of Jesus

Crucifixion. Contemporary stained-glass window.

The Gospel describes in graphic detail the brutality of Jesus' death. Historical records support what the Gospel says about the cruelty with which the Romans treated those condemned to die.

Crucifixion was meant to be a terrifying public spectacle. It was a savage form of capital punishment that was intended to deter others from rebelling against the power of the Roman state.

Jesus Truly Died

Jesus truly died a real physical death. Jesus stopped breathing and entered the dwelling place of the dead. From the time that he died on the cross until his resurrection, he experienced the condition of death—separation of his soul from his body.

The Gospel meticulously describes how Jesus was taken down from the cross and buried in a nearby tomb (see John 19:38–42). There is no reason to think that Jesus merely pretended to be dead. Scripture tells us that by the grace of God he tasted death for everyone (see Hebrews 2:9).

Why is the fact of Jesus' death so important to Christians?

Descent into Hell

Another puzzling aspect of Christ's death is his descent into hell. Every time we pray the Apostles' Creed we say:

> He suffered under Pontius Pilate, was crucified, died, and was buried.
> He descended into hell.

After Jesus died but before he was raised from the dead, Jesus descended into hell—the place where the souls of the dead live separated from God. Actually, what confuses us about this event is the word *hell*, a place generally associated with damnation and endless suffering. The word *hell* in this instance is a translation of the Hebrew word *sheol*, which simply means "the abode of the dead."

Upon his death, Jesus entered sheol, the house of the spirits, where he joined the souls of all who had preceded him in death. The First Letter of Peter teaches, "[T]he gospel was preached even to the dead" (1 Peter 4:6).

Christ's descent into hell vividly demonstrates his love for and sensitivity to all people. His first act after death is to reunite himself with those who have already died. Imagine the intense joy felt by these just women and men who had gone before him as he opens heaven's gates for them to enter.

Explain what Christians are referring to in the Apostles' Creed when they say that Jesus "descended into hell."

Jesus' death made amends for the sins of humankind. It reconciled human beings with God. From his descent into hell we learn that God does not wish to exclude anyone from his kingdom.

Did you Know...

A wonderfully poetic, ancient homily read in the Liturgy of the Hours on Holy Saturday night captures the meaning of Jesus' descent to the regions of the dead:

> Today a great silence reigns upon earth, a great silence and a great stillness.
> A great silence because the king is asleep.
> The earth trembled and is still because God has fallen asleep in the flesh and he has raised up all who have slept ever since the world began. . . .
> He has gone to search for Adam, our first father, as for a lost sheep. . . .
> "I order you, O sleeper, to awake. I did not create you to be a prisoner in hell. Rise from the dead, for I am the life of the dead."

WHAT DIFFERENCE DOES FAITH MAKE?

How does the fact that Jesus died change your understanding of the meaning of the death of someone?

_____

_____

_____

WHAT DIFFERENCE

Does This Make in Our Church?

Church of the Holy Sepulchre, Jerusalem.

Stations of the Cross

Catholics profess their faith in the meaning of the Crucifixion for their lives by praying the Stations of the Cross. Making the Stations of the Cross is a minipilgrimage. A pilgrimage is a spiritual journey to a specific place to remember a special event that occurred there.

Pilgrimages to the Holy Land became very popular in the Middle Ages. Many liturgical practices were brought back to local churches from the pilgrimages to the Holy Land. The procession of palms and veneration of the cross grew out of practices that had originated in Jerusalem.

In 1342 the Franciscans took over the care of the shrines in the Holy Land. They promoted a great devotion to these sacred places. Since the number of Christians who were able to visit the Holy Land was very limited, shrines or stations commemorating the important events in the life of Jesus—especially his passion and death—were placed in local churches.

Jesus died for our sins. By freely choosing to suffer death for our sins, he redeemed us and reconciled us with God and with one another. Because he journeyed the way of the cross, we proclaim:

> Lord, by your cross
> and resurrection
> you have set us free.
> You are the Savior of the world.

FROM *ROMAN MISSAL*,
MEMORIAL ACCLAMATION

Dominus Flevit ("The Lord Wept"), Jerusalem. Pilgrims remember Jesus' weeping over Jerusalem.

Saint Leonard of Port Maurice (1676–1751), a Franciscan, promoted this devotion very enthusiastically. He set up more than 572 sets of the Stations of the Cross and became known as the "preacher of the Stations of the Cross." The most famous place he set up the Stations of the Cross is in the Colosseum of Rome. Each year during Holy Week, Pope John Paul II prays the Stations of the Cross there.

Popular custom has set the number of stations, or stops, on the Way of the Cross at fourteen. Today a fifteenth station, the Resurrection, is often added to emphasize that the Passion of Christ and the Resurrection "have set us free."

How does your parish help you "walk through" the Passion, death, and resurrection of Jesus?

Pope John Paul II. Good Friday procession inside The Colosseum, Rome, Italy, April 2, 1999.

Pope John Paul II. Good Friday sermon, Palatine Hill, April 13, 1990.

WHAT
DIFFERENCE

Does It Make in My Life?

Jesus' passion and death was a time of pain and grief for Jesus' followers. You can imagine how especially difficult it must have been for his mother, Mary, to see her son suffer and die.

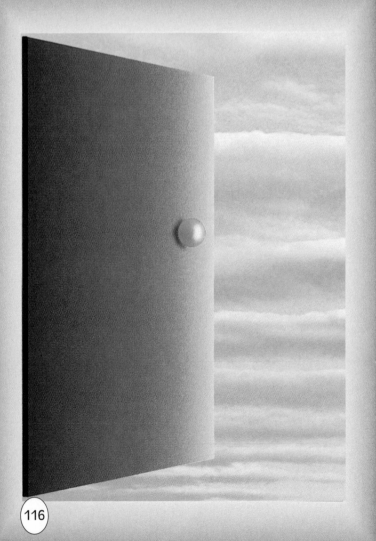

Sadness and Hope

Sadness and death are a part of everyone's life. When someone you love dies, you feel very sad. You may be filled with deep feelings that you have never experienced before. What do you do with those feelings and memories? What do you do with your grief? You want these feelings to go away and leave you alone. You want your friends to be with you but you do not want to talk about what you are feeling.

Grief is a time of sorrow. As Christians we believe that the person you loved now lives in a new way with God. In the Funeral Liturgy we talk about life not ending but changing. We sing alleluia. All this may seem like a contradiction, but it is not. It is based on our faith in Jesus' promise of life everlasting.

On a spiritual level you can believe your loved one is with God. At the same time, on a physical and emotional level you miss them and want them here with you. Remember you are made up of your body, mind, spirit, and emotions. You have to be good to yourself and grieve the death of a loved one on all these levels.

What Can You Do?

There are some things that will help you as you move through the grieving process.

1. **Share your feelings.**
   Sharing your grief with someone you trust is called the talking cure. It helps to talk about the person who died. Even if you cry it is okay.

2. **Face your feelings.**
   Feelings will come and go like waves rolling over you. Sometimes they are strong and seem to knock you down. Other times they are gentle and peaceful. Try to let yourself "feel" the feelings instead of ignoring them. Go with the flow.

3. **Pray.**
   Pray to your loved one to help you handle the feelings you are experiencing. Ask the Holy Spirit to give you hope and strength. Remember that God loves you and is always with you.

4. **Keep a journal.**
   You may want to write a letter to the person who has died and share what's in your heart. You can then put the letter in a special place. Writing love letters or angry letters or I miss you letters can help you get your feelings out and feel a little bit better.

5. **Process your grief.**
   Grief is a process. Take time to move toward healing; it cannot be rushed. Healing takes as long as it takes. You cannot run or hide from grief. Just try to walk through it.

6. **Express your feelings.**
   Expressing feelings in a healthy way is not a sign of weakness but a sign of strength.

faith decision

- Are you able to name your feelings? Some people use colors to express how they feel. For example, gray may depict feelings of sadness. What colors would you use to depict your different feelings?

- Think of a particular situation. Use color to express how you feel. Draw and share your picture with a partner.

This week I will think about God's promise of everlasting life. This will help me

_____

_____

_____

_____

_____

_____ .

Faith Vocabulary

Define each of these terms:

1. original sin
2. moral evil
3. redemption
4. expiation

People and Places and Events

Identify these people, places, and events:

1. Adam and Eve
2. Satan

Main Ideas

Choose either (a) or (b) from each set of items. Write a brief paragraph to answer each of your choices.

1. (a) Describe the results of Adam and Eve's free choice to go their own way.

   (b) Why do Christians call Jesus the new Adam?

2. (a) Describe the connection between the mystery of moral evil in the world and the suffering and death of Jesus.

   (b) How does Jesus' suffering and death help us deal with the crosses in our own lives?

3. (a) Why is Jesus' death so important for all people?

   (b) Explain the meaning of Jesus' descent into hell.

Critical Thinking

Using what you have learned in this chapter, briefly explain this statement:
   God can make "all things work for good."

Family Discussion

Often people say that everyone has their own crosses to bear. What crosses has our family had to bear and how has God helped us to cope with and understand these difficult times?

Visit our web site at www.FaithFirst.com

The Paschal Mystery: Jesus' Resurrection and Ascension

10

WE PRAY

Father, all-powerful and
　　ever-living God,
we do well always and
　　everywhere to give you
　　thanks
through Jesus Christ our
　　Lord. . . .

In him a new age has dawned,
the long reign of sin is ended,
a broken world has been
　　renewed,
and man is once again made
　　whole.

FROM *PREFACE, EASTER IV*

Through the events of the
Paschal mystery—the mystery
of Jesus' death-resurrection-
ascension—a new age has
dawned. Explain what the
Gospel tells us about the
resurrection and ascension
of Jesus Christ?

*Christ, that Morning Star,
　who came back from
　　the dead,
and shed his peaceful light
　on all mankind.*

FROM *ROMAN MISSAL,
EASTER PROCLAMATION*

FAITH FOCUS

Why is Jesus' resurrection our greatest source of hope?

FAITH VOCABULARY

Resurrection

Ascension

particular judgement

Last Judgment

Three days after Jesus' crucifixion, his disciples were proclaiming, "Jesus is risen! Jesus is risen!" Jesus' resurrection changed their lives. No other event in human history has ever changed the lives of people more.

The Resurrection of Jesus

The mystery of Jesus' resurrection from the dead resides at the heart of Christian faith. The **Resurrection** is Jesus' being raised from the dead to a new glorified life. It is the reuniting of his human self to a new and glorified body.

The Resurrection is a historical event that can never be directly proven with scientific evidence. There were no pictures taken by television cameras. There were no eyewitnesses to Jesus actually being raised from the dead. None of the evangelists describes the actual occurrence. No one can say how it happened on the physical level. Jesus' passover from death into life is recorded in history, yet it goes beyond human history into the realm of divine mystery where God shares his life and love with us.

Why do we say that the Resurrection is a historical event?

The Work of the Trinity

The Resurrection took place in time (it is a historical event), but it also transcends time. The raising of Jesus from the dead was not observed. It was not seen through human eyes. It escapes space and time.

The Resurrection is a true mystery of our faith. It is the work of the Trinity. All three divine Persons act together to effect Jesus' history-shattering Easter miracle. The Father's power "raised up" Jesus. By so doing, the glorified Son's humanity is brought into the life of the Trinity. Once raised from the dead, the glorified Son of God joins with

Road to Emmaus. Stained-glass window.

The Risen Jesus and Mary Magdalene. Stained-glass window.

the Father to send, as promised, the gift of the Advocate, the Holy Spirit, to his disciples.

Describe the Resurrection as the work of the Trinity.

The Testimony

History records the event through the testimony of those who saw, talked to, walked with, and ate with the risen glorified Christ. Around the year 56, Paul the Apostle testified in writing:

> For I handed on to you as of first importance what I also received: that Christ died for our sins in accordance with the scriptures; that he was buried; that he was raised on the third day in accordance with the scriptures; that he appeared to Cephas [Peter], then to the Twelve. After that, he appeared to more than five hundred brothers at once, most of whom are still living.
>
> 1 CORINTHIANS 15:3–6

The accounts of the Gospel list by name many of those who actually saw the Risen Christ. The holy women who first went to anoint his body at dawn on Easter Sunday testified that Jesus' tomb was empty. Peter and the other disciples immediately rushed to the burial chamber and verified the absence of Jesus' body. The Gospel according to John tells that when John himself saw the empty tomb and the burial cloths rolled up in a separate place, "he saw and believed" (John 20:8).

What testimony do we have about the Resurrection?

The gospel accounts, as well as the Acts of the Apostles and other New Testament letters, refer to those who met firsthand with the Risen Christ. They saw and touched him. They ate and spoke with him. Despite the efforts of nonbelievers since that first Easter Sunday to discredit these witnesses and their testimony, the authenticity of that testimony is simply a matter of record.

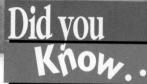

The Risen Jesus and Thomas. Stained-glass window.

"My Lord and My God"

WHAT DIFFERENCE DOES FAITH MAKE?

How does your belief in the resurrection of Jesus help you live as his follower?

_____

_____

_____

_____

Forty days after the Resurrection, Jesus met with his disciples on a mountain in Galilee. Remember that it was in Galilee that Jesus began his public ministry. Here is what happened:

[A]s they [the apostles] were looking on, he was lifted up, and a cloud took him from their sight. While they were looking intently at the sky as he was going, suddenly two men dressed in white garments stood beside them. They said, "Men of Galilee, why are you standing there looking at the sky? This Jesus who has been taken up from you into heaven will return in the same way as you have seen him going into heaven."

ACTS OF THE APOSTLES 1:9–11

Jesus' Return to His Father

In John Maesfield's *The Trial of Jesus,* the following fictional conversation takes place between a soldier who stood guard at Jesus' cross and the wife of Pontius Pilate. Pilate was the Roman leader who handed Jesus over to be crucified.

"Do you think he is dead?"

"No, lady, I don't."

"Then where is he?"

"Let loose in the world, lady, where . . . [no one] can stop his truth."

By leaving the physical presence of his disciples and taking his place at his Father's right hand, the Risen Christ paradoxically is "let loose in the world." We call the return of the Risen Christ to his Father, to the world of the divine, the **Ascension.**

What is the Ascension?

Jesus with Us

We might think that it would have been nice if the Risen Christ had stayed around on earth for all to see and listen to forever. The truth is that he is present with us. In one sense, the Risen Jesus remained for

forty days, during which he ate and drank with his disciples and taught them about the kingdom. After this time, he left them. A "cloud took him from their sight" (Acts of the Apostles 1:9). By ascending to the Father, Jesus accomplishes many things for us.

The arrival of the Holy Spirit. Jesus' return to his Father is a necessary prelude to the sending of the Holy Spirit, who is now with us as Advocate and Teacher, available to us anywhere, anytime.

Access to the "Father's house" (John 14:2). By going before us, Jesus has opened up for us the way to eternal life and happiness with God. His ascension gives us confidence that where he has gone, there we will follow.

Intercession on our behalf. Imagine that you have a friend, one who remembers her friends, who becomes a world leader. When you bring to her attention matters that are truly important, she does what she can to address them. In a far more effective way than any friend could do, the risen glorified Christ intercedes on our behalf. Jesus takes his place beside his Father, "that he might now appear before God on our behalf" (Hebrews 9:24).

Inauguration of a new age. We have heard of the age of space exploration and the information age. Jesus' ascension signifies that the kingdom that he preached during his earthly ministry truly has begun.

Despite all the discord and conflict we see occurring on the world's stage, his kingdom is taking hold and "will have no end" (Nicene Creed).

Explain the meaning of the Ascension in God's plan for us.

The Church sets aside a holy day of obligation to celebrate the ascension of Jesus. In the Preface for the feast of the Ascension we pray:

> Christ, the mediator between God and man,
> judge of the world and Lord of all,
> has passed beyond our sight,
> not to abandon us but to be our hope.
> Christ is the beginning, the head of the Church;
> where he has gone, we hope to follow. FROM PREFACE, ASCENSION I

Ascension of Jesus. Contemporary stained-glass window.

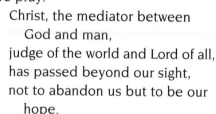

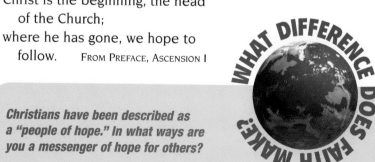

Christians have been described as a "people of hope." In what ways are you a messenger of hope for others?

_____

_____

_____

123

The New Jerusalem. Fabric art.

What will become of us when we die? Christians have found the answer to the mystery of human death in the Pascal mystery of Christ. At death, life is not ended but changed!

Life Is Changed, Not Ended!

When you attend a Catholic funeral liturgy, you will hear the words "Life is changed, not ended" (Preface, Christian Death I). This expresses both our hope and our faith in the meaning of the death-resurrection-ascension of Jesus for our life. When we die, our lives change rather than

end. Jesus says it best: "[W]hoever believes in me, even if he dies, will live, and everyone who lives and believes in me will never die" (John 11:25–26).

Life After Death

Sacred Scripture and Tradition give us many insights into understanding the mystery surrounding the nature of our life after death. Here are a few:

Insight 1: The particular judgment. At death our souls separate from our bodies. At the moment of our death Jesus will assign our souls to their final destiny. The basis of this assignment, or judgment, is based on what we have done in our lives. We call that our **particular,** or individual, **judgment.**

At the particular judgment we either receive:

- **Heaven:** eternal life and happiness with God and the saints forever.
- **Purgatory:** an opportunity to purify and strengthen our love for God before we enter heaven.
- **Hell:** the immediate and everlasting separation from God and the saints.

What is the particular judgment?

Insight 2: We will never die again. Jesus' resurrection and ascension to the Father is a sign that we also will live forever. The Risen Jesus did not return to earthly existence as he was before he was raised. Instead, he passed from death into another state, a new glorified life beyond space and time. Jesus is the source and principle of our resurrection. He is God's promise that we too will pass into a state beyond space and time where we will never die again.

Why do we believe that our death is a transition to everlasting life?

Insight 3: The last day. At the resurrection on the last day, the souls of everyone who ever lived will be reunited with their bodies (see 1 Corinthians 15:35–51). This resurrection of all the dead, of both the just and the unjust (see Acts of the Apostles 24:15), will precede the **Last Judgment.** The Last Judgment is the judgment at which all humans will appear in their own bodies, give an account of their deeds, and Christ will show his identity with the least of his brothers and sisters (see Matthew 25:31–46).

Describe what Catholics believe will happen at the end of time on the last day.

Insight 4: A new heaven and earth. On that last day, Christ will reveal himself as the Lord of history. God's loving plan of goodness for his creatures will be re-created and restored. The kingdom of God will come in all its glory. Those who had accepted God's grace, who had cared for Christ in the person of his "little ones," will reign with him forever.

Describe the kingdom of God.

God will transform the cosmos into a realm of justice and peace. In this new heaven and earth, there will be no more tears, suffering, and death. (See Revelation 21:1–4.)

WHAT DIFFERENCE DOES FAITH MAKE?

How does your belief that you will give an accounting of your life to God affect the way you treat others?

_____

_____

_____

WHAT DIFFERENCE

Does This Make in Our Church?

The Resurrection and Ascension reveal to us the meaning of Jesus' suffering and death. God raised him from death and exalted him as the Savior of the world. Through Christ's saving deeds death has been destroyed. Each year we proclaim this faith as we begin our celebration of the Easter Vigil:

> This is the passover of the Lord:
> if we honor the memory of his
>   death and resurrection
> by hearing his word and
>   celebrating his mysteries,
> then we may be confident
> that we shall share his victory
>   over death
> and live with him for ever in God.
>
> FROM *ROMAN MISSAL*,
> THE SERVICE OF LIGHT,
> EASTER VIGIL

A Cheerful Saint

Our belief in the resurrection of Christ and our own hope of life forever gives us the power to see the world in a new light. We celebrate that vision in many ways, one of which is seeing the good side of things. Saint Philip Neri (1515–1595) exemplified this trait.

Philip was born in Florence, Italy, and lived most of his life in Rome. Philip lived in Rome during a time in the history of the Church when the life of the Church needed "a resurrection," a rebirth into new life.

Raised by a loving step-mother, his family trained him for a career as a merchant. Living his life in such a career, however, was not among Philip's career goals. At one point, while living in Rome, Philip became overcome—perhaps somewhat depressed—at the disarray of the Church. He decided to get on with his life and move away from Rome and serve the Church as a missionary. This, however, was not in God's plan. A wise old advisor told him that his work was to take place in Rome. Philip's outlook on his own life and on the life of the Church in Rome changed. He committed himself to living a life of holiness and cheerfulness.

Philip became a priest in 1551. In 1564 he gathered many of his followers and fellow priests into an oratory, a place of prayer, connected to a local church. They joined together and formed a religious community. They prayed and ate together. They celebrated the Eucharist and preached regularly. They flooded the streets of Rome with living examples of holiness and cheerfulness.

Philip's sense of humor and spirit of cheerfulness became well known. He told the young men who crowded his oratory, "I will have no sadness in my house." To those who took themselves too seriously, he advised, "Don't be forever dwelling on your sins. Leave a little something for the angels." Philip's fondness for laughter and pranks earned him many critics, who thought of him as a fool and a clown. Nevertheless, the "fool" influenced many of the church leaders of his day. They delighted in his friendship and sought his advice, such that he became known as the "Apostle of Rome."

In the face of widespread corruption and attacks on his holiness, he stood as a champion of positive

The Campo Vaccino, Rome. Antonio Joli (1700–1777), Italian artist.

thinking and a real, living spirituality. He was a messenger of hope and new life at a time when the Church really needed that vision. This holy clown of God founded forty-five oratories and a religious order, the Oratorians. Philip was canonized a saint in 1622.

What can you do to make your living a life of holiness more cheerful and affirming?

Modern-day Oratorians embrace the spirit of Saint Philip Neri.

WHAT DIFFERENCE

Does It Make in My Life?

Our faith tells us that Jesus' resurrection to new life had a tremendous impact on his disciples. Their faith was renewed and their lives were changed forever. The Resurrection gave them the perseverance to continue forward and spread the Good News.

Our lives too have been changed forever. You are called to make many transitions to new life each day. There are times when you may feel defeated. You may have worked hard to achieve a goal and yet somehow failed. What you need to remember is that God loves every attempt you make at trying to do your best. God will give you the strength and courage to renew your commitment and try again.

Whenever you meet major obstacles, you'll want to remember that your life is not ended but through renewed effort you can pick yourself up, change what needs to be changed, and continue on.

Renewed Effort and Perseverance

Think of some obstacles you have faced in your life so far. What did you need to do to get up and try again? Did you give it a renewed effort? Did you try to give it your best shot? Here are some skills that may help you make that transition and put forth your best effort once again.

1. **Use positive self-talk.** Self-talk is something we do all the time in the privacy of our own minds. Self-talk is either positive or negative. It's either going to build you up or tear you down. For example: You fail a math test. Do you say to yourself, "You stupid thing, you're never going to pass math." You drop a glass of juice on the kitchen floor. Do you say, "I can't do anything right."

   Negative self-talk is the negative message that will make you feel even worse. It will keep you down and make you feel that it is not worth trying to do any better. Negative self-talk stifles perseverance.

   Positive self-talk is changing the negative message to a positive one. For example: "Okay, I failed that test but I know I can study harder or I can ask someone to help me understand that concept better. I can do better on the next test." Positive self-talk is more of a positive affirmation.

teamwork. Constructive criticism is meant to help you, not to hurt you or put you down. It's easy to become defensive and not accept constructive criticism for what it is. Constructive criticism can in fact be a gift. It can help you learn and grow in many ways, but only if you're open to it.

2. **Cancel or delete negative messages.** One way to try to get rid of negative messages in your head is to say after the negative thought, "Cancel" or "delete." After you cancel the negative message, replace it immediately with a positive thought. You may have to cancel the "put-down message" many times as you practice this new skill. For example: Someone calls you a "loser." In your head cancel that remark and say to yourself, "I am okay" or "I am very capable of doing many things." Again you need to practice doing this every time you hear yourself or someone else put you down.

3. **Accept constructive criticism.** When a friend, a parent, a coach, or a teacher asks you to look at your behavior or something you might want to change to be a better person, learn from their criticism. For example: Your coach may say to you, "You are not passing the ball—let's have some teamwork." Hopefully you wouldn't cancel that but instead would try to work harder on

faith decision

ff

- List several negative messages that you say to put yourself down. Then change each negative message to a positive one.

- Try to be consistent in practicing positive self-talk. Before you know it you will find yourself becoming your own best friend.

This week I will ask Jesus to help me change any negative self-talk to positive messages by

_____

_____

_____

_____

_____

_____ .

Faith Vocabulary

Define each of these terms:

1. The Resurrection
2. The Ascension
3. particular judgment
4. Last Judgment

Main Ideas

Choose either (a) or (b) from each set of items. Write a brief paragraph to answer each of your choices.

1. (a) Why do we believe that the Resurrection was a historical event?

   (b) Explain the Resurrection as the work of the Trinity.

2. (a) Describe what the Acts of the Apostles tells us about the Ascension.

   (b) Explain the meaning of the Ascension in God's plan of salvation.

3. (a) Explain what Christians believe is the meaning of the death-resurrection-ascension of Jesus for our life.

   (b) Describe the Christian belief that at the end of time there will be a new heaven and earth.

Critical Thinking

Using what you have learned in this chapter, briefly explain this statement:
At the moment of our death, life is changed, not ended.

Family Discussion

Who are the members of our family who have died?
What do we do and say that shows we believe they are alive and live in a new way?

Visit our
web site at
www.FaithFirst.com

Breakfast at the Lake

A Scripture Story

WE PRAY

God our Father,
may we look forward with hope
  to our resurrection,
for you have made us your sons
  and daughters,
and restored the joy of our youth.
Amen.

*FROM OPENING PRAYER,
THIRD SUNDAY OF EASTER.*

After Jesus was raised from
the dead, he appeared to his
disciples. Retell a story of
the Risen Lord with his
disciples.

*Jesus revealed himself again
to his disciples at the
Sea of Tiberias.* JOHN 21:1

Bible Background

FAITH FOCUS

What is the importance of Jesus appearing to the disciples after the Resurrection?

FAITH VOCABULARY

resurrection stories

Breakfast can be one of the best meals of the day—it can also be one of the most rushed. A good breakfast gets us off to a good start. Touching base with our family at breakfast helps us focus on the day. Whether we have breakfast at home, at the drive-in, or at school, we need a good breakfast.

The Voice from the Shore

Would it surprise you that there is a well-known breakfast story in the Gospel? Well, there is. You can find it in John 21:1–14. Before you read it, let's talk a little about the background to the story.

The sun was rising over the eastern shore of the Sea of Tiberias, which is another name for the Sea of Galilee. Peter, Thomas, Nathanael, James, John, and two other disciples were finishing up their night's work of fishing on the lake. Their empty boat and nets were all they had to show for their efforts. Suddenly, the silence over the lake was broken. "Cast your nets over the right side," a voice from the shore called out to them. "You will find fish there." A good catch and a good breakfast were just what the disciples needed.

Testimonies to Jesus' Resurrection

There are many stories in the Gospel that tell us of Jesus appearing to his disciples after his resurrection. The breakfast story at the Sea of Tiberias is one of these **resurrection stories.** Each of the resurrection stories gives the testimony of the Church to the fact of Jesus' resurrection. Here is a list and a brief description of those stories:

- Matthew 28:8–17. The Risen Christ appears to the disciples and the women on a mountainside in Galilee.
- Mark 16:9–18. The Risen Christ appears first to Mary Magdalene; second, to two disciples walking; and third, to eleven disciples at table. All of these appearances take place in Jerusalem.
- Luke 24:1–49. The Risen Christ appears first to Peter. He next appears to two disciples walking on the road to Emmaus. Then he appears to the eleven disciples in Jerusalem.
- John 20:11–31. The Risen Christ first appears in Galilee to Mary Magdala and then to the disciples, without Thomas. A week later he appears again to the disciples. This time Thomas is with them.
- John 21:1–23. The Risen Christ appears to seven disciples at the Sea of Tiberias.

Choose one of the gospel accounts of the Risen Christ appearing to his disciples. Look it up and read it. What testimony does it provide for Jesus' resurrection?

Replica of a first century fishing boat.

The Structure of the Resurrection Stories

Keeping the following four points in mind will help you understand the meaning of the resurrection stories.

Pattern: There is a common pattern to each story. First, the disciple initially does not recognize Jesus. Second, Jesus does something, for example, like addressing a disciple by name. This helps the disciple or disciples recognize Jesus. Third, the disciple comes to know that it is truly the Risen Lord.

Describe the pattern used in the writing of the resurrection stories.

Audience: Each account of the Gospel was first written to a particular community, or audience. It was important that an eyewitness well known to each community tell the story of Jesus' resurrection to that community.

Why is the disciple who witnesses the Risen Christ important to the story?

Setting or Location: The Jerusalem and the Galilean communities of early Christians told the resurrection stories using places that would have local familiarity. The story would have a greater interest and the people would be better able to remember the story if it took place in a location they knew well.

Explain the importance of the setting of each resurrection story.

Faith Testimonies: The gospel accounts of the appearances of the Risen Jesus to his disciples are testimonies to the event of the Resurrection itself. The variances in each story help make the story more understandable and memorable to the people who are reading or listening to the story.

Summarize the importance of the gospel accounts of Jesus appearing to the disciples after the Resurrection.

Did you Know...

Today we would call the Sea of Galilee a lake because it is totally surrounded by land.

Each resurrection story paints a vivid picture of the personal interaction between the Risen Christ and an individual disciple or group of disciples. Each time the disciples are assured that Jesus who had died and was buried had truly been raised from the dead.

WHAT DIFFERENCE DOES FAITH MAKE?

What are the questions you would ask to find out more about Jesus' resurrection?

_____

_____

_____

Reading the Word of God

FAITH FOCUS

Why did the disciples recognize the man calling them to be Jesus?

Second Miraculous Draught of Fishes. James J. Tissot (1836–1902), French artist.

Peter and other disciples of Jesus were fishermen by trade. They came from Galilee and from families who made their living fishing on the Sea of Galilee. It is no surprise then that after Jesus' death, we find them back home at work. This resurrection story opens with Peter and the others doing what they had always done before they first met Jesus—fishing by casting their nets into the waters.

The Appearance to the Seven Disciples

The Gospel according to John begins the account of the

appearances of the Risen Christ to the disciples this way:

After this, Jesus revealed himself again to his disciples at the Sea of Tiberias. He revealed himself in this way. Together were Simon Peter, Thomas called Didymus, Nathanael from Cana in Galilee, Zebedee's sons, and two others of his disciples. Simon Peter said to them, "I am going fishing." They said to him, "We also will come with you." So they went out and got into the boat, but that night they caught nothing.

When it was already dawn, Jesus was standing on the shore; but the disciples did not realize that it was Jesus. Jesus said to them, "Children, have you caught anything to eat?" They answered him, "No." So he said to them, "Cast the net over the right side of the boat and you will find something." So they cast it, and were not able to pull it in because of the number of fish.

So the disciple whom Jesus loved said to Peter, "It is the Lord." When Simon Peter heard that it was the Lord, he tucked in his garment, for he was lightly clad, and jumped into the sea. The other disciples came in the boat, for they were not far from shore, only about a hundred yards, dragging the net with the fish.

When they climbed out on shore, they saw a charcoal fire with fish on it and bread. Jesus said to them, "Bring some of the fish you just caught." So Simon Peter went over and dragged the net ashore full of one hundred fifty-three

large fish. Even though there were so many, the net was not torn. Jesus said to them, "Come, have breakfast." And none of the disciples dared to ask him, "Who are you?" because they realized it was the Lord. Jesus came over and took the bread and gave it to them, and in like manner the fish. This was now the third time Jesus was revealed to his disciples after being raised from the dead.

JOHN 21:1–14

Describe what happened when the disciples recognized the Risen Lord on the beach.

We can learn much about the disciples and their relationship to the Risen Lord from the gospel account of the appearance of the Risen Jesus on the shore of the Sea of Tiberias. Jesus calls us to be fishers of men and women. We are to bring others to know and recognize that Jesus was raised from the dead and lives. Jesus is the Lord.

WHAT DIFFERENCE DOES FAITH MAKE?

In what ways can you share with others the good news that Jesus was raised from the dead and lives?

_____

_____

_____

_____

_____

Understanding the Word of God

FAITH FOCUS

How does reading or listening to this story strengthen our faith in Jesus?

What does that expression "Seeing is believing" mean to you? When might you use that expression?

Seeing Jesus

In the Gospel according to John, "Seeing is believing" has a unique meaning. John's account of the Gospel is filled with stories about the people who at first did not know who this person was whom they were seeing (looking at and listening to). After conversation with him or seeing his work, they came to see (believe in) that the person was the Risen Jesus.

John 21:1–14 uses this movement from seeing to believing. The disciples who first "did not realize that it was Jesus" came to believe it was Jesus, who had truly risen.

There is a charming simplicity to the story of Jesus appearing to the disciples at the shore. On one hand it is a warm story of the reunion of Jesus with his friends. On the other hand the story reveals the mystery of the person in whom they placed their hopes and dreams.

What does "seeing" mean in the Gospel according to John?

Symbols in the Story

We have already learned that John's account of the Gospel is filled with symbols and signs. Identifying these symbols and their meaning in John 21:1–14 helps us understand the faith meaning of the story.

136

The Number Seven

In this resurrection story the Risen Jesus appears to seven disciples. Why seven and not eleven? The number seven would have a meaning for the original audience for whom John's account of the Gospel was written. The number seven was a symbol for perfection and completeness. The seven disciples in turn represent all Christians. All Christians believe in the Resurrection.

Give one explanation of the meaning of the number seven in John 21:1–14.

Light and Darkness

The image of movement from darkness to light is a theme used here and at other times by John. Part of the setting of the story is the movement of the disciples from darkness (fishing all night) to light (dawn). During the night they had no success. At dawn the Risen Christ (the Light of the World) appears to them. At his word the disciples cast their nets into the water once again. Their fishing is successful beyond their wildest expectations.

At the moment of their success they recognize the man who had called out to them was "the Lord" (John 21:7). The disciples see (believe) and go to the shore to meet Jesus. They move from darkness to light, from failure to success. The disciples' faith in the Lord is strengthened.

How do the disciples recognize Jesus as the Risen Lord?

The Breaking of Bread

Breaking of bread is another image that early Christians used to identify their faith in Jesus and his presence with them. In this story Jesus "took the bread and gave it to them" (John 21:13). It is in this same action through which the disciples who traveled and conversed with the stranger on the road to Emmaus finally recognized the Risen Christ. Reading this part of the story would strengthen the faith of its readers in the presence of Christ with them.

Describe the meaning of the symbol breaking of bread.

The resurrection stories in the Gospel help us come to know who Jesus is. We, in turn, courageously and shamelessly share with others our faith in the Risen Lord.

In this story Peter "tucked in his garment, for he was lightly clad, and jumped into the sea" (John 21:7). According to Jewish law greeting someone is a religious act, and to perform a religious act one must be clothed. Peter put on his tunic and tucked it into his loincloth so that he could be the first of the disciples to greet the Risen Jesus and acknowledge him as Lord.

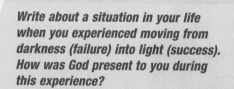

WHAT DIFFERENCE DOES FAITH MAKE?

Write about a situation in your life when you experienced moving from darkness (failure) into light (success). How was God present to you during this experience?

_____

_____

_____

_____

_____

_____

_____

WHAT DIFFERENCE

Does This Make in Our Church?

John's account of the Gospel is filled with signs and symbols. Each of these signs and symbols help us, in its own unique way, grasp the deeper meaning of the life of Jesus. In the gospel story of the Risen Lord appearing to his disciples on the shore of Lake Tiberias, John uses many signs and symbols. Light and darkness are among the symbols John uses to describe the meaning of faith in Christ. Christians use light and darkness to tell the story of our faith in other ways too. One form of such faith sharing is the stained-glass window.

Rose window, Notre Dame Cathedral, Chartres, France.

Stained-Glass Windows

Christians were making stained-glass windows as early as the fourth century. The best examples of stained glass were made in Europe, especially in France, during the twelfth and thirteenth centuries. Stained glass became important in churches during the Middle Ages (ca. A.D. 500–1500) for two main reasons.

First. Stained-glass windows were a source of brilliant light. Since there was no electricity, churches depended upon natural light. The bubbles, flaws, and irregularities of stained-glass windows diffuse the light and make the glass sparkle.

Second. Stained-glass windows were perfect for sharing the faith. The symbolism of light and darkness permeates our faith. The complex truths of good and evil, knowledge and ignorance can better be understood through pictures and symbols illuminated with color and light. For example, in the Middle Ages, when many people could not read, the pictures in the windows passed on the story of our faith from generation to generation. In the cathedral of Chartres, France, the entire Bible story, from Genesis to Revelation, is depicted in the rich glass hues of reds and blues.

The Life of Christ,
**stained-glass window.
Notre Dame Cathedral,
Chartres, France.**

The brilliance of the colors intertwining and reflecting off floors and walls surrounded people of faith with the presence of God. Imagine how easily believers could put themselves in the pictures and become part of the many stories that were unfolded before their eyes.

How can you share your faith in the Risen Jesus in a way that would capture the attention of people today?

**Interior of Notre Dame
Cathedral, Chartres, France.**

WHAT DIFFERENCE

Does It Make in My Life?

In this chapter you heard some of the gospel stories about Jesus appearing to his disciples after the Resurrection. Each of these stories is a testimony of faith that Jesus was raised from the dead and seen by his disciples. The impact this had on the faith of the disciples in Jesus was tremendous. As you know they were so filled with faith that they began to share it with others. This news was just too good to keep to themselves. They became real faith sharers.

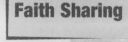

Faith Sharing

As disciples of Jesus today, we too are called to share our faith with others. At our baptism we received a wonderful challenge and responsibility not only to "keep the faith" but to "spread the faith." Just like the early followers of Jesus, we have good news to tell! Jesus was raised from the dead. He is our Lord and Savior. If we follow him and live according to his law of love, then we too will live forever in happiness and peace.

You probably know people who seem to have little trouble sharing their faith. They do so with great enthusiasm and purpose. However, some people have difficulty honestly sharing what they believe about God and the impact this has on their lives. You might be one of those people. There are various reasons why you might hesitate to accept the challenge of sharing your faith with others. You may feel uncertain about what you really believe. Or you might be afraid that your friends will think you're strange or weird. Or you may not realize how important it is for Christians to share their belief in Jesus.

As you grow in your faith it is important to find ways to overcome these obstacles and work at the challenge. You may need to grow in understanding your faith and in the courage to pass it on. This doesn't

mean you will have to preach on street corners or become a TV evangelist, and you certainly don't have to act strange or weird. Just remember that faith is shared each and every day by what we do as well as by what we say.

Faith Sharing Words and Actions

Here are a few suggestions of ways you can share your faith with others.

† Have a discussion with a friend or family member about what you believe and what your faith means to you.

† Make a habit of reading the Bible at least once a week and sharing what you've read with someone else.

† Be especially attentive and respectful at Mass and during prayer times.

† Volunteer to work on a parish or community project or committee that reaches out to help those in need.

† Participate in your religion classes by sharing your thoughts, questions, concerns.

† Help organize and participate in a prayer service, retreat day, or special Mass in your parish or school.

† Volunteer to be a reader at Mass.

† Help a younger brother or sister learn their prayers or read them a Bible story.

† Be willing to stand up for what is right even when it means going against the crowd.

faith decision

In a small group talk about why you find it easy or difficult to share your faith with others. Talk about ways you can overcome any obstacles you might have to sharing your faith. Promise to support and encourage one another in doing this.

This week I will share my faith with others by

_____

_____

_____

_____

_____

_____

_____

_____

_____ .

Faith Vocabulary

Define the term *resurrection stories*.

Main Ideas

Choose either (a) or (b) from each set of items. Write a brief paragraph
to answer each of your choices.

1. (a) Explain the importance of Jesus appearing to the disciples after
   his resurrection.

   (b) Summarize some of the events in the different resurrection stories
   in the Gospel.

2. (a) Describe what happened when the Risen Jesus called out to his disciples
   from the shore of the Sea of Tiberias.

   (b) Explain the meaning of the setting of the resurrection story in
   John 21:1–14.

3. (a) Explain the use of the images of light and darkness in John 21:1–14.

   (b) Explain the use of the image of breaking of bread in this resurrection story.

Critical Thinking

Using what you have learned in this chapter, explain the importance of the expression
"Seeing is believing" for followers of Christ.

Family Discussion

How do we help one another see the part Jesus
plays in our family life?

**Visit our
web site at
www.FaithFirst.com**

THE CHURCH
UNIT 3

PARENT PAGE—UNIT 3

FAITH

This third unit of *Creed and Prayer* presents the teachings of the Catholic Church named in the third part of the Apostles' Creed, which begins "I believe in the Holy Spirit, the holy catholic Church." Your child will learn about the Holy Spirit, whom the Father sent in Jesus' name to guide and teach the community of his followers, the Church, as they continue Christ's work in the world until he comes again in glory at the end of time.

The Church is first and foremost the New People of God. We are a community of believers joined to Christ and one another in Baptism. We are a people working in every place and in every age announcing God's plan of salvation in Christ and preparing for the coming of God's kingdom. Guided by the Holy Spirit, all the baptized—laypeople, ordained ministers, and those who consecrate their lives by vowing to live lives of gospel poverty, obedience, and chastity—work together as the Body of Christ in the world.

Reading about the shipwreck of Paul the Apostle will add drama to your child's understanding of his or her own call to share their faith in Christ with others. A closer look at Christian art, the work of your parish council, and the election of a pope will also concretize your child's appreciation of some of the many ways the Spirit leads and guides the Church to fulfill our mission of building up the Church until Christ comes again in glory. At that moment, the kingdom announced by Christ will come about. All people will live together with God and one another in peace and happiness forever.

WHAT DIFFERENCE
DOES IT MAKE?

In Unit 3 your child will learn that the Church is the Body of Christ and the Temple of the Holy Spirit. It is through the Holy Spirit, present in the Church and in each of the baptized, that the work of Christ in the world is continued until the end of time. Through the gifts of the Holy Spirit Christians are empowered to live a life of loving service of God and others. We continue the work of Christ and help prepare for the coming of the kingdom of God.

Your family has a special opportunity to participate in the work of the Church. Joined to Christ in Baptism, each member of your family is called to use the gifts of the Holy Spirit to build up the Body of Christ, the Church. Together as a family you face situations each day that invite you to work together and for one another. These are opportunities for seeing these situations through the eyes of faith. These moments of cooperating, compromising, and solving problems are moments for growing as a Christian family and sharing with others God's loving plan of goodness for the world.

Perhaps there is a particular goal or concern that your family is working on right now. Talk together about how you all might use the skills discussed on these pages to achieve that goal or solve a problem. Before you begin and all throughout the process of working toward achieving your goal, invite the Holy Spirit to be part of that work. Ask the Holy Spirit to open your eyes to the ways you can grow in love and commitment to one another.

You and your child can join with the larger church community and bring Christ's message to a waiting and needy world beyond your family. Make the time to join with members of your parish family in one of the numerous ways they reach out to people in need. By working with you and your parish family, your child will see and experience the optimism faith in Christ brings to you and others. This will help your child see that by joining with Christ and other believers, we can make the world a better place. We can continue the work of rebuilding the world according to God's plan.

By acting on your faith with your child, your son or daughter learns ways to make faith-centered decisions and choices. By living your faith through your clear, concrete actions, you are making faith come alive. You are inviting your child to open his or her eyes of faith and to live the Christian values of love and service of others.

The Gift of
the Holy Spirit

12

Come, Holy Spirit, fill the hearts
of your faithful.
And kindle in them the fire of
your love.
Send forth your Spirit and they
shall be created.
And you will renew the face of
the earth. . . .
Lord, by the light of the Holy
Spirit
you have taught the hearts of
your faithful.
In the same Spirit help us to
relish what is right
and always rejoice in your
consolation.

FROM *A BOOK OF PRAYERS*

When you pray the Apostles'
Creed, you pray, "I believe in
the Holy Spirit." What is your
understanding of the role of
the Holy Spirit in God's plan?

*And suddenly there came
from the sky a noise like
a strong driving wind. . . .
Then there appeared
to them tongues as of fire. . . .
And they were all filled
with the holy Spirit.*

ACTS OF THE APOSTLES 2:2–4

145

The Spirit: The Giver of Life

FAITH FOCUS

What was the work of the Holy Spirit prior to Jesus' birth?

FAITH VOCABULARY

Holy Spirit

Annunciation

advocate

charism

Movements of air fascinate us. Cool breezes refresh and renew us on hot summer days. Violent gales frighten us as twisters bear down on our communities, or hurricanes stalk, ghostlike, toward our coastlines. Children lie outdoors on their backs and watch clouds scuttle across the sky. Whether delightful or devastating, the power of moving air has the ability to fascinate us.

The Spirit of God at Work in God's Plan

Ruah is the Hebrew word that means "breath" or "wind." In English, *spirit* translates *ruah* and designates the **Holy Spirit,** the third Person of the Holy Trinity. If you think of the Spirit this way, you get some idea of the Spirit's powerful yet mysterious presence in our lives.

Throughout the pages of the Old Testament, you will find few direct references to the Holy Spirit before the birth of Jesus. But that does not mean that the Spirit was not at work in the world bringing about God's plan of goodness. The Spirit was hidden, but at work, a part of God's promise that would be fully

revealed. Often as invisible as breathing and breezes, the Spirit was at work throughout the ages before the birth of Jesus.

Why does the image of wind or breath of life describe the Spirit's work?

The Spirit of the Covenant

The Spirit revealed God's presence countless times to the children of Abraham. Whether in the burning bush or in a flash of lightning or the visit of mysterious strangers, the Holy Spirit was breathing energy into God's people.

After the Israelites settled in the land promised them by God, they chose kings to lead them. Some of these kings guided the Israelites in faithfully living their covenant with God. Others misled them, even allowing the worship of their neighbors' false gods. This infidelity eventually led to the destruction of the center and heart of the nation, the Temple in Jerusalem. Tragically, the Israelites were forced into living in exile.

These unfaithful leaders proved to the people that only God could truly rule over them in the age to

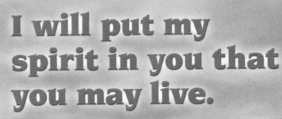

I will put my spirit in you that you may live.

Ezekiel 37:14

come. One prophet after another spoke out against what they saw happening. To the faithful Israelites they pledged God's loyalty and faithfulness. An anointed one, a messiah, would come who would be a faithful shepherd to Israel.

Describe the work of the Spirit among God's people of the Old Covenant.

The Giver of Life

Other prophets spoke of a divine spirit who would be poured out into the hearts of all the people. This spirit would be the source of new life for God's people. We read:

The hand of the LORD came upon me, and he led me out in the spirit of the LORD and set me in the center of the plain, which was now filled with bones. He made me walk among them in every direction so that I saw how many they were on the surface of the plain. How dry they were! He asked me: Son of man, can these bones come to life? "Lord GOD," I answered, "you alone know that.". . . Then he said to me: Son of man, these bones are the whole house of Israel. . . . Therefore, prophesy and say to them: . . . I will put my spirit in you that you may live, and I will settle you upon your land; thus you shall know that I am the LORD. I have promised, and I will do it, says the LORD.

EZEKIEL 37:1–3, 11, 12, 14

Describe the Spirit as the Giver of Life.

The Spirit breathed life into the people of the Old Testament. However, it was only through Christ that the Spirit's role becomes clear.

WHAT DIFFERENCE DOES FAITH MAKE?

How might you remember the Spirit's presence with you each day?

_____

_____

_____

_____

Ezekiel and the Dry Bones.

The Spirit in the Gospel

The Gospel often presents Jesus and the Spirit together. While distinct Persons of the Holy Trinity, the Son and the Spirit are indeed inseparable. Their role in God's plan of salvation is always connected. Whenever God the Father sends the Son, he always sends the Spirit.

The Spirit and the Son

In the gospel story of the **Annunciation** (a word meaning "announcement"), Jesus and the Spirit are linked together. The angel Gabriel announced to Mary that God would implement his plan in her through the Holy Spirit (see Luke 1:35). With these words of the angel, the mission of the Holy Spirit begins to be revealed. The Holy Spirit prepared Mary to be the mother of our redeemer, Jesus. The Spirit brings the Father's plan for our salvation to fulfillment. The Spirit manifests, or shows, Jesus to be the Son of God, who is now also son of Mary. Finally, through Mary the Holy Spirit begins the great

FAITH
FOCUS

Why is the Spirit called our advocate?

Have you ever known two people who are so close that it is hard to imagine one without the other? See one of them and you know that the other is nearby. Such closeness gives us an insight into the inseparable relationship between Jesus, the Son of God, and the Spirit.

work of connecting the human family together in Jesus Christ, her only son.

In the gospel story of the Annunciation, what does Luke tell us about the Spirit?

The Advocate and Helper

Jesus assured his disciples that his heavenly Father would "give the holy Spirit to those who ask him" (Luke 11:13). In the same vein, Jesus promised the apostles that they would be put on trial. He told them that when the time came "[I]t will not be you who speak but the Spirit of your Father speaking through you" (Matthew 10:20).

As Jesus' own trial approached, he pledged that the Spirit would be their **advocate** (see John 14:26). An advocate is one who stands by a person's side, speaking for them, standing up for them. The Spirit would come and be with them forever.

Describe what the Gospel tells us about the work of the Spirit.

The Spirit in Our Lives

The Holy Spirit is our advocate too. So close is he to us that we are temples of the Holy Spirit. He is like our breath, which is a vital element for our survival. Very often we do not even realize we are breathing because it is so much a part of our lives—so necessary for us to live. The Spirit is like that.

- Given to us at Baptism, the Spirit dwells within us.
- The Spirit teaches us to pray.
- The Spirit gives us the courage to live as disciples of Christ.

- The Spirit is our teacher and he is present with us, reminding us of Christ and instructing us in everything.
- The Spirit calls us to cooperate with him in using our gifts to build the Church.

Describe ways the Holy Spirit is present in your life.

The Spirit of Life

Jesus tells his friend Nicodemus that "no one can enter the kingdom of God without being born of water and Spirit" (John 3:5). When Jesus discloses that his own body will be food for the world, Jesus calls the Spirit the Giver of Life (see John 6:63).

Describe why Christians call the Holy Spirit the Giver of Life.

Little by little, Jesus unveiled the reality and work, or mission, of the Holy Spirit. Eventually Christians would come to understand that the Spirit is the third Person of the Trinity.

Christians have expressed their faith in the Holy Spirit in the gospel story of John baptizing Jesus at the Jordan River. The image of a dove represents the Holy Spirit. The voice from heaven represents the Father. You can read this story in Matthew 3:13–17. The story is also told in Mark 1:9–11, Luke 3:21–22, and John 1:31–34.

Did you Know...

Pentecost. Contemporary stained-glass window.

How might the Holy Spirit be your advocate and helper right now?

WHAT DIFFERENCE DOES FAITH MAKE?

_____

_____

_____

Why is the Spirit so important to the Church?

If you wondered how the Church has thrived for nearly two thousand years, look no further than the Holy Spirit. Just as Christ and the Church are inseparable, so also are the Church and the Spirit. The Church's mission is the very mission of Christ and the Spirit.

The Church Begins Its Mission

On the day of Pentecost, Jesus' mission on earth is fulfilled and the work of the Spirit, in a sense, takes center stage. With the coming of the Spirit, the Church was born. The Holy Spirit plays many roles in the Church.

Lifeforce of the Church

The Spirit breathes life in each of us and in the Body of Christ, the Church. Christ, the Head of the Church, constantly pours out his Spirit on the Church. The Spirit nourishes the People of God, heals the Church, and helps the members of the Church act in harmony. The Spirit draws us to the message of the Gospel and he prepares our hearts as we follow Jesus.

The Holy Spirit is the principle agent of the Church's mission. It is the Spirit who shows us the Risen Lord, recalling Christ's words and opening our minds to understand the Paschal mystery of his death and resurrection and ascension to the Father. The Spirit guides the popes and bishops in their ministry of serving the Church as its leaders. Through the power of the Holy Spirit, Christ is present in the sacraments, especially in the Eucharist and in the word of God proclaimed in Scripture.

The Spirit of God dwells within you.

The Spirit enables the Church to become one with God and empowers us to create a better world. By being members of the Church, we participate in the works of God being performed here and now, in and through the Church.

Describe the role of the Holy Spirit in the life of the Church.

Source of Unity

The Holy Spirit is the source of the Church's unity. The Spirit unites all of the Church's different parts into a unified whole, so that everything works together according to God's plan.

The Spirit works in every member of the Church and he is the source of the many **charisms** that enable the Church to carry on its mission in the world. Charisms are gifts or graces freely given to individual Christians for the benefit of building up the Church. The greatest of these charisms is the charism of love or charity (see 1 Corinthians 13:13).

Out of the enormous diversity of the gifts and talents given to the Church, the Spirit brings a remarkable harmony and peace. The Spirit ensures that Christ is the Head of the Body, animating and directing the Church to continue bringing about God's plan of creation and salvation until the end of time.

Explain the Church's belief that the Spirit is the source of the Church's unity.

Temple of the Spirit

Saint Augustine of Hippo said, "What the soul is to the human body, the Holy Spirit is to the Body of Christ, which is the Church." Augustine reworded what Paul the Apostle said even more directly: "Do you know that you are the temple of God, and that the Spirit of God dwells in you?"(1 Corinthians 3:16). "[W]e are the temple of the living God" (2 Corinthians 6:16). Without the Holy Spirit, the Church would not exist.

Describe the Church as the temple of the Holy Spirit.

The Church's mission is to announce, bear witness to, and make present the life of the Trinity. To help the Church fulfill this role in the world, the Spirit constantly builds up, inspires, animates, and blesses the Church until Christ comes again in glory at the end of time.

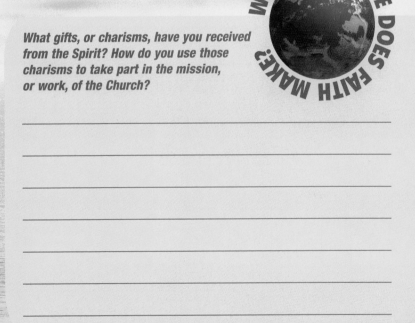

WHAT DIFFERENCE DOES FAITH MAKE?

What gifts, or charisms, have you received from the Spirit? How do you use those charisms to take part in the mission, or work, of the Church?

_____

_____

_____

_____

_____

_____

WHAT DIFFERENCE

Does This Make in Our Church?

The Spirit of God has always been at work in the world—at creation, among the people of God of the Old Testament, with Jesus during his life on earth, at the first Christian Pentecost, among us today. Until the end of time, the Spirit is the lifeforce of God's work in the world.

The Spirit is our advocate and teacher helping us remember all Jesus said and did. He is the Giver of Life blessing the Church with the many gifts to build up the Body of Christ in the world until Christ comes again in glory at the end of time. The Spirit has blessed us with the gift of creativity. One of the many ways Christians have expressed this gift to build up the Body of Christ is through art.

Pieta. Michelangelo Buonarroti (1475–1564), Italian sculptor, painter, architect, and poet.

Christian Art

Can you remember when you were younger and your parents took you to church? Do you remember what you saw? Maybe you were fascinated by the sights and colors in the church. Perhaps the huge statues caught your eye or your attention was drawn to the brilliant colors in the windows or the other art throughout the church.

From the beginning of the Church, Christians have shared their faith with others through the visual arts.

Early Christian art used statues and mosaics to depict images of Christ and the miracles that demonstrated the saving power of God. In the seventh and eighth centuries, Irish missionaries needed liturgical books. Artistic centers arose where monks copied books and lavishly illustrated them with colors and gold.

Saint Francis of Assisi. Paint on wood.

During the Renaissance the popes commissioned artists to work for the Church. In 1503 Pope Julius II began a rebuilding of Saint Peter's Basilica and commissioned Michelangelo to paint the ceiling of the Sistine Chapel and to create other major sculptures and monuments. Painters like El Greco captured the spiritual fervor of the Church. Architects and stone masons and sculptors used their gifts to raise magnificent grand cathedrals in praise of the grandeur of God. All these masterpieces of faith continue to be admired by both Christians and non-Christians to this day.

Many Christian artists saw their work as their prayer to God. For Michelangelo art and prayer could not be separated. They were one and the same activity. For artists like Michelangelo art becomes their prayer to God. It expresses their innermost thoughts, feelings, and faith.

Pope John Paul II, in a letter to artists dated April 4, 1999, invited artists to rediscover the depth of the spiritual and religious dimension which has been typical of art in its noblest forms in every age. Future Christian artists will continue to use the Spirit's gift of creativity to celebrate and share their faith in God until Christ comes in glory at the end of time.

Pope John Paul II celebrates Mass in Sistine Chapel, Vatican, Rome, Italy.

What forms of Christian art help you deepen your faith in God?

Elizabeth Anne Seton.
Bronze statue.

153

WHAT DIFFERENCE

Does It Make in My Life?

At Baptism we received the gift of the Holy Spirit to help and guide us to be open to God's grace in our lives. We became vibrant living temples of the Holy Spirit. Confirmation and Eucharist continue to fill us with the gifts of the Holy Spirit to help us live as followers of Christ and to build up the Body of Christ, the Church.

Understanding

Courage

Reverence

Wonder and Awe

The Gifts of the Spirit

What does it mean when we say someone is full of spirit or someone has great spirit? Well, as Christians, we are called to be spirited people—that is, people filled with the Holy Spirit and filled with God's love. The Holy Spirit gives us certain "gifts" to help us live as people filled with God's love.

Gifts for Life

There are seven special gifts that the Holy Spirit showers upon us. These gifts are freely given and fill us with grace to help us and to benefit the whole church community. These gifts are wisdom, understanding, knowledge, right judgment, courage, reverence, and wonder and awe. They help you listen to the prompting of the Holy Spirit luring you to make good choices, live good lives, and be true followers of Christ.

154

Let's look at how we can really live the Gifts of the Holy Spirit each and every day.

➤ **WISDOM** is the gift of knowing the right choices to make to live a holy life. It helps you avoid the things that could lead you away from God.

➤ **UNDERSTANDING** is the gift of comprehension, the ability to grasp the teachings of our religion. It is the gift that helps you be tolerant and sympathetic of others. It helps you sense when someone is hurting or in need of compassion.

➤ **KNOWLEDGE** is the gift of knowing and enlightenment. It enables you to choose the right path that will lead you to God, and it encourages you to avoid obstacles that will keep you from him.

➤ **RIGHT JUDGMENT, OR COUNSEL**, is the gift of prudence. This gift helps you make choices as a follower of Jesus.

➤ **COURAGE, OR FORTITUDE**, is the gift that helps you stand up and overcome any obstacles that would keep you from practicing your faith.

➤ **REVERENCE, OR PIETY**, is the gift of reverence for and confidence in God that inspires you to joyfully want to serve God and others.

➤ **WONDER AND AWE, OR FEAR OF THE LORD**, is the gift of wonder and respect that encourages you to be in awe of God. It is not to fear God but to so love him that you do not want to offend him by your words or actions.

Knowledge

faith decision

Name three changes that would happen in the world if Christians really tried to use the gifts of the Holy Spirit in their lives.

_____

_____

_____

This week I will ask the Holy Spirit to help me live the gift of _____ in order to help me

_____

_____

_____

_____ .

Right judgment

Wisdom

Faith Vocabulary

Define each of these terms:

1. Holy Spirit
2. Annunciation
3. advocate
4. charism

Main Ideas

Choose either (a) or (b) from each set of items. Write a brief paragraph to answer each of your choices.

1. (a) What insight does the Hebrew word *ruah* give us into the work of the Holy Spirit among us?

   (b) Describe the work of the Spirit among the People of God in the Old Testament.

2. (a) Discuss the relationship between the work of Jesus and the work of the Spirit.

   (b) Explain how the Holy Spirit is our advocate.

3. (a) Discuss the work of the Spirit as the lifeforce of the mission of the Church.

   (b) Describe the work of the Spirit as the source of unity for the Church.

Critical Thinking

Using what you have learned in this chapter, briefly explain what you profess in the Nicene Creed when you say:
"We believe in the Holy Spirit, the Lord, the giver of life."

Family Discussion

How can we cooperate with the Spirit to be the lifeforce and source of unity and harmony in our family?

Visit our web site at www.FaithFirst.com

The Church: The People of God

13

WE PRAY

God our Father,
by the promise you made
in the life, death, and
    resurrection of Christ your
    Son,
you bring together in your
    Spirit, from all the nations,
a people to be your own.
Keep the Church faithful to its
    mission:
may it be a leaven in the world
renewing us in Christ,
and transforming us into your
    family.

FROM *ROMAN MISSAL,
MASS FOR THE UNIVERSAL CHURCH, B*

We use the word *church* in
many ways. What do you
mean when you use the
word *church*?

*[G]race to you and peace
from God our Father
and the Lord Jesus Christ.*

EPHESIANS 1:2

157

Gathered in Christ's Name

Abraham Leaving Home for Canaan.
Adrian Kupman (1910–), Austrian artist.

FAITH FOCUS

Why do we call the Church the new People of God?

Having friends and belonging to groups is important to all people—young and old. "Belonging" just seems to be part of who we are. To what groups do you belong? Why do you belong to those groups? Which of the groups to which you belong is your favorite? Why is it your favorite?

FAITH VOCABULARY

Church

Born in the Heart of God

Everyone who is baptized belongs to the **Church.** The Church is the sacrament of salvation—the sign and instrument of our reconciliation and communion with God and one another. The origin of the Church lies deep within the plan of God from the very beginning of time. It was the design of God in creation to share his own divine life with those he created and to "call together in a holy Church those who should believe in Christ" (*Constitution on the Church,* 2).

The gathering of God's children began as soon as sin destroyed God's original plan. The Book of Genesis first describes the chaos that sin brought into the world. We read about:

- the accusations of Adam and Eve against one another (see Genesis 3:8–13),
- the rift between Cain and Abel (see Genesis 4:1–16),
- the spread of sin that covered the world prior to the flood (see Genesis 6:5–6),
- and the confusion of human speech brought on by the sin of Babel (see Genesis 11:1–9).

Even in the face of sin, God did not abandon the human race. To Noah he promised a universal covenant with all people. Next God promised Abraham that he would be the father of a great nation (see Genesis 12:2), foreshadowing the future gathering of all nations into one people.

God elected the people of Israel to be his people. He entered a covenant with them on Mount Sinai and gave his Law to them through

Moses. Later the prophets announced that God would make a new and everlasting covenant (see Jeremiah 31:31–34) with all people—just as he had promised.

Describe the origin of the Church in God's plan.

The New and Everlasting Covenant

The promise of the New Covenant was instituted in Jesus Christ (see Luke 22: 14–20). Jesus called his first followers, who became known as the Twelve, to be the foundation of this new People of God. They symbolized and represented the twelve tribes of the Israelites and served as the foundation stones for the new Jerusalem (see Revelation 21:1, 10–14).

The New People of God

When his redemptive work was accomplished on earth, the risen glorified Christ returned to his Father in heaven. As he promised, the Father sent the Holy Spirit in his name. It is the Spirit who forms the followers of Jesus into the new People of God, the Church. The word *church* means "convocation, those called together."

It is God's plan that all people are called to belong to the new People of God so that in Christ they can form one family, the one People of God. In the new dispensation of the Holy Spirit, acceptance of the Church is inseparable from belief in God.

Describe the Church as the New People of God.

The Church is on pilgrimage as the People of God until the end of time. Then all God's children will be gathered together in fulfillment of God's plan. The Church will be the shining Bride of Christ (see Revelation 22:17). There will be "one flock, one shepherd" (John 10:16).

WHAT DIFFERENCE DOES FAITH MAKE?

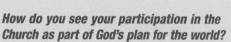

How do you see your participation in the Church as part of God's plan for the world?

_____

_____

_____

_____

_____

FAITH
FOCUS

Why is the work of the Church the work of all the members of the Church?

Civic organizations, school clubs, theater companies, athletic teams—no matter what type of group you think of, each usually has a variety of members. Each of the members, in turn, have some responsibility for the work the group does. Think of a club or organization to which you belong. Who are the members? How is the responsibility for the work, or mission, of the group divided? What are the responsibilities of the officers? Of members leading and serving on committees? Of the general membership?

The People of God

The visible Church on earth is made up of many people too. Each has responsibility for the work, or mission, of the Church. Joined to Christ in Baptism, each is called to share in the Paschal mystery of Christ and to be happy with him forever. This is the vocation, or calling, of all Christians.

The Holy Spirit blesses the People of God with talents and gifts and responsibilities to live that vocation and to help build up the Body of Christ on earth. Paul the Apostle wrote:

There are different kinds of spiritual gifts but the same Spirit; there are different forms of service but the same Lord; there are different workings but the same God who produces all of them in everyone. To each individual the manifestation of the Spirit is given for some benefit.   1 CORINTHIANS 12:4–7

Laypeople

At Baptism all the newly baptized receive the gift of the Spirit and are anointed with the blessed oil called chrism. The presider prays:

He [God the Father] now anoints you with the chrism of salvation, so that, united with his people, you may remain for ever a member of Christ who is Priest, Prophet, and King.

FROM RITE OF BAPTISM

After their anointing, the newly baptized receive a lighted candle, a symbol of Christ. They are to live as lights of Christ in the world.

Most of the baptized are members of the laity, or laypeople. Laypeople light up the world. They are lights of faith, hope, and love in their families and among their friends, in their communities and in their workplaces, and in their parishes. They are living witnesses of Christ at the very heart of the human community.

Explain how laypeople live their vocation as members of the People of God.

Ordained Ministers

Bishops, priests, and deacons are ordained to serve the whole Church. Through the ordained ministry, especially of bishops and priests, the presence of Christ as Head of the Church is made visible in the midst of the church community. Bishops are helped by their co-workers, priests and deacons, in their work of teaching the faith, celebrating divine worship, and guiding the faithful entrusted to their care. All ordained ministers of the Church are clergy.

How do the clergy live out their vocation?

The Consecrated Life

Laypeople and ordained ministers sometime consecrate themselves more intimately to God's service and to the good of the Church.

They vow or promise to live the evangelical counsels of poverty, chastity, and obedience in a way of life approved by the Church. They can live out their consecration publicly in religious communities, or even privately as cloistered religious do. In whatever way these members of the Church live out their consecration, they are living signs of God's saving love at work in the world. Their lives remind us to keep our focus on living the Gospel.

How do those in the consecrated or religious life live out their baptismal promises?

Laypeople, ordained ministers, and those who live the consecrated life each have different roles and responsibilities in the Church. Joined to Christ and one another in Baptism and anointed with the Spirit, all cooperate with the Spirit and with one another to build up the Church until Christ comes again in glory.

WHAT DIFFERENCE DOES FAITH MAKE?

Describe a symbol you would use to demonstrate your understanding of how the work of the Church is the work of all its members.

_____

_____

_____

Every group has leaders. Sometimes we even join a group because we like its leader. For example, athletes try out for certain teams because they think a certain coach will help them best develop their skills. What good leaders do you know? What are some of the qualities of a good leader?

Christ, the Good Shepherd

A person becomes a member of the new People of God, the Church, by faith in Jesus and by Baptism. Christ is the head of his Body, the Church. The Church on earth also has visible leaders, whom God chooses to serve the Church. The Gospel clearly tells us that the Lord Jesus gave his Church on earth a structure. He chose the Twelve with Peter as their leader. After finishing breakfast with his disciples, the Risen Jesus said to Peter:

> "Simon, son of John, do you love me more than these?" He said to him, "Yes, Lord, you know that I love you." He said to him, "Feed my lambs." He then said to him a second time, "Simon, son of John, do you love me?" He said to him, "Yes, Lord, you know that I love you." He said to him, "Tend my sheep." He said to him the third time, "Simon, son of John, do you love me?" Peter was distressed that he had said to him a third time, "Do you love me?" and he said to him, "Lord, you know everything; you know that I love you." [Jesus] said to him, "Feed my sheep." JOHN 21:15–17

Jesus, the Good Shepherd, gave Peter the ministry and responsibility of being the shepherd, the servant and leader, of the whole Church.

To whom did Jesus give the authority and ministry of serving the Church as its leaders?

The Pope and Other Bishops

The pope and other bishops in our Church today are the successors of Peter and the apostles. Together they form the college of bishops. They are the visible source and foundation of unity within the Church. The pope is also the bishop of Rome. He is the shepherd and the servant-leader of the whole Church and the head of all the bishops. Bishops are chosen by the

pope to lead local churches in every part of the world. As the leader and chief pastor for his local church, a bishop stands in the place of Christ.

Bishop as Teacher

The first duty of the bishop is to preach the Good News. This duty is based on the command of Jesus: "Go into the whole world and proclaim the gospel to every creature" (Mark 16:15). Guided by the Spirit the bishop, as a successor of the apostles, passes on, preserves, and defends the truth of the Gospel by teaching authoritatively on matters of faith and morals. The faithful are called to believe what the Church teaches.

Bishop as Sanctifier

Helped by priests, their co-workers, and deacons, bishops sanctify the Church by their prayers and work, by their ministry of word and sacrament, as well as by their personal example of holiness. Bishops have the responsibility and authority to see to it that the sacraments are celebrated reverently with the faithful in their care. Bishops are stewards of the grace of Christ, especially of the Eucharist over which they preside or delegate to priests as co-workers.

Bishop as Pastor

The bishop leads and serves the faithful by following the example of Christ the Good Shepherd (see Luke 22:26).

He should not refuse to listen to his subjects whose welfare he promotes as of his very own children. . . . [T]he faithful . . . should be closely attached to the bishop as the Church is to Jesus Christ, and as Jesus Christ is to the Father.

CONSTITUTION ON THE CHURCH, 27

Describe the threefold ministry of the bishop.

The cross is to be central in their lives, just as it was in the life of Christ. In other words, the Good Shepherd who was willing to lay down his life for his sheep is the model for every bishop. Those chosen to lead the Church are to serve others as Jesus served (see John 13:1–17).

Crosier (also spelled crozier) is the name given to the staff carried by a bishop or archbishop while walking in procession during the celebration of the liturgy. The top of the crosier is curved like the top of a shepherd's staff. The crosier resembles the staff often carried by shepherds while shepherding their flocks. The crosier reminds us that the bishop is the shepherd who serves the members of the Church entrusted to his care. The crosier carried by a pope has a crucifix at the top of it.

WHAT DIFFERENCE DOES FAITH MAKE?

In what ways can you be a Christian leader, one who leads by serving others?

_____

_____

_____

WHAT DIFFERENCE

Does This Make in Our Church?

The Conclave of Cardinals, 1978. Election of Albino Cardinal Luciani, archbishop and patriarch of Venice, Italy, who took the name John Paul I.

Through Baptism we are joined to Christ and become members of the Body of Christ, the Church. Christ is the Head of his Body. The visible Church on earth is made up of many members—ordained ministers, laypeople, and those who consecrate their lives by vowing lives of poverty, chastity, and obedience. The pope, the bishop of Rome, is the visible head of the whole Church on earth. He is the successor of Saint Peter, whom Jesus gave the responsibility of being the shepherd, the servant-leader, of his followers.

The Naming of a Pope

Catholics believe that the naming of a pope is the work of the Holy Spirit. The Spirit is the Advocate and Teacher sent by Christ to guide his followers in fulfilling their mission until the end of time. It is the work of the Spirit working side by side and through the leaders of the Church that a pope, the successor of Saint Peter the Apostle, is chosen.

After a pope dies, how is the new successor of Saint Peter chosen? The choosing, or election, of a pope takes place at a special gathering, or conclave, of the cardinals of the Church. The title *cardinal* is usually given to a bishop—although nonbishops have been named cardinals. Cardinals belong to the College of Cardinals. They serve the Church by advising the pope and electing the pope.

Guidelines for Electing a Pope

The guidelines for electing a pope have changed over the years. The current guidelines include:

- No cardinal over eighty years old is eligible to elect a new pope.
- The maximum number of papal electors is 120. This means that at any one time, there cannot be more than 120 cardinals under the age of eighty.
- Two-thirds majority of votes is required. If no one is chosen after thirty ballots, the cardinals may then elect a pope by simple majority.
- All voting is silent.
- The conclave takes place in the Sistine Chapel. The papal electors are housed in a location 350 meters from the Sistine Chapel until they elect a new pope.

Electing a New Pope

When the papal electors enter the conclave, they take an oath to follow the rules of the conclave and obey the rules of secrecy about the voting and the discussions. These rules of secrecy include: There is to be no contact between the cardinals in the conclave and the outside world either by phone, television, papers, or mail. The penalty for breaking this secrecy is automatic excommunication.

The papal electors take seats around the wall of the Sistine Chapel and are given a paper ballot on which is written, "I elect as supreme Pontiff . . ." They write a name on the ballot, fold it, and place it in a chalice on the altar. The ballots are counted and if there is no majority, the ballots are burned with straw and chemicals to give off a black smoke—the sign that no pope has been elected. The cardinals vote twice each morning and once each afternoon until a new pope is chosen.

When a new pope is elected, the paper ballots are burned without the chemical additive. This creates white smoke—the sign to the crowds gathered in Saint Peter's Square and the whole world that a new pope has been elected. The Dean of the College of Cardinals asks if the newly elected pope accepts his election and, if so, by what name he wishes to be called as pope. The cardinals then pledge their obedience to the new pope.

The new pope then puts on the official papal vestments—the white cassock and white skull cap. The Dean of the College of Cardinals moves to the main balcony of the Vatican, overlooking Saint Peter's Square. The Dean announces to the world, "Habemus Papam!" or "We have a pope!" The newly elected pope appears on the balcony and gives his blessing to the world, as the crowds jubilantly shout, "Viva il Papa!" or "Long live the pope!"

Imagine that your class was given the opportunity to nominate one of the cardinals to be the pope. What qualities would you want the new pope to have?

The Conclave of Cardinals, 1978. Cardinals voting.

WHAT DIFFERENCE

Does It Make in My Life?

Vocations in Life

There are different vocational choices for you to consider. Your first and basic call is to love: love God, love yourself, and love others. This love can be lived out through marriage and family life, the single life, a consecrated life as a member of a religious community, or an ordained minister. The word *vocation* comes from a Latin word that means "to call." Throughout our lives, God calls each of us to follow him in a special way. How we will respond to God's call is up to us. To help you respond you need to discover your own gifts and talents so you can determine the best way to serve God and others. How will you know what vocation God wants you to choose?

At your baptism, you were called to live in relationship with God and others throughout your life. The way you attain this is through the vocation or lifestyle you choose. Your vocation is God's invitation to you to live, love, and serve him and others.

Right now your calling is to be a student, finish school, and then decide what you will do with the rest of your life. Do you have any idea what you want to be or what you want to do with your life?

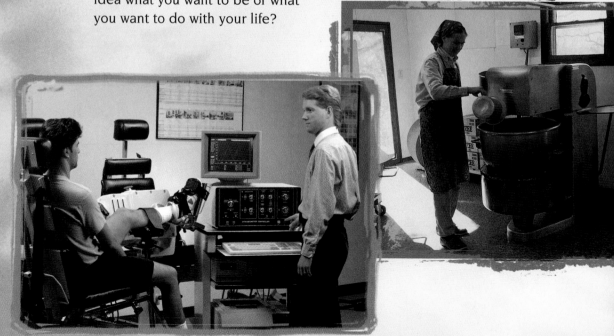

Discernment

According to the dictionary, discernment is a way or a quality of understanding something that is not yet clear. According to the Catholic Church, it is a way or a process that Christians use to comprehend and figure out what God is calling them to do. Discernment is a prayerful way to gain insight into and to learn more about yourself, your gifts and skills, so you can recognize or determine your vocation in life. This is an ongoing process. It takes thought and prayer throughout our lives. Here are a few steps to help you practice discernment.

- Set aside time to be quiet. Ask the Holy Spirit to open your mind and heart to listen to what God is saying to you about your life.

- Be open to different possibilities. What do you enjoy doing? What do you do especially well? While many people choose to marry, it is important to consider the possibility that God may be calling you to be ordained, to live in religious life, or to be single.

- Talk to people who seem to be living God's call to holiness and wholeness:
  —a married couple,
  —a religious brother or sister,
  —a deacon, priest or bishop,
  —a single person.

- Think about your unique personality, gifts, and talents, and the best way you can use them.

- Remember that discernment is an ongoing process. The more time you give to it, the better you will become at listening to who God is calling you to be.

faith decision

f

Discuss the following questions.

- How can the discernment process help you right now in your life?

- How can you get to know yourself and your gifts even better?

- Plan an interview with someone who is living his or her vocation as
  —a single person
  —a married person
  —a religious brother or sister
  —a bishop, a priest, or a deacon

  Write down two or three questions you would like to ask each person that would help you better understand each vocation.

This week I will think about what God is calling me to do with my life. I will set aside some time to practice the steps of discernment. I will do this on

_____
(date)

from _____ to _____.
(time)

Faith Vocabulary

Define the term *Church*.

Main Ideas

Choose either (a) or (b) from each set of items. Write a brief paragraph to answer each of your choices.

1. (a) Why do we say that the origin of the Church lies deep within the plan of God from the very beginning of time?

   (b) Describe the Church as the new People of God.

2. (a) Describe the role of laypeople in the Church.

   (b) Describe the role in the Church of those who live the consecrated life.

3. (a) Explain the ministry of the pope in the Church.

   (b) Describe the threefold ministry of the bishops of the Church.

Critical Thinking

Using what you have learned in this chapter, briefly explain this statement:
The Church is both human and divine.

Family Discussion

How can our family be a sign that reminds others that God calls all people to be one family, the People of God?

Visit our
web site at
www.FaithFirst.com

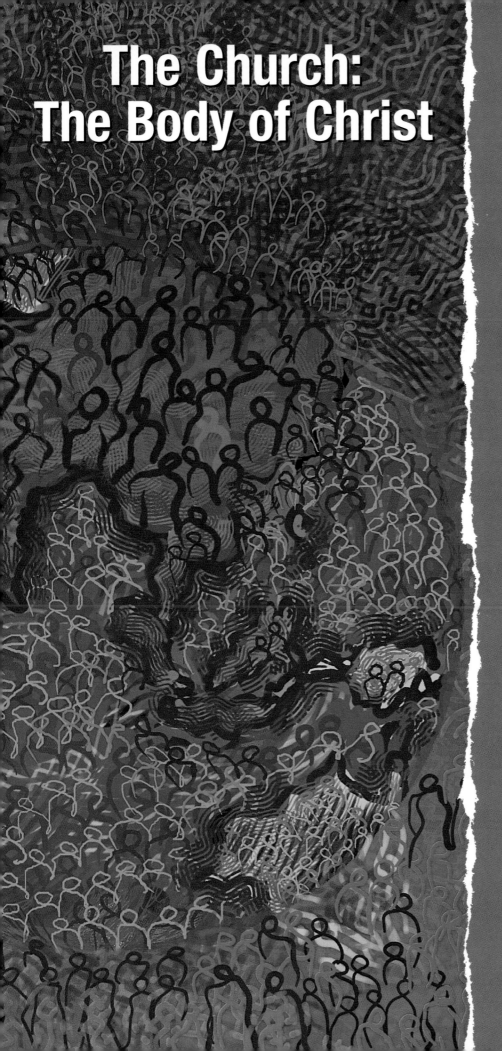

The Church: The Body of Christ

14

WE PRAY

God our Father,
may your Church always
    be your holy people,
united as you are one with the
    Son and the Holy Spirit.
May it be for all the world a
    sign of your unity and
    holiness,
as it grows to perfection in
    your love.

FROM *ROMAN MISSAL*,
MASS FOR THE UNIVERSAL CHURCH, C

When someone talks about
the Church, what images
come to your mind? Imagine
that you have been asked to
talk with a group of second
graders who are preparing for
First Eucharist. Your topic is
"The Church." What would
you tell the second graders?

*[There is] one Lord, one faith,
one baptism; one God and
Father of all, who is over all
and through all and in all.*

EPHESIANS 4:5–6

169

The Mystery of the Church

How do images help us understand the mystery of the Church?

Body of Christ

Temple of the Holy Spirit

marks of the Church

apostolic succession

Magisterium

infallibility

People sometimes say, "It's all a mystery to me." What do you think someone who says this might mean? Some situations are very difficult to understand or even seem to be "beyond" our understanding. Some problems seem too difficult to solve. We sometimes call these situations and problems mysteries.

What Is a Mystery?

As Catholics we believe in many mysteries of faith. A mystery of our faith is something we believe because God has revealed it and the Church teaches it. It is a truth of our faith that we will never be able to understand fully, so vast is its meaning.

We can learn a great deal about a truth of our faith, a religious mystery, and still not begin to exhaust all there is to know about it. We can never learn all there is to know about a mystery of faith. The Church is a mystery in just this

sense. No matter how much we learn about it, there will always be more than we can understand.

One reason this is true of the mystery of the Church is that the Church is made up of both a visible, or human, reality and an invisible, or spiritual, reality. The Church is a community of people with a hierarchical structure. The Church is also an invisible communion of love, a spiritual community that mirrors the unity of the Holy Trinity. The Church is an earthly reality that exists here and now, with both a history and a future. The Church is also a reality that exists beyond time and space in heaven, where the Lord reigns in glory surrounded by all the saints.

Explain the meaning of the word mystery *as it applies to the Church.*

Images of the Church

Because the Church is so vast a mystery, we use many images to help us understand that mystery. Each image in its own way can capture only part of the mystery of the Church. In Chapter 13 we used the image of the People of God to deepen our understanding of the Church. The images of the Body of Christ and the Temple of the Holy Spirit also help us grow in our understanding of the Church.

Las Manos y Los Pies de Jesus. ("The Hands and Feet of Jesus"). Cement slab created by parishioners of Saint Gabriel the Archangel Catholic Community, McKinney, Texas, during mission trip, Sabrinas, Mexico, October 1999.

The Body of Christ

In Baptism we have been joined to Christ so fully that the Church is also called the **Body of Christ.** The image of the Body of Christ compares the Church to the functioning of the human body. Paul the Apostle uses this image. He writes:

> Now you are Christ's body, and individually parts of it.
>
> 1 CORINTHIANS 12:27

As the parts of a physical body are united one to another, so Christians are united with one another in Christ. Christ is "the head of the body, the church" (Colossians 1:18). Christ directs and gives life to us. Together we make up the "whole Christ."

How does the image of the Body of Christ help us understand the mystery of the Church?

Temple of the Holy Spirit

The image of the Church as a temple, the **Temple of the Holy Spirit**, is used to describe the indwelling of the Spirit in the Church and within the hearts of the faithful. Paul used this image in his First Letter to the Corinthians (see 1 Corinthians 3:16 and 6:19). Paul reminds us that the Spirit is the source of the richness of the Church's charisms (see 1 Corinthians 12:27–31), or gifts to be used "so that the church may be built up" (1 Corinthians 14:5).

Describe the Church as the Temple of the Holy Spirit.

Family Plan.
Diana Ong (1940–),
Chinese/American artist.

From the earliest days of the Church, Christians have used images to describe the nature and work of the Church. Each image in its own way tells us a partial truth about the mystery of the Church.

WHAT DIFFERENCE DOES FAITH MAKE?

Illustrate the images you can think of that help you understand what you have learned about the Church.

_____

_____

_____

_____

_____

The Church is one, the one Body of Christ. We might ask, "What are some essential signs of the unity of the pilgrim Church on earth?" The visible bonds of unity that unite Christ's followers as "one" include:

1. profession of one faith received from the apostles;
2. common worship, especially Baptism, the Eucharist, and the other sacraments; and
3. direct succession of bishops from the apostles through the sacrament of Holy Orders.

These bonds of unity within the Church are found most fully in the Catholic Church.

Throughout the history of the Church, Christians have separated themselves from the Catholic Church. Non-Catholic Christians who do not share fully with us in these bonds of unity today are joined to us "in some, although imperfect, communion" (*Decree on Ecumenism*, 3). We recognize in these non-Catholic Christian communities many elements of holiness and truth that are truly means of salvation for their members.

All Christians must make Jesus' prayer their own prayer. We must pray and work for the restoration of the unity of the Church. We call this work of the Church ecumenism.

Ecumenisim is directed precisely to making the partial communion existing between Christians grow toward full communion in truth and charity.

FROM JOHN PAUL II,
THAT ALL MAY BE ONE, 14

How does the mark of the Church that it is one help us understand the mystery of the Church?

Pope John Paul II and Bartholomew I, Ecumenical Patriarch and Archbishop of Constantinople.

FAITH FOCUS

How do the marks of the Church "one" and "holy" help us understand the mystery of the Church?

Each Sunday at Mass after the homily you stand with the worshiping assembly and pray the Nicene Creed. You say, "We believe . . . in one holy catholic and apostolic Church." What are you professing you believe about the Church? "One holy catholic and apostolic" are the four **marks of the Church**, or the essential characteristics of the Church founded by Jesus Christ.

The Church Is One

Jesus founded one Church. At the Last Supper Jesus prayed to his Father that the Church, the community of Jesus' followers:

"may all be one, as you, Father, are in me and I in you, that they also may be in us, that the world may believe that you sent me."

JOHN 17:21

The Church Is Holy

The Church is holy because in Baptism we are joined to Christ, become adopted children of the Father, and receive the gift of the Holy Spirit. We share in the life and love of God, the Holy One. We receive the grace to live a life of holiness.

All the baptized are on the road to holiness. The best way to grow in holiness is to cooperate with the

*Saint Thérèse of Lisieux.
Stained-glass window.*

Holy Spirit and strive to live the Great Commandment as Jesus taught us to do. As the People of God, the Body of Christ, we support one another on this journey. The following guide us and give us strength for our journey:

1. the word of God, the Scriptures;
2. the Tradition and teachings of the Church;
3. the writings and lives of the saints;
4. the liturgy and prayer life of the Church, especially the Eucharist.

WHAT DIFFERENCE DOES FAITH MAKE?

What are some of the ways you are a sign of the oneness and holiness of the Church?

_____

_____

_____

FAITH
FOCUS

How do the marks of the Church "catholic" and "apostolic" help us understand the mystery of the Church?

The Church Is Catholic

The Church of Christ that we profess in the Nicene Creed to be "one holy catholic and apostolic" can be found in its fullest in the Catholic Church, which is led by the pope and the bishops in communion with him. The word *catholic* means "universal." It is the mark of the Church that tells us that in God's plan all people are to become one people of God, joined to Christ, the Head of the Body of Christ, the Church.

Before he ascended into heaven, the Risen Jesus gave his disciples this mission: "Go, therefore, and make disciples of all nations" (Matthew 28:19). Being "catholic" and announcing the Gospel to all peoples go hand in hand. This means that the Church is missionary by nature. This is a vocation in which all the baptized share. Paul wrote, "[God] wills everyone to be saved and to come to knowledge of the truth" (1 Timothy 2:4). Jesus is "the way and the truth and the life" (John 14:6) in whom salvation is found.

What about all those people who are not baptized? The Church believes and trusts that God's love has no limits. People who through no fault of their own do not come to faith in Christ and his Church can still achieve eternal salvation by seeking to follow God's will according to their conscience. Their salvation comes about as a result of the grace of Jesus Christ, whose death on the cross has won forgiveness of sins and reconciliation with God for the entire human race. It is in this sense that the Church teaches that all salvation—even the salvation of the unbaptized—comes from Christ through his Body, the Church.

How does the mark of the Church that it is catholic *help us understand the mystery of the Church?*

The Church Is Apostolic

Apostolic means "from the time of the apostles." The Church is apostolic because it has its origin and foundation in the life of the original apostles chosen by Jesus. Ever since that time, leadership in the Church has been handed down from Peter and the other apostles to the popes and bishops. The bishops are the successors of the apostles. Catholics believe that bishops stand in a long line of apostles whose roots go all the way back to Peter. This connection of all popes and bishops back to Peter and the first apostles is called **apostolic succession.**

The Pope and the College of Bishops

Jesus made Peter the visible foundation, or rock, on which he would build the Church (see Matthew 16:18–19). Peter and his successors would be the "rock" and source of the unity of the Church founded by Jesus. The Church uses the term *college of bishops* to name the unity of all the bishops (the successors of the

Jesus Sending. Contemporary stained-glass window.

apostles) and the special leadership, or primacy, of the pope (the successor of Peter) among the bishops.

Why does the Church use the term college of bishops?

The Magisterium

Paul wrote to his disciple Timothy, telling him, "Guard this rich trust [that is, the deposit of faith he had received from the apostles] with the help of the holy Spirit that dwells within us" (2 Timothy 1:14). The Church uses the term **Magisterium** to name the teaching authority of the Church, entrusted to the pope and the bishops by Christ. When the pope and the bishops act together in their capacity as the college of bishops, they exercise supreme and full teaching authority over the universal Church. The pope as the successor of Peter and head of the college of bishops also has a special authority in the Church. He has "supreme, full, immediate, and universal power in the care of souls."

What is the Magisterium of the Church?

Paul's conviction that the Holy Spirit would guide him and Timothy as teachers of the faith continues today in the Church. **Infallibility** is the charism of the Spirit given to the Church that guarantees that the official teaching of the pope or the pope and bishops on matters of faith and morals is without error. This charism is at work when:

1. the pope teaches officially as the supreme pastor of the Church, or
2. the college of bishops teaches together with the pope.

The Catholic faithful are required to accept such teachings with the "obedience of faith" (Romans 16:26).

How does the mark of the Church apostolic *help us understand the mystery of the Church?*

Saint Peter's Basilica, Vatican. Pope John Paul II addresses bishops from North America and South America. Opening of Synod of Bishops, November 16, 1997.

WHAT DIFFERENCE DOES FAITH MAKE?

What can you do to learn what the pope teaches? What your bishop teaches?

_____

_____

_____

WHAT DIFFERENCE

Does This Make in Our Church?

The Church is a mystery of faith. The Church is the Body of Christ and the Temple of the Holy Spirit. The Church founded by Jesus Christ is one, holy, catholic, and apostolic. We call these four characteristics of the Church the marks of the Church. Together all the baptized are called to work together to build up the Church. One way we do this work is through parish councils.

Parish Councils

All the people of a parish have gifts to share for the building up of God's kingdom in our midst. An important way for the local church to employ and benefit from these gifts is the parish council. A parish council is made up of representatives of the parish family. These representatives are either appointed by the pastor or elected by parishioners.

Parish councils in the Church today have their origins in the "Decree on the Apostolate to the Laity" (1965) of Vatican Council II. Vatican II calls for the involvement of laypeople in parish responsibilities. In the first decade after Vatican II (1962–65), more than ten thousand parish councils were founded. By the late 1980s approximately 75 percent of parishes in the United States of America had a council in place.

Sharing Our Gifts

Imagine a typical parish community. Often it contains a whole host of talented people whose skills can enrich the entire church family. For example, parishioners who are social workers, artists, nurses, skilled laborers, merchants, business leaders, secretaries, lawyers, doctors, educators, and so on, can use their gifts to help create vibrant faith communities. Among the issues that councils tackle are the continuing need for parish volunteers, youth education, developing and implementing parish mission statements, care for the needy, parent education, and the challenges of the shortage of priests.

The Work of Parish Councils

Parish councils help the pastor with his managerial and pastoral tasks, by working with him in such areas as finance, justice, education, and service. Parish councils foster an enthusiastic sense of community by developing and promoting programs and outreaches that touch the lives of church members and members of the wider community as well. Acting as consultants and sounding boards to the pastors, councils are often organized into dynamic committees. Examples of these committees include: finance, administration, education, social justice, spiritual development, ecumenism, evangelism, and parish activities.

How does your parish council help the Body of Christ thrive in your local community?

177

WHAT DIFFERENCE

Does It Make in My Life?

Through Baptism you have the wonderful gift and responsibility to participate in the Church's mission of telling others about Jesus Christ. You have the wonderful job of showing others that we are all God's children. We all belong to the family of God. One of the ways you do this is through the many groups to which you belong.

Belonging to Groups

As humans, we all have a basic need to belong. We were not made to live in isolation; we need other people. Yes, there are times when we choose to be alone, but we all like to belong to a certain group where we are accepted, have fun, and work together.

Throughout your life you may belong to many different kinds of groups. Your own families, your parish, classes in school, teams, clubs, and organizations are only a few examples. Members of a group share things with others, learn to trust each other, recognize one another's gifts and talents, and learn how to work together.

Sometimes it is a challenge to work with a group. From your own experience give an example of why you think this can sometimes be

difficult. If you said there are times you have to give in or compromise, or you believe your way of doing something is better, or you would rather work on something yourself, you are naming some of the reasons being an active group member can be difficult. To be a vibrant member of any group you have to learn how to get along, how to play fair, and how to work together for the common good of the group.

Skills for Working in Groups

Here are some suggestions to help you be a valuable member of any group. First of all, to be a vibrant member of a group you have to want to be there and to belong. You need:

1. to have a spirit of cooperation and an open mind;
2. to be willing to compromise when necessary;
3. to be respectful of other members of the group and their ideas;
4. to express your opinions honestly, in a give and take of ideas;
5. to be a part of the planning, the brainstorming of ideas, or the solution of problems;
6. to decide who will do what, when tasks will be accomplished, and how to achieve the group goals cooperatively;
7. to work for the good of the group or the project by taking responsibility for doing your part.

faith decision

- Name the groups to which you now belong. Describe the best group to which you ever belonged. Write the number of each point from the list on this page that you feel was part of your experience in that particular group.

- Choose one thing from the list that you can work on to help you be a more active member of your parish community.

This week I will contribute to the work of my parish community by

_____

_____

_____

_____

_____.

179

Faith Vocabulary

Define each of these terms:

1. Body of Christ
2. Temple of the Holy Spirit
3. marks of the Church
4. apostolic succession
5. Magisterium
6. infallibility

Main Ideas

Choose either (a) or (b) from each set of items. Write a brief paragraph to answer each of your choices.

1. (a) Explain why we use images to help us understand the mystery of the Church.

   (b) Describe how the image of the Body of Christ helps us understand the mystery of the Church.

2. (a) Explain how the mark of the Church "one" helps us understand the mystery of the Church.

   (b) Explain how the mark of the Church "holy" helps us understand the mystery of the Church.

3. (a) Explain how the mark of the Church "catholic" helps us understand the mystery of the Church.

   (b) Explain how the mark of the Church "apostolic" helps us understand the mystery of the Church.

Critical Thinking

Using what you have learned in this chapter explain your understanding of this statement:

God invites everyone to salvation.

Family Discussion

How are these marks of the Church signs of our family? How is our family "one"? How is it "holy"?

Visit our
web site at
www.FaithFirst.com

The Shipwreck of Paul

A Scripture Story

15

WE PRAY

Lord,
may your Spirit who helped
Paul the apostle
to preach your power and glory
fill us with the light of faith.

FROM *MASS OF THE CONVERSION OF PAUL,
APOSTLE, PRAYER OVER THE GIFTS*

The Church has spread the
Gospel of Jesus to all the
nations. This work, which
the apostles began, has
continued for two thousand
years. What stories do you
remember about the apostles
spreading the Gospel?

*Paul . . . called to be
an apostle and set apart
for the gospel of God, . . .
the gospel about his Son.*

ROMANS 1:1, 3

Bible Background

FAITH FOCUS

How did Paul spread the Gospel throughout the Roman Empire?

FAITH VOCABULARY

missionary

People often take trips. All trips share one thing in common: We go some place for a reason, or purpose. For example, we might visit relatives or go on vacation. Some trips are just what we expected. Other trips are full of surprises, even with unexpected adventures. Think about a trip you took that didn't go as you planned. How did you feel? What did you do?

Saul's Trip to Damascus

The Acts of the Apostles tell about the trips made by Paul the Apostle. Before he became known as Paul the Apostle, he was known as Saul. Saul was a faithful Jew who thought that the believers in Jesus were doing harm to the religion of the Jews. Saul was zealous about his faith and its teachings about God. He set out on a trip to the city of Damascus for the sole purpose of stopping the followers of Jesus from preaching about Jesus (see Acts of the Apostles 9:1–2).

The trip did not go as Saul planned. We are told that as Saul approached the city of Damascus, a light flashed from the sky. He was literally thrown to the ground and temporarily blinded by a bright light.

He heard a voice call to him from the light, "Saul, Saul, why are you persecuting me?" (Acts of the Apostles 9:4). It was the voice of Christ calling Saul to become his disciple.

The purpose of Saul's trip changed. He proceeded on to Damascus, where he was baptized, changed his name to Paul, and became a zealous disciple of Jesus (see Acts of the Apostles 9:10–30).

Describe what happened to Saul on his trip to Damascus.

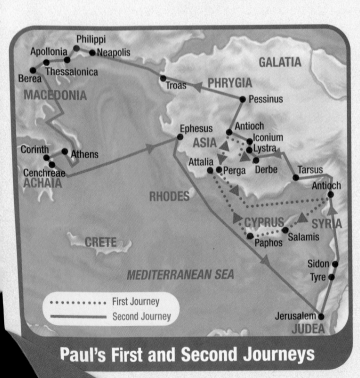

Paul's First and Second Journeys

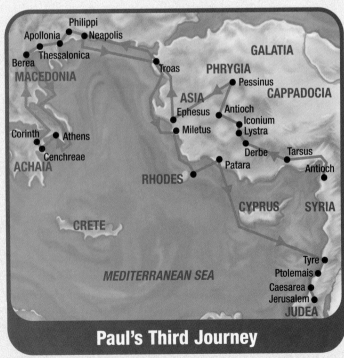

Paul's Third Journey

Paul the Apostle and Missionary

Saul became Paul the Apostle, the great **missionary** to the Gentiles, or people who were not Jewish. A Christian missionary is one who carries out Christ's mission to preach the Gospel to all nations. As a missionary, Paul made many other journeys that brought him to the towns and cities and regions all around the Mediterranean Sea. He traveled by land and by sea. He traveled from Jerusalem to Asia, Greece, and eventually to the city that was the center of all civilization at that time—Rome. All his journeys had one purpose: to bring disciples to Jesus.

The Acts of the Apostles tells us that Paul made four missionary journeys to spread the Gospel. The first three took Paul throughout Syria, Asia Minor, and Greece. His fourth and last journey took him to Rome, where he was finally martyred. On this journey to Rome Paul was shipwrecked.

Describe the missionary journeys of Paul.

Paul's Sea Adventure

The story of Paul's shipwreck in the Acts of the Apostles follows a popular type of ancient adventure story— the sea voyage. The story of the shipwreck of Paul has all the drama and adventure of one of these tales.

It also has one major difference. Usually the hero in these stories did not stand up to explain the importance of all of the adventures. Paul did. The hardships and terrors of the sea only proved that there was a divine plan for the journey that Paul was making. God saved Paul from the perils of the sea so that he could continue the real reason for the journey—to ceaselessly spread the Gospel to all people, all the way to Rome.

Paul zealously carried out Jesus' command to his disciples to preach the Gospel and "make disciples of all nations" (Matthew 28:19). Beginning in Jerusalem, he traveled to Rome, the heart and center of the Roman Empire. There he would be put to death for his faith in Christ.

Did you Know...

According to tradition, Saint Paul was beheaded on the Ostian Road outside of Rome and was buried in a cemetery nearby. Excavations have verified that there was a pagan cemetery dating from the first and second centuries on this same Ostian Road. In the fourth century, Constantine the Great erected the Basilica of Saint Paul Outside the Walls over the tomb of the apostle Paul. The current basilica was completed in 1854.

WHAT DIFFERENCE DOES FAITH MAKE?

How does knowing about Saint Paul help you live your faith in Jesus?

_____

_____

_____

_____

_____

_____

_____

_____

_____

Reading the Word of God

Saint Paul Arriving at Malta.
Peter Mulier (1637–1701), Dutch painter.

FAITH FOCUS

Why is it important for the Church to retell the story of Paul's shipwreck?

Paul's fourth and final journey took him to Rome. Paul had been in prison in Jerusalem for two years. As a Roman citizen, Paul was able to appeal his case directly to Caesar and request a trial in Rome. So he set sail for Rome, escorted by a Roman centurion.

Paul's Journey to Rome

It was late autumn of A.D. 60 and very close to when sea travel stopped because of winter storms. Paul foresaw great danger in continuing the voyage.

> Much time had now passed and sailing had become hazardous because the time of the fast had already gone by, so Paul warned them, "Men, I can see that this voyage will result in severe damage and heavy loss not only to the cargo and the ship, but also to our lives." The centurion, however, paid more attention to the pilot and to the owner of the ship than to what Paul said. Since the harbor was unfavorably situated for spending the winter, the majority planned to put out to sea from there in the hope of reaching Phoenix, a port in Crete facing west-northwest, there to spend the winter. ACTS OF THE APOSTLES 27:9–12

Why did Paul advise the centurion not to sail on to Rome?

As they traveled on, a storm, a northeaster, struck. It was hard to control the ship. Spare cargo and even the ship's tackle was thrown overboard to lighten the ship. The hurricane force storm blew so fiercely that people started to lose hope. Paul addressed them:

> "I urge you now to keep up your courage; not one of you will be lost, only the ship. For last night an angel of the God to whom [I] belong and whom I serve stood by me and said, 'Do not be afraid, Paul. You are destined to stand before Caesar; and behold, for your sake, God has granted safety to all who are sailing with you.' Therefore, keep up your courage, men; I trust in God that it will turn out as I have been told." ACTS 27:22–25

What was Paul's message of hope to the men on the ship?

The storm got worse and some of the sailors tried to abandon the ship. Again, Paul spoke:

> "Today is the fourteenth day that you have been waiting, going hungry and eating nothing. I urge you, therefore, to take some food; it will help you survive. Not a hair of the head of anyone of you will be lost." When he said this, he took bread, gave thanks to God in front of them all, broke it, and began to eat. They were all encouraged, and took some food themselves. In all, there were two hundred seventy-six of us on the ship. ACTS OF THE APOSTLES 27:33–37

The ship finally ran aground on a sandbar. But Paul's faith saved everyone.

> But they struck a sandbar and ran the ship aground. The bow was wedged in and could not be moved, but the stern began to break up under the pounding [of the waves]. The soldiers planned to kill the prisoners so that none might swim away and escape, but the centurion wanted to save Paul and so kept them from carrying out their plan. He ordered those who could swim to jump overboard first and get to the shore, and then the rest, some on planks, others on debris from the ship. In this way, all reached shore safely. ACTS OF THE APOSTLES 27:41–44

How does Paul's faith save the people on the shipwrecked boat?

Paul soon reached safety on the island of Malta. Three months later he again set sail for Rome. When he arrived there, he proclaimed the kingdom of God. Paul continued to teach about Jesus Christ until he was martyred for his faith in Christ.

WHAT DIFFERENCE DOES FAITH MAKE?

What are some times it is difficult to give witness to your faith? How does the story of Paul help you?

_____

_____

_____

_____

Jesus' disciples and to live by the Spirit. By the end of the first century, Christian communities could be found in all the large cities from Jerusalem to Rome.

A Mission to All People

The Church today continues to carry out the mission Jesus first gave to the apostles. God sent his Son for the salvation of all people. It is our mission as a Church, as the Body of Christ, to announce that invitation to everyone.

We bring Christ and the Gospel to all people. We live out that mission in our families and in our communities and neighborhoods. We share our faith in Christ in our schools and in our parks and in our neighborhoods. We proclaim the Gospel throughout our own countries, and we travel far and wide, as Paul did, sharing it with peoples of all cultures and nations. We will do this until the end of time when Christ comes again in glory.

What does it mean to say that the Church is a missionary Church?

FAITH FOCUS

How does the Church carry out its missionary work?

The story of the shipwreck of Paul is in some ways the story of the Church in a nutshell. Paul's adventures on the high seas not only recount an event in his life but also tell about the life and mission of the Church.

The Missionary Church

Before he ascended into heaven, Jesus gave his followers a mission. He told them:

> "Go, therefore, and make disciples of all nations, baptizing them in the name of the Father, and of the Son, and of the holy Spirit, teaching them to observe all that I have commanded you."
> MATTHEW 28:19–20

Spreading the Gospel and making disciples of all nations is exactly what the apostles did. They courageously and tirelessly preached about God's plan of salvation accomplished in Jesus. They welcomed others to become

The Missionary Spirit

Paul the Apostle's missionary journeys teach us what it means to be a missionary Church.

1. Paul showed God's love for everyone when the boat was in danger. This is what the missionary spirit is all about—the energy and vitality of sharing the Gospel of salvation with everyone without exception.

How do Paul's actions as a missionary guide us in our mission to preach Christ today?

Paul the Apostle zealously and tirelessly carried out his mission to tell everyone about Jesus and to invite them to become disciples of Jesus. Every baptized Christian is charged with being a missionary. The Church today continues the mission given to the Church by Christ.

2. During the violent storms, when the ship was about to sink, everyone seemed to totally lose hope. Paul did not.

3. The meal that Paul shared with the crew is very similar to the Eucharist. Paul "took bread, gave thanks to God in front of them all, broke it, and began to eat. They were all encouraged, and took some food for themselves" (Acts of the Apostles 27:35–36). This meal reminded the early Christian readers of the Eucharist. Jesus is present in the Eucharist. He is with us to help us through the rough times.

WHAT DIFFERENCE DOES FAITH MAKE?

How can you invite others to live as disciples of Jesus?

_____

_____

_____

_____

_____

_____

WHAT DIFFERENCE

Does This Make in Our Church?

Paul the Apostle traveled by land and by sea to announce the Gospel to all people. Wherever he went, Paul preached the message of God's love for everyone revealed in Jesus Christ. The Church continues this missionary work today. Some Christians—laypeople, religious, and clergy—dedicate their entire lives to this work as missionaries. Others respond to the missionary call of the Church by working on special projects.

Church Youth on Mission

Saint Mary of the Lake

The high school youth group of Saint Mary of the Lake parish in White Bear Lake, Minnesota, participates in a mission project each summer. The youth make a journey to a different place in the United States to repair homes for people living in poverty.

On two occasions the group has traveled to Appalachia where families were living in homes that had leaky roofs and broken doors and windows. If it was raining outside, it was also raining inside. The repairs to these houses made a big difference in people's lives! The group has also traveled to the home of the Lakota Sioux in South Dakota, which is the poorest county in the nation. They have also traveled to the Arapaho living in Wyoming.

These missionary journeys are much more than just one summer week spent away from home. The group begins planning and preparing in September by learning about the culture of the people they will be serving. To remember the real purpose of their mission the youth pray and reflect on the works of mercy. Money is also raised for materials and transportation. This makes the whole parish part of the mission.

The week that the students spend on mission is more than just labor. The group experiences firsthand the results of living in poverty, neglect, and prejudice. In the evenings the youth spend time reading and reflecting on the Scriptures. They call on the Spirit to guide them in following the loving example of Jesus in all they say and do.

Mission Mexico

The Catholic community of Saint Gabriel the Archangel in McKinney, Texas, sponsors Mission Mexico. Mission Mexico is made up of youth and advisors who travel to Sabinas, Mexico, where they visit Casa Hogar and work with children whose parents are unable to care for them. Some parents are in prison, others are ill; most are living in such poverty they cannot adequately care for their children.

Before the group departs, everyone spends time planning the trip. They gather regularly in prayer, asking the Spirit to guide them on the mission to be "the hands and feet of Jesus"—the motto that appears on their T-shirts.

While at Casa Hogar, the youth clean, paint, and make general repairs to the dormitories. Most importantly they spend time with the children making friends. After the work of the day is done, everyone dances to Spanish and American rhythms. Saying good-bye to the children is the most difficult work of all.

The youth return from the mission with a lifetime of memories and a lifetime lesson of spiritual growth. On all their journeys the youth receive much more than they are able to give.

What youth groups do you know about that do missionary work? How can you support or become an active member of one of these mission projects?

WHAT DIFFERENCE

Does It Make in My Life?

Saul was a zealous, faithful Jew who persecuted the followers of Jesus. When Saul was converted to Christianity, he, Paul, used that same zeal to spread the Gospel. In both cases his zeal was intense love in action. Paul, and the other zealous disciples, missionaries, and true believers, preached the Gospel far and wide and enabled the Catholic Church to be established and grow throughout the centuries and into our present day.

Living with Zeal and Optimism

Zeal is eagerness, an intensity of action, which drives someone to act with determination. In a religious sense, it means the zeal, the enthusiasm, the intensity a person has, inspired by the love of God, to do good works and to promote God's honor and glory. Zeal is love in action. Every baptized person is called to use his or her energy, vitality, and zeal to share the teachings of Jesus and the message of God's love and care for us.

Optimism

Optimism comes from the Latin word *optimus*, meaning "best." Optimism is an attitude or an emotional inclination or belief that things are good and that all will work out for the best. For Christians, optimism is based on our belief that God is always there for us. We believe in a God who loves us and offers us everlasting life. This is what the Christian virtue of hope is all about.

Ask Yourself

What things do you get fired up about? Do you give your all when you play sports? When you play music, or work at a hobby, do you bring energy and vitality to it? What is your attitude toward the way things are going? Do you believe things are going to work out for the best or are you convinced of doom and gloom? Do you believe you are meant to be happy, or do you feel like a victim or that things will always go wrong? If you always think the worst or if you are sure something will go wrong, you are bringing negativity to your thinking and actions.

Optimism is not simply magical thinking. It is a trust in God's love and a belief that God wants you to be happy and he wants the very best for you and all people. It is a spirit of confidence and cheerfulness that things are going to work out.

Optimism affects your attitude and your relationship with others. It also affects your mood. Your attitude will either build you up or tear you down.

No one likes to be around someone who always seems to be negative. You probably don't even like yourself when you are feeling and acting like this. And the scary part is that negativity and pessimism are contagious. The good news is that zeal and optimism are also contagious.

When you are worried, or praying for someone, or praying for something to turn out in a certain way, you need a positive attitude. Write a prayer, asking God to help you stay positive and helpful when you are faced with a difficult situation.

As a Christian you are called to be a person of zeal and hope. God wants this for you, but you have to choose to accept this gift.

faith decision

- How can an optimistic attitude help you in your relationship with God and with others?

- With a partner think of one thing you can do in your school or neighborhood to show others that you are a zealous follower of Christ.

Write your plan here.

_____

_____

_____

_____

_____

This month try to put your plan into action.

Faith Vocabulary

Use the word *missionary* correctly in a sentence.

People and Places and Events

Identify each of the following:

1. Saul
2. Paul
3. Damascus
4. Rome

Main Ideas

Choose either (a) or (b) from each set of items. Write a brief paragraph to answer each of your choices.

1. (a) Explain why Paul went on missionary journeys.

   (b) Discuss how the adventure stories of the sea voyage are used in the Acts of the Apostles.

2. (a) Recount the story of Paul's shipwreck on the sea.

   (b) What was the message of hope that Paul brought to the people on the ship?

3. (a) Why does the Church have a mission to announce salvation to all people?

   (b) What can the missionary journeys of Paul teach us today?

Critical Thinking

Using what you have learned in this chapter, briefly explain this statement: The Church by its very nature is missionary.

Family Discussion

What can we as a family do to help spread the Gospel to others?

Visit our web site at www.FaithFirst.com

Your Kingdom Come!

16

WE PRAY

God our Father,
may we love you in all things
and above all things
and reach the joy you have
prepared for us
beyond all our imagining.

FROM *ROMAN MISSAL,*
OPENING PRAYER,
TWENTIETH SUNDAY IN ORDINARY TIME

People find happiness in many ways. The Gospel often teaches about the kingdom of heaven—a happiness that never ends. Think about the meaning of happiness. What is the connection between our search for happiness on earth with our happiness in heaven?

O God, you are my God—
for you I long! . . .
I will bless you as long as
I live;
I will lift up my hands,
calling on your name.

PSALM 63:1, 5

The Church: A Communion of Saints

FAITH FOCUS

How does the image of the communion of saints help us further understand the mystery of the Church?

FAITH VOCABULARY

communion of saints

physical death

beatific vision

Sometimes during September and October the budget fight between the members of Congress and the president threatens to shut down the government. Everyone seems to have a different opinion on how to divide up the tax dollars to serve the common good of the country. Imagine you are a member of Congress. What would be the three most important items in your budget?

The Common Good of the Church

The Acts of the Apostles describes how the very first generation of believers devoted themselves to the common good of the Church.

> They devoted themselves to the teaching of the apostles and to the communal life, to the breaking of the bread and to the prayers. . . . All who believed were together and had all things in common; they would sell their property and possessions and divide them among all according to each one's need.
>
> ACTS OF THE APOSTLES 2:42, 44–45

The early Christians held all things in common. They shared their spiritual blessings—the teachings of the apostles and prayer. They also shared their material blessings—their possessions according to each one's need.

The sharing of material and spiritual blessings is the heart of the life the People of God share with God and with one another in Christ. The "communal life" (Acts of the Apostles 2:42) of the Church is also known as the **communion of saints.** The communion of saints is the communion of holy things and holy people that make up the Church.

The Communion of Saints

In the liturgies of some of the Eastern Catholic Churches the presider before distributing Holy Communion raises the Eucharist for all to see and announces, "Holy gifts for God's holy people." This phrase captures in a wonderful way what we mean when we describe the Church as a communion of saints.

A Communion of Holy Things

There is a deep solidarity among the people that God has made holy by sharing his life with us. The Church is:

- **A communion in the faith.** There is a sharing in the precious treasure of the faith handed down from the apostles.

- **A communion in the sacraments.** There is a sharing in the Paschal mystery that binds us to one another in the Lord Jesus.
- **A communion in the Spirit.** The Church is enriched by spiritual gifts of the Holy Spirit (see 1 Corinthians 12–14).
- **A communion of charity, or love.** After explaining that the greatest spiritual gift is love, Paul writes, "[S]eek to have an abundance of [spiritual gifts] for building up the church" (1 Corinthians 14:12).

Describe the communion of saints as a communion of holy gifts.

A Communion of Holy People

The Church is also a community, or communion, of holy people. It is a communion of all the faithful who are living on earth and those who live in a new way after their bodily death. This communion of holy people includes:

1. **The faithful on earth** who are pilgrims and are still journeying toward our heavenly home.
2. **The faithful who are being purified** after death so as to be made worthy of heaven.
3. **The faithful in heaven** who are enjoying their life with God forever.

Describe the members of the communion of saints.

The Church is a living communion of all the faithful, both those living on earth and those living after death. The Church on earth continues to pray for those being purified after their bodily death. The faithful in heaven intercede with God on behalf of those on earth who are still journeying toward eternal life.

WHAT DIFFERENCE DOES FAITH MAKE?

Name one of the saints who might help you live as a follower of Christ. Why did you choose that saint?

_____

_____

_____

_____

_____

Video games, movie and video "thrillers," the yearly immersion into Halloween conjure up images of the dead. Many young people's imaginations are filled with repulsive images of the dead, created by the media. Compare those images with how the Church has traditionally represented the faithful who have died—people whose life is not ended but is changed; people who rest in peace. How Christian is your imagination?

Life Is Changed, Not Ended

Physical death is the separation of our immortal soul from our mortal body. It is not the end of our life. With the death of our body, our life is changed not ended. Without the soul, its life-force, the human body no longer lives. It dies and so begins the natural process of its corruption and decay.

Funeral Liturgy,
Final Commendation
and Farewell.

We have one life to live. We begin living that life here on earth and will continue to live it in a new way forever after our physical death. We will not be reincarnated and returned to earth to live another life in a different body. The Letter to the Hebrews teaches that "it is appointed that human beings die once, and after this the judgment" (Hebrews 9:27).

The Forgiveness of Sins

The knowledge that our lives will be judged is a gift. It helps us appreciate God's saving love for us. Christ, the Son of God, died to free all humankind from sin and death. The Spirit is always inviting us to share in the life and love of God through the forgiveness of our sins.

Jesus explicitly entrusted to his Church the power to forgive sins.

- First, the Church exercises that power in the sacrament of Baptism in which all sin, both original sin and personal sins, are forgiven.
- Second, the Church celebrates the sacrament of Reconciliation, or Penance, also called second baptism, with those who sin after Baptism. "By Christ's will, the Church possesses the power to forgive the sins of the baptized and exercises it through bishops and priests normally in the sacrament of Penance" (*Catechism of the Catholic Church*, 986).

- Third, throughout our lives we celebrate the sacrament of the Eucharist. Venial sins are forgiven, our unity with God and one another is strengthened.
- Fourth, God's forgiveness of punishment due to sin is offered to us after death.

In Matthew 25 Jesus teaches that there is punishment connected with sin. That punishment may be eternal, or last forever. It may also be temporal, or temporary. Through indulgences the faithful can obtain remission, or release from, the temporal punishment due to our sins. They can do this for themselves or for the souls being purified after death.

Describe the belief of the Catholic Church in the forgiveness of sins.

Life Everlasting

Our life after death will reflect the way we have chosen to live our life on earth. Jesus was very clear about

that (see Matthew 25:31–46). We shall know the ultimate meaning of the whole work of creation and understand the wonderful ways by which God's Divine Providence has led all things towards the final end. Justice will triumph over all of the injustices committed by his creatures. We will come to see that God's love is stronger than death.

The Resurrection of Jesus. Stained-glass window.

How can you show your gratitude to God for the gift of life everlasting?

_____

_____

_____

Madonna and Child. By unknown apprentice of Antonio Rosellino (1427–ca. 1479), Italian sculptor.

Mary's exemplary life of faith on earth is the model of living for all believers. Her assumption, body and soul, into heaven is a sign of our hope and of our own life after death. We believe and hope that we will enter the blessedness of heaven and "look upon [God's] face" (Revelation 22:4) and "see him as he is" (1 John 3:2).

The Church has called this seeing God face-to-face in heavenly glory the **beatific vision.** In that vision we will be drawn into communion with the Most Holy Trinity in a way that brings us perfect happiness.

Why is Mary a promise and the sign of the future that God has prepared for us?

Heaven

Heaven is beyond all description and understanding. It is a mystery in the sense explained in Chapter 14. It is so rich in meaning that we will never be able fully to comprehend its mystery (see 1 Corinthians 2:9).

Heaven and the beatific vision will be the fulfillment of the happiness we are searching for on earth. We will live in an everlasting relationship of love with God and with all who love God—with the Virgin Mary, with the angels and saints, and with all of our loved ones who have gone before us in Christ's love. In heaven we will clearly see the wonderful creation God has made us. There will be nothing more that we lack, nothing more we could desire.

Mary, the Mother of the Church

Mary, our heavenly Mother, is the model of what it means to belong to the communion of saints. Mary's holiness stems from her unique gifts of grace and the perfect way in which she cooperated with God in the work of our redemption. In Mary we see the future of the Church and our future in heaven. We pray:

Holy Mary, Mother of God,
pray for us sinners,
now and at the hour of our death.

FROM HAIL MARY

A New Heaven and a New Earth

The entire cosmos will also share in the fulfillment of God's plan. Just as the resurrection on the last day will reunite our souls to our risen bodies, there will also be a corresponding transformation of the visible universe. There will be "a new heaven and a new earth" (Revelation 21:1). The kingdom Jesus proclaimed will finally be established for all eternity.

The efforts that we make here on earth to better the human condition in some mysterious way contribute to the coming of God's kingdom. Working with the poor and powerless against oppression, struggling to build a world on the gospel values of peace and justice, these and all of our just human labors have profound spiritual value. They truly prepare for God's kingdom. While earthly progress and the growth of God's kingdom are not identical "such progress is of vital concern to the kingdom of God" (*Pastoral Constitution on the Church in the Modern World*, 39).

Compare the kingdom of God with a just and peace-filled society on earth.

When we live our faith in Jesus, we too proclaim the coming of the kingdom of God. Our words and actions share in and continue the work God the Father began, Jesus himself restored, and the Holy Spirit continues until the end of time. God's loving plan of creation and salvation will be realized, ushering in the advent of a new heaven and a new earth!

WHAT DIFFERENCE DOES FAITH MAKE?

How can you prepare yourself and help others prepare for the coming of the kingdom of God?

_____

_____

_____

WHAT DIFFERENCE

Does This Make in Our Church?

Basilica of the National Shrine of the Immaculate Conception, Washington, D.C.

The Church is a communion of saints. We are the community of the People of God, both living and dead. Sharing in the life of God we build that community here on earth and prepare for the eternal life with God, the Virgin Mary, and all the saints.

The Saints

While all the faithful are called to be saints, we also speak of saints in a special way. These are the members of the communion of saints whom the Church has officially recognized, or canonized, as living with God in heaven.

Each of the canonized saints serve as models of living for us. During their life on earth, they lived their lives as faithful followers of Christ, standing up for their beliefs. Their actions and words help us live as the faithful People of God and followers of Christ. Many remained faithful even in the face of death. We honor those who gave their lives for their faith as martyrs.

The saints living in heaven care about us and care for us. They serve the faithful on earth as our intercessors before God in heaven. This faith moves us to pray to them and to learn about their lives on earth.

The Blessed Virgin Mary

The greatest of the saints is the Blessed Virgin Mary, the Mother of God, the mother of Jesus, and the mother of the Church. Catholics of the Americas honor Mary in a special way. Under the title Our Lady of Guadalupe we pray to Mary and look to her as the patron of the Americas. Catholics in the United States of America honor Mary as the patron of our country under the title of the Immaculate Conception.

**Our Lady of Guadalupe
Patron of the Americas**

In 1531 Mary first appeared to Juan Diego and then to his dying uncle, Juan Bernardino, in Tepeyac near Mexico City. Then from a cloak on which her image had miraculously

Mary Immaculate
Patron of the United States
of America

Catholics believe that Mary, from the very first moment of her existence (from her conception) and all throughout her life, was sinless. Through the gift of God's special grace Mary never lost the gift of original holiness. She was always free from sin—from original sin and all personal sins.

In 1846 the bishops of the United States of America chose Mary under the title of her Immaculate Conception as the patron of their country. We look to Mary and her life on earth as a model of faith. We seek the grace of courage and wisdom to live our faith by saying yes to God as she did. We pray to her, asking her to intercede for us that we might live as faithful children of God and followers of her son, Jesus Christ. We pray that we will one day join her and all the saints in heaven.

Create a prayer to Mary, asking her to help you live your faith courageously.

appeared, Mary, the Mother of God, spoke to the bishop.

Mary, our Lady of Guadalupe, spoke a message of hope during a time of great suffering for Juan Diego and his people. In 1521 they had been defeated by the Iberians in a bloody war. During this time of death and suffering, Mary spoke in Nahuatl, the native language of Juan, about love and compassion, about hope and new life. The heart of her message is symbolized in the image that appeared on Juan's cloak. In the painting Mary is pregnant and the Nahuatl symbol for new life appears over her womb. Mary, Our Lady of Guadalupe, was named patron of the Americas by Pope Pius XII in 1945.

Our Lady of Guadalupe Cathedral, old and new. Mexico City, Mexico.

WHAT DIFFERENCE

Does It Make in My Life?

You are a member of the communion of saints. You are part of the faithful on earth who are journeying toward our heavenly home. How you live this journey, your words and actions and the choices you make each day show others what being a Christian really means.

Standing Up for What is Right

If you were on trial and you were accused of being a good Christian, would you be convicted? How much evidence would your prosecutors have against you? How many witnesses would they call to prove you were indeed guilty as charged?

Values

One school had a motto that read "If to be right means to be different, then by all means be different." "Different" in this motto does not mean strange. It means to have the courage to stand up for your values and beliefs.

Your values are inner beliefs that are really important to you. They are convictions by which you live your life. Your values are beliefs you choose to act on. If something is of value to you, you will stand by it even when other people put you down for standing up for it.

What do you really value right now in your life? Prioritize the items on this list by ranking them in order. Mark as number one the thing you value most. Cross out things you do not value.

____ I value being number one.

____ I value looking good.

____ I value great clothes.

____ I value my family.

DO NOT ENTER

DETO

_____ I value being with the "in" crowd.

_____ I value a good education.

_____ I value my religious beliefs, my faith.

_____ I value the music I listen to.

_____ I value my friends.

Are there any other values you would stand up for in your life right now? Add them to the list.

_____ _____

_____ _____

Courage and Integrity

Christians are often called to be "countercultural." This means that we sometimes have to choose against certain values our society or culture is telling us to live by.

Being countercultural and standing up for what you believe makes you stand out. You run the risk of rejection, being laughed at, assaulted, or even being abused verbally or physically. It takes courage and integrity to stand up for your values.

Courage is a virtue, an inner strength, that enables you to withstand danger or threats and overcome fear. It gives you the strength not to cave in to peer or any other kind of pressure. It gives you the will power to express yourself honestly even when others disagree with you.

Integrity is honesty. It is the quality of a person who holds on to one's moral values and beliefs. Integrity means you try to be the best that you can be. You say or do the right thing whether someone is watching or not.

faith decision

Our society has certain values and beliefs. Select a topic from the list below and discuss in a small group whether your values and beliefs go against what society promotes.

Would you and could you stand up for your beliefs even if they are different?

TOPICS FOR DISCUSSION

- TV programs, movies and movie ratings, gun control laws, curfews, alcohol and drugs, sex and violence.

- What are three values you live by?

This week keep a record of how many times you are called upon as a Christian to go against what others are saying or doing and stand up for what you believe.

_____

_____

_____

_____

YIELD

JR SPEED LIMIT

DEAD END

Faith Vocabulary

Use each of these faith terms correctly in a sentence.

1. communion of saints

2. physical death

3. beatific vision

Main Ideas

Choose either (a) or (b) from each set of items. Write a brief paragraph to answer each of your choices.

1. (a) Describe how the early Christians devoted themselves to the common good of the Church.

   (b) Describe the Church as a communion of saints.

2. (a) Explain the Christian belief that at the time of our physical death our life is not ended but changed.

   (b) Explain the ways Jesus entrusts the Church with the power to forgive sins.

3. (a) Explain what the Church teaches about heaven.

   (b) How are the kingdom of God and our belief that there will be a new heaven and a new earth similar?

Critical Thinking

Using what you have learned in this chapter, briefly explain this statement:
"A man can have but one life and one death, / One heaven, one hell."
(From "In a Balcony," Elizabeth Barrett Browning [1806–1861], English poet.)

Family Discussion

In what ways is our family a communion of saints?

Visit our
web site at
www.FaithFirst.com

THE PRAYER OF THE PEOPLE OF GOD
UNIT 4

PARENT PAGE—UNIT 4

FAITH

Prayer is an expression of faith and trust in God. The words of our prayers describe our relationship with God. In Unit 4, "The Prayer of the People of God," your child will learn more about the Christian tradition of prayer. This fourth unit of *Creed and Prayer* begins with a presentation of the Psalms, especially Psalm 23. While the Psalms give expression to the faith and trust of Israel in the Lord God, they are also models for the prayer of the Church. Built upon the tradition of prayer found in the Scriptures, the Church names five forms of prayer: blessing and adoration, petition, intercession, thanksgiving, and praise.

By examining the lives of Abraham, Moses, the prophets, and Jesus, your child will rediscover that prayer is spending time with God, talking and listening to him. He or she will learn the importance of choosing one or several of the many ways Christians express their prayer and of developing a daily rhythm of praying. Having a regular rhythm to our prayer life, like having a regular rhythm to our breathing, strengthens our life with God and with the other members of the Church.

Jesus is the model of prayer for Christians. He gave us the Lord's Prayer, or the Our Father, as a model for our conversation with God the Father and for living the Gospel. The final chapter of this unit opens up the meaning of the petitions of the Our Father for you and your child.

WHAT DIFFERENCE DOES IT MAKE?

In this unit your child will learn about the many ways we can build our relationship with God through prayer. As in any relationship, our relationship with God can only grow and deepen if we devote time and attention to God. Through prayer in all its many forms, we grow in our understanding and commitment to live as followers of Christ.

Praying together as a family can be a powerful means toward helping each family member grow in his or her personal relationship with God. Family prayer also deepens relationships among the members of the family and strengthens the family's ability to witness the Christian faith to others. Prayer takes time, but prayer can move mountains, change hearts, and build solid foundations for family life. By praying together families can stay focused on their Christian commitment to live and serve as Jesus did.

As you reflect on the chapters in this unit you might reflect on your call as a parent to be your family's shepherd. Pages 216 and 217 point out that the image of the Good Shepherd can be applied to all of us today. A good shepherd is one who loves, cares for, and protects those entrusted to his or her care. Your child also has opportunities to care for and love others. Talk with your child about each person's call to be responsible, trustworthy, compassionate, and gentle—all attributes of the Good Shepherd, Jesus.

The many forms of prayer discussed in this unit can help your family build a stronger prayer life. Journal writing and meditation are two ideas discussed in detail. You might consider integrating one of these forms of prayer into your family's schedule. Begin by reviewing the journal writing ideas on pages 228 and 229 together with your family. In addition to individual journals, the family might keep a family journal in which people could write down thoughts, feelings, or concerns that all family members might remember in their prayers. These journal entries might become a source of family prayer each evening.

Meditation, while a private time with God, can be incorporated into family prayer. Use the ideas on pages 240 and 241 to get started. Reading the Bible, singing a hymn, or praying a decade of the rosary might help to lead the family meditation time. Perhaps start out by setting aside a few minutes once a week for family meditation. Choose a time when as many members of the family as possible can be present. If family prayer time is a new idea for your family, it may take time to become a part of your routine, but the time will be well worth it.

God Is Our Shepherd

A Scripture Story

17

WE PRAY

Give to the Lord, you heavenly
    beings,
    give to the Lord glory and
    might;
Give to the Lord the glory due
    God's name.
    Bow down before the Lord's
    holy splendor!

PSALM 29:1–2

There are many times
throughout the day that
we turn to God in prayer.
What are some of the times
and situations during the
day that lead you to prayer?
How do you address God in
your prayer?

*The Lord is my shepherd;
there is nothing I lack.*
PSALM 23:1

Bible Background

FAITH FOCUS

How do psalms help us express our faith and trust in God?

FAITH VOCABULARY

psalms

Psalter

laments

prayers of blessing and adoration

prayers of petition

prayers of intercession

prayers of thanksgiving

prayers of praise

Think of a time when you were so happy you just wanted to burst into song. When the home team scores the winning point, the gym breaks out in a rousing chorus of the school victory song. Singing has always been used as a way to express feelings. What are some feelings other than joy that songs can convey?

Songs of Feeling

The Bible is filled with songs that express the feelings of the People of God. We call these songs **psalms.** Psalms are prayer-songs that God's people have used from the time of King David right up to the present day.

Most of the psalms in the Bible are found in the Book of Psalms, which contains 150 psalms. Flowing from the heart of God's people, psalms express their deepest feelings of trust and faith in God and his faithful presence with them in all their life's experiences.

What do psalms express?

Organization of the Book of Psalms

The Book of Psalms is sometimes called the **Psalter.** It is arranged into five books, or sections. This five-part division, in keeping with an ancient Jewish tradition, is in imitation of the five parts of the Torah, or Pentateuch. The Pentateuch is the first five books of the Bible. It contains the law God revealed to Moses. The five sections of the Book of Psalms are:

- Psalms 1 to Psalm 41,
- Psalm 42 to Psalm 72,
- Psalm 73 to Psalm 89,
- Psalm 90 to Psalm106, and
- Psalm 107 to Psalm 150.

Each of the five sections ends with a doxology, or an expression of praise to God. The final section of the Book of Psalms, Psalm 146 to Psalm 150, begins with the words "Praise Yahweh." Together this entire section also makes up the doxology for the whole Psalter as well.

Psalm 34. Nineteenth-century Fraktur painting, Rev. George Geistweite.

Hymns

A hymn is a song of praise to God. Psalms of praise follow a simple structure. Each begins with a call to praise or worship. This is followed by a telling of the great deeds or activities of God for which the people are praising God.

The psalm concludes with a repetition of the call to praise. Most of the psalms of praise were written to be used in the worship and liturgy of Israel. They were, of course, also used for individual prayer.

Laments

Nearly a third of all psalms are **laments.** A lament is a prayer of trust and hope in God during a time of suffering or great trial.

The structure of each psalm of lament is not exactly the same. The common elements each lament shares are:

- a direct calling of God's name,
- a vivid description of the complaint or suffering,
- a plea or petition for help or deliverance from the suffering,
- a vow or promise to offer praise or sacrifice in gratitude for God's help, and
- a statement of praise to God.

There are community laments, used when the people gathered for official worship, and individual laments, which were probably responses to personal misfortunes.

Thanksgiving Psalms

Thanksgiving psalms flow from the confidence and gratitude of God's people in God. A thanksgiving psalm is a proclamation of what God has done for his people. Psalms of thanksgiving have two simple parts:

- an expression of praise and
- a description of what God has done.

Explain the difference between psalms of praise, psalms of lament, and psalms of thanksgiving.

There are many other ways people have classified the Psalms. No matter what classification is used, each in some way expresses the faith and trust of God's people in his love and faithfulness to them.

WHAT DIFFERENCE DOES FAITH MAKE?

What feelings do you express to God? How can praying the psalms help you?

_____

_____

_____

_____

_____

_____

_____

Reading the Word of God

Shepherd with his Flock (with a view of the Confrane Hill, Pyreness Mountains, France). Auguste-François Bonheur (1824–1884), French landscape and animal painter.

FAITH FOCUS

How does Psalm 23 express the faith and trust of God's people in God?

Images help people express their relationship with one another. We use the image "land of the free and home of the brave" to help us express the heart of the relationship that unites citizens of the United States. What other images do you use to describe your relationship with others? For example, how does your school mascot image who you are as a school community?

Images for God

The sacred writers of the Bible used many images to describe the relationship of God to his people. Among the images used in the Book of Psalms is the image of God as the Shepherd of his people.

Psalm 23 is a Psalm of David, the shepherd boy who became king. It describes God as the Lord, Shepherd of his people.

The LORD is my shepherd;
    there is nothing I lack.
In green pastures you let me graze;
    to safe waters you lead me;
    you restore my strength.
You guide me along the right path
    for the sake of your name.
Even when I walk through a dark
    valley,
    I fear no harm for you are at
    my side;
    your rod and staff give me
    courage.

David the shepherd.

David was the shepherd boy who became king. The description of the king as shepherd was not new to the Israelites. As early as the third millennium B.C. Sumerian kings referred to themselves as the shepherd of their people. This image emphasized the leadership of the king who would look after and protect his people. It was also common for kings to give a huge, sumptuous banquet for all the people on special occasions. David and the Israelites saw God as their true shepherd and only true king. Yahweh, the God of Israel, was seen as the protector of Israel.

You set a table before me
   as my enemies watch;
You anoint my head with oil;
   my cup overflows.
Only goodness and love will
    pursue me
   all the days of my life;
I will dwell in the house of the LORD
   for years to come.

Describe the psalmist's relationship with God.

Anointing of David.

David the king.

What other image or images help describe your relationship with God?

FAITH FOCUS

How can praying the Psalms help us express our prayers to God?

The beauty of the Psalms is that they primarily speak to God rather than about God. Flowing from the heart of God's people, they express the trust of God's people in God their Shepherd. Through the Psalms God's people share all their experiences of life—all our hope, all our sorrow, all our joy—with God. Through them God is acknowledged as the source of every blessing.

The Church's Prayer

While the Psalms give expression to the faith and trust of Israel in the Lord God, they are also models for the prayer of the Church. Built upon the tradition of prayer found in the Scriptures, the Church names five traditional forms of prayer: blessing and adoration, petition, intercession, thanksgiving, and praise.

Blessing and Adoration

Our **prayers of blessing and adoration** declare that God is our almighty creator. We bless God, who is the source of all blessings. We adore God our creator. With the psalmist we pray:

> Enter, let us bow down in worship;
> let us kneel before the LORD who made us. PSALM 95:6

Our prayers of blessing and adoration are a gift of the Holy Spirit. Filled with the Spirit's gift of awe and wonder, we bless and adore God who made us.

Petition

Through our **prayers of petition** we express our faith and trust in God. We ask, beseech, plead, invoke, entreat, cry out, and even struggle in our prayer. We ask for God's forgiveness and pray "thy kingdom come. Thy will be done on earth as it is in heaven." Trusting that God knows our every need, we pray in faith, never doubting. Filled with the Spirit's gifts of knowledge and wisdom, we pray that God will fulfill our truest needs—everything we need to reach the kingdom of heaven.

Being thankful is synonymous with being a Christian. Christians are people of thanksgiving. God is the source of every blessing. He is the Giver of Life. Our **prayers of thanksgiving** express our gratitude to God for his unlimited blessings.

Praise

Prayers of praise give glory to God simply because he is God. He is the holy One, deserving of our praise and respect. Our prayers of praise give glory to God not only for what he has done for us but because he is the One who is always with us in our good times and bad times.

Name and describe the five traditional forms of prayer used by the Church.

Intercession

Prayers of intercession are a form of prayer of petition that flow out of love for others—all others. Prayers of intercession truly have no limits. They reach out to God as Christ taught us. We pray for all others, those we know and those we have never met—even those who have harmed us.

Thanksgiving

Paul the Apostle wrote:

In all circumstances give thanks, for this is the will of God for you in Christ Jesus. I Thessalonians 5:18

We are a believing and praying Church. These forms of prayer have been passed on through the church community from the days of the apostles and the first disciples of Christ. Our prayers give witness to our faith and strengthen our life with God and with one another.

WHAT DIFFERENCE DOES FAITH MAKE?

Choose a psalm verse you can make part of your daily prayer. Write it here.

_____

_____

_____

WHAT DIFFERENCE

Does This Make in Our Church?

Pope John XXIII

Angelo Giuseppe Roncalli was born in 1881 in northern Italy to a farm family. After he was ordained his many responsibilities prepared him to serve the whole Church as pope. After serving the people as a parish priest, he became a chaplain in the Italian army during World War I. He worked at the Vatican reorganizing the Society for the Propagation of the Faith. He was a diplomat for the Vatican for twenty-five years, first in Bulgaria, and then in Turkey, Greece, and France. Finally for six years he was the patriarch of Venice, Italy.

Father Angelo Giuseppe Roncalli (center) with two fellow priests, while studying in Rome, 1901.

Psalms have been described as "songs of feelings." Psalms are the prayer-songs of the People of God through which they express their many feelings to God. Characteristic of all the psalms is the trust they express in God, whom they look upon as their shepherd.

Among the many shepherds of the Church who led us to trust in God is Pope John XXIII. Pope John XXIII is among the most beloved popes of modern times. His warm, outgoing personality made him easily accessible to all people.

Father Angelo Roncalli in the uniform of the Italian army, 1915.

Archbishop Angelo Giuseppe Cardinal Roncalli was elected pope in 1958 when he was seventy-seven years old. John XXIII said we must read "the signs of the time" and be alert to the work of the Holy Spirit in the world today. And he did listen to the Holy Spirit. To his own surprise and the surprise of the world, he announced, on January 25, 1959, his plans for an ecumenical council for the Church.

With his characteristic energy and enthusiasm John XXIII said that the purpose of the council was *aggiornamento*, an Italian word meaning "bringing up to date." This word has since become synonymous with the Second Vatican Council, through which the Church called for a new openness on its part to the world and other churches, both Christian and non-Christian.

When John XXIII realized that he probably would not be able to live to see the conclusion of the Second Vatican Council, he said to a friend, "At least I have launched this big ship—others will have to bring it to port." Pope John XXIII died on June 3, 1963. The sorrow felt throughout the world was best expressed by a newspaper drawing of the earth shrouded in mourning with the caption, "A Death in the Family."

Explain how Pope John XXIII was a shepherd to the Church. What modern-day shepherds are helping the Church today?

Pope John XXIII.
October 29, 1958.

Background photo:
Vatican Council II in session.

WHAT DIFFERENCE

Does It Make in My Life?

February Morning.
Charles Neal (1951–),
British painter.

Shepherds

In the Old Testament there are many stories of some very bad shepherds who really didn't care for their sheep. But Psalm 23 and the image Jesus showed us, "I am the good shepherd" (John 10:11) proved to us what a truly good shepherd is all about. Jesus loves us, cares about us and what happens to us, knows us intimately, and calls us to follow him.

Good Shepherd

The idea of a shepherd is a very strong, consoling, and loving image. It brings with it a very real responsibility and a high level of care. A shepherd must bond with his sheep so they will recognize his voice and only follow that voice. If a stranger tries to lure the sheep away, they will not respond. They only answer their shepherd's voice whenever they are called.

The beautiful message of Psalm 23 assures us that the Lord is our shepherd, our protector. We can put our faith and trust in him because he loves us and will always take care of us. He will lead us to safety and we will find our way home to God.

Sheep must be taken care of and constantly be led away from danger. They rely totally on their shepherd (and of course the sheep dog is an essential helper) to provide for them and lead them to safety. A good shepherd will do whatever it takes to rescue his sheep. He will make sure that none of them stray away or get lost or are in danger.

He will go to great lengths to keep them safe. Jesus the Good Shepherd had all these qualities; and in addition, he did the ultimate act of love—and died for us.

Qualities of Shepherds and Caregivers

You may never be called upon to be a shepherd but you are called upon each day to care for others. Here are some qualities to think about and incorporate into your life.

1. **Be a responsible person.** As followers of Jesus you are asked to love and take care of people in your life and also animals and all created things on earth.
2. **Be trustworthy.** Be a person your family and friends can depend on when they need your help.
3. **Be compassionate.** By your kind words and caring actions show others how to follow Jesus.
4. **Be gentle and a sign of peace to others.**

faith decision

ff

Discuss these questions in a small group.

- How can you recognize false, or bad, shepherds who may try to lead you astray?

- How can you be a good shepherd, or caregiver, to others?

This week I will choose to be a "good shepherd," or caregiver, to _____.

I will do this by _____

_____

_____

_____

_____

_____

_____

_____

_____.

Winter at Ferme L'Aumone. Charles Neal (1951–), British painter.

Faith Vocabulary

Define each of these terms:

1. psalms
2. Psalter
3. laments
4. prayers of blessing and adoration

5. prayers of petition
6. prayers of intercession
7. prayers of thanksgiving
8. prayers of praise

Main Ideas

Choose either (a) or (b) from each set of items. Write a brief paragraph to answer each of your choices.

1. (a) Explain the form or structure of hymns of praise, psalms of lament, and psalms of thanksgiving.

   (b) Why do we say that psalms are prayers that express the feelings of God's people?

2. (a) Describe what the psalmist expresses in Psalm 23.

   (b) Explain why the psalmist would describe God as a shepherd.

3. (a) Why would the Church model its prayers on the Psalms?

   (b) Name and describe the five traditional forms of prayer used by the Church.

Critical Thinking

Using what you have learned in this chapter, briefly explain this statement:
God, the Good Shepherd, guides and protects his people.

Family Discussion

We are called to be people of prayer. How is prayer a part of our family life?

Visit our
web site at
www.FaithFirst.com

The Call to Prayer

18

WE PRAY

Lord Jesus Christ, Son of God, have mercy on us sinners.

ANCIENT PRAYER OF THE SPIRITUAL MASTERS OF THE SINAI, SYRIA AND MOUNT ATHOS

What has been your personal experience of prayer? What is the earliest experience of prayer that you can remember? How many different ways of praying are you familiar with?

LORD, hear my prayer; . . .
Show me the path I should walk,
for to you I entrust my life.

PSALM 143:1, 8

A Living Relationship of Love

Spending time together—that pretty much can summarize our day. Take the time to answer these questions: Who do you spend your time with? Where do you spend your time? What do you spend your time doing? When you look at your answers, ask yourself why you spend your time that way. Your answer will give you a glimpse of who and what is important to you.

Spending Time with God

FAITH VOCABULARY

prayer

Prayer is spending time with God, talking with and listening to him. Saint John Damascene described that time with God, or prayer, as "the raising of one's mind and heart to God or the requesting of good things from God." Spending time with God—sharing our life with him and listening to him—is at the heart of our relationship with God.

Our time with God is so vital that he does not wait for us to come to him in prayer. The Spirit tirelessly reaches out to everyone, calling us to meet him in prayer. You might say that God gives all of his time, which is the same as saying he gives all of himself, inviting us to spend time with him. The mystery and wonder of prayer is that God always begins our conversation with him. The Holy Spirit first invites us to pray and teaches us to pray. He silently awaits us to join in that conversation.

In your own words describe prayer.

Prayer as Covenant

The truth is that we are so connected with God that life without him is not possible. God has created us and entered into a covenant with us. He is with us in every moment of our lives. Through Baptism we are joined to Christ. We are united in Christ with the Father and the Holy Spirit. Christian prayer is an expression of that covenant relationship with God.

Prayer as Communion

What would our relationship with our friends be like if we never spent time with them, talking with them and listening to them? Sharing hopes and dreams, joys and sorrows, likes and dislikes is a sign that a friendship is alive.

Our prayer is a sign that our life as children of God is alive. In Baptism we are united with Christ. We receive the gift of the Holy Spirit and new life as adopted children of God. In prayer we talk and listen to God as Jesus, the only Son of God, did. When we pray we are living, in a very important way, our relationship with God the Father, with his Son, Jesus Christ, and with the Holy Spirit.

Explain prayer as both an expression of our covenant and communion with God.

Obstacles to Prayer

For some reason, days often seem to go by without God hearing a word from us—or our giving God a moment to listen to him. While prayer needs to become as natural

Did you Know...

The Gospel often describes Jesus in prayer with his Father. Here are several passages in which you can read about Jesus at prayer:

Matthew 14:22–23

Mark 1:35

Luke 5:15–16

Luke 6:12–13

John 17:1–26

to us as breathing, there are very few people for whom prayer seems to come that easy. The truth is that communicating with God on a regular basis each day just seems to take practice and hard work. If prayer is so important to our spiritual life— as important as breathing is to our physical life—why do we struggle with prayer? There are many reasons. Some of them are:

1. We misunderstand what prayer really is. We might feel that prayer takes us away from the important things we need to do. We don't quite see how prayer can lead to our being successful in the real world. What we need to do is become more aware of God's loving presence with us. When we do, prayer might just become more natural. How better could we spend our time than building our relationship with God—a relationship that will last forever?

2. We become discouraged when we pray and don't see results. We feel abandoned by God, who just doesn't seem to be listening. When this happens, take a few moments to believe and trust in your relationship with him. Remember the faith stories of the People of God. Over and over again they felt abandoned too. We know the opposite was true. God was always with them.

3. Sometimes we are so busy and distracted that God cannot get a word in. So much in our life pulls our attention away from God. When that happens, take a time-out. We need to turn our hearts to God and think for a moment how God might be talking to us through the very things that seem to be drawing our attention away from him.

When we feel that our prayer is not heard or that we do not have the time just now, we need to remember and believe that above everything else we are children of God.

Describe some of the obstacles to prayer.

More than anything else prayer will change our lives. It has the power to help us see God in the people around us and in the ordinary events of our daily lives. It has the power to help us remember that we are children of God with whom he shares his life and love.

WHAT DIFFERENCE DOES FAITH MAKE?

What can you do to be more aware of the presence of God in your life?

_____

_____

_____

FAITH FOCUS

How does the story of God's people help us understand prayer?

The Scriptures, in one sense, are the story of the prayer life of God's people. In the Scriptures we listen to the story of the many conversations between God and his people. The prayers of God's people found in the Scriptures express the faith and trust of God's people in him. Above all else, these conversations express God's love for us.

Moses and the Burning Bush. Henry Osswa Tanner (1859–1937), American painter.

Abraham

We call Abraham our "father in faith" (Eucharist Prayer I) for good reason. When Abraham was seventy-five years old, God said to him, "Go forth from the land of your kinsfolk and from your father's house to a land that I will show you" (Genesis 12:1). Then God made a covenant with Abraham:

> "I will make of you a great nation, and I will bless you;
> I will make your name great, so that you will be a blessing."
> GENESIS 12:2

Solely on God's promise to them, Abraham and Sarah and their family packed up all their belongings. In faith they did what God asked. From the descendants of Abraham and Sarah the People of God would be born. The offer of divine love and friendship first made at creation was renewed.

Explain how the story of Abraham shows us why faith is important in our prayer.

Moses

When the Israelites felt abandoned in slavery in Egypt, God reached out to them. Moses listened:

> "Remove the sandals from your feet, for the place where you stand is holy ground. I am the God of your father, . . . the God of Abraham, the God of Isaac, the God of Jacob." EXODUS 3:5–6

From that first moment of his approaching the burning bush, God and Moses went back and forth in conversation. The Scripture tells us:

> The LORD used to speak to Moses face to face, as one man speaks to another. EXODUS 33:11

Those face-to-face meetings with God, or moments of contemplative prayer, transformed Moses' life. The sacred writer tells us that even Moses' physical appearance changed each and every time he went up the mountain to be alone with God. It was during these moments of prayer that Moses opened his heart to God and interceded for his people. Moses would always come down confident and assured of God's love for his people.

Describe two dimensions of the prayer of Moses.

God's People

David, the shepherd-king of God's people, knew that God alone was the one true king of the Israelites. So David drew up plans to center the life of his people around God. He would build a temple in which the people would gather in prayer in the presence of God. David would never see his plan come true. His son Solomon, after he became king, would build the Temple in Jerusalem.

The Prophets

The Scriptures are also filled with many conversations the prophets had with God—conversations that refocused the attention of God's people on God and living their covenant with him.

As the nation grew in power and prestige, God's people became too busy building and maintaining their nation. There seemed to be no time left for God. In the midst of their search for success and the sufferings

that searching brought, God reached out to his people. Isaiah, Jeremiah, Elijah, and the other prophets of Israel heard God. They sometimes resisted and wanted to turn a deaf ear to God but, in the end, they listened and responded. They pleaded with God on behalf of his people. In God's name they pleaded with God's people to change their hearts, promising God's unbroken love for them. God's people listened. They too responded to God.

Explain how the prophets help us understand the importance of prayer in our lives.

The prophet Jeremiah.

The prophet Isaiah.

The prophet Elijah.

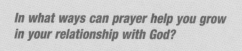

WHAT DIFFERENCE DOES FAITH MAKE?

In what ways can prayer help you grow in your relationship with God?

_____

_____

_____

223

Jesus in the Garden of Gethesemane Outside Jerusalem. Artist unknown.

The Prayer of Jesus

Jesus most fully reveals the way of prayer. Jesus taught us to pray, "Our Father in heaven." He invited us to approach God in prayer and trust God as "Abba," a loving Father whose most driving concern in life was the good and well-being of his children.

Throughout his life on earth, Jesus did just that. Time and time again Jesus spent time alone with his Father before making important decisions. During these conversations with his Father he came to see more clearly the work his Father sent him to do. He also received the courage and wisdom to do that work.

The Gospel also describes Jesus praying with his disciples and others. He prayed with them in the Temple and in the synagogue. He prayed with them at the Passover meal, blessing and thanking God as Jews have done for centuries.

Prayer was at the very center of his Paschal mystery. Jesus prepared for his death and resurrection in communion with his Father by praying first for others and then for himself. Before leaving the upper room where they celebrated their final Passover meal together, Jesus prayed:

"I pray not only for them, but also for those who will believe in me through their word, so that they may all be one, as you, Father, are in me and I in you, that they also may be in us, that the world may believe that you sent me."

JOHN 17:20–21

To prepare for his imminent suffering and death, Jesus invited his disciples to join with him in prayer outdoors in the quiet of the night. Going off to be alone with his Father, he turned to his Father and spoke of his fears and his trust:

"My Father, if it is possible, let this cup pass from me; yet, not as I will, but as you will."

MATTHEW 26:39

Getting up, Jesus returned to his disciples, who had fallen asleep. He said to Peter:

"So you could not keep watch with me for one hour? Watch and pray that you may not undergo the test. The spirit is willing, but the flesh is weak." Withdrawing a second time, he prayed again, "My Father, if it is not possible that this cup pass without my drinking it, your will be done!" Then he returned once more and found them asleep, for they could not keep their eyes open. He left them and withdrew again and prayed a third time, saying the same thing again. MATTHEW 26:40–44

Strengthened with his trust in his Father's love, Jesus faced his arrest, his public ridicule and scourging, and his brutal death on the cross. At the moment of death, he reached out and shared his suffering with his Father. He cried out in unconditional love and trust:

> "Father, into your hands
> I commend my spirit."
>
> LUKE 23:46

Jesus' whole life was a life of prayer. He lived his life on earth in continuing conversation with his Father. Jesus acknowledged his Father as God. He blessed and thanked his Father as the source of all blessings. He prayed for himself and others, confident in his Father's love for him, for his disciples, and for all people.

How does Jesus teach us to pray?

The Prayer of the Church

The whole life of the Body of Christ, the Church, is a life of prayer as the life of Jesus was. Our whole life— our thoughts, our words, our actions, and our silences—is a sign that we live in communion with God. Because God blesses us, we bless him who is the source of every blessing. We thank and praise God. We pray for ourselves and for others.

Prayer and living our life in Christ are inseparable. It is always possible to pray because God is always present with us, inviting us to share our life with him as he shares his life with us. Wherever we are, whatever we are doing, whomever we are with, God is with us.

Paul the Apostle reminds us of how vital prayer is for our life. He writes:

> Pray without ceasing. In all
> circumstances give thanks,
> for this is the will of God
> for you in Christ Jesus.
>
> I THESSALONIANS 5:17–18

Why do we say that the life of a Christian is a life of prayer?

Christian prayer rises out of faith, out of hope, and out of love for God who has revealed himself to us most fully in Jesus Christ. Our prayer ascends in the Holy Spirit through Christ to the Father. God's blessing in turn descends upon us through Christ in the Spirit, showering upon us his many gifts.

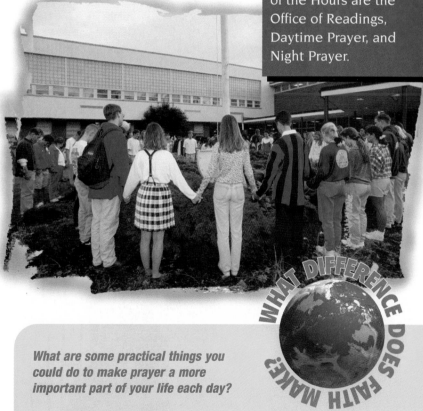

WHAT DIFFERENCE DOES FAITH MAKE?

What are some practical things you could do to make prayer a more important part of your life each day?

225

WHAT DIFFERENCE

Does This Make in Our Church?

Saint Francis of Assisi.

Prayer and living our life in Christ are inseparable. The whole life of the Church, the Body of Christ, is a life of prayer as the life of Jesus was. Christian prayer arises out of faith, hope, and love for God. We do not pray on our own. The Holy Spirit first invites us to pray and teaches us to pray. He silently awaits us to join in that conversation. Living our life in response to the Spirit is called spirituality.

Forms of Spirituality

The history of Catholic spirituality reveals how numerous groups in various times and regions came to live the life of Christ authentically and integrally. There is no one way of living our life in Christ. There are different paths along which women and men continue to follow Jesus. Here is an overview of four of the many paths, or forms, of Christian spirituality.

Monastic Spirituality

Monastic spirituality is a form of religious life in which men and women take vows of poverty, chastity, and obedience. These individuals separate themselves from society either singly (as hermits) or in communities known as monasteries, abbeys, or priories. The goal of monasticism is to pursue, under the guidance of a common rule (such as the Rule of Saint Benedict), a life devoted to prayer and work for the glory of God and the good of the Church and the world.

Saint Dominic de Guzman.

Dominican Spirituality

Dominican spirituality is a mode of life and prayer that was founded by Saint Dominic de Guzman (1170–1221). Dominic wanted to recapture the enthusiasm of the apostles as presented in the Gospel according to Saint Matthew. Commissioned by Jesus, the apostles went far and wide to preach the Good News. Members of the Dominican order are dedicated to preaching, communal living, and private prayer.

Lay Spirituality

Lay spirituality addresses the daily challenges of men and women who live their lives in Christ in the midst of the world. It keeps living one's relationship with God at the heart of raising families, attending school, pursuing careers, and so on. Lay spirituality is supported in many ways. These include Bible study groups, prayer groups, retreat programs, men's and women's organizations, small faith communities, outreach programs to the poor, and Catholic action programs.

How can you develop your own spirituality?

Franciscan Spirituality

The spirituality of the followers of Saint Francis of Assisi (ca. 1181–1226) puts its emphasis on imitating the total obedience and self-giving of Jesus to his Father. Followers of Francis choose, as Francis did, to live their lives in a way that emphasizes their total dependence on God. They live humble lives of thanksgiving and poverty, recognizing that all blessings have been given to us by God out of his love for us.

WHAT DIFFERENCE

Does It Make in My Life?

There are different schools of spirituality and there are different forms of prayer. Spirituality is your relationship with God right here, right now where you are, being the person you are. You acknowledge God's love and friendship in your life. You recognize that God is here with you. He is in every person you meet and every situation you encounter.

Thursday, August 17th

Dear God, this morning some thing happened that I thou... would never happen to me. My best friend real... let me down, we've be... friends since 3rd. Gr... I really want to forgive... but it's really hard. I...

Journal Writing

Journal writing is a form of prayer that helps you discover God's daily working in your life. Keeping a journal helps you write down any special feelings you have, or special events of each day where you feel God's presence in your life. A spiritual journal is different from a diary and yet there are similarities. You usually write very personal things in your diary—thoughts, feelings, fears, and joys. The wonderful thing about keeping a spiritual journal is that you are sharing all those very special thoughts, feelings, fears, and joys with God.

You write these things in your journal so you can deepen your relationship with God.

You can write about things that remind you of God's love and presence in your life. On a certain day you may wonder where God is in your life because things do not seem to be going well. When you may feel lonely or sad, writing in your journal may help you talk to God. Tell him how you feel and ask for his help to get you through this hard time. Reading over what you wrote on other days may lift your spirit and help you feel more hopeful.

Your Dialogue with God

Your journal is your dialogue with God, your personal prayer. You can write words, sentences, thoughts, or feelings. You can scribble, write fast and not worry about grammar or misspelled words. Remember that God knows what's in your heart and what you are sharing with him.

You can also write quotes, good ideas, thoughts from reading Scripture, lines of a poem you heard or read, and of course you can create your own poems, prayers, or songs. You can draw pictures; you can paste in pictures or newspaper clippings—anything you want to remember that day. Each day or each time you choose to write in your journal, it helps you bring the daily events of your life to prayer. Writing in your journal can deepen

❖ Just begin to write. Write quickly and don't worry about punctuation or spelling. Be aware of your inner thoughts, feelings, beliefs, and any new insights you discover.

❖ Write anything that comes to your mind. Use your writing as your personal dialogue with God and listen to God's response in your heart.

your spirituality and help you gain a new awareness of God revealing himself in your life.

How Do You Begin?

Here are a few basic steps to get you started.

❖ Find the right book (a book of blank pages or a notebook) or paper (loose leaf or legal pads), and the pen or pencil you want to use. Keep these in one special place.

❖ Decide how often you will write in your journal. If daily, you can establish a routine, a daily form of prayer.

❖ Find a time and a place to write, free of noise and interruption.

❖ Relax and ask the Holy Spirit to enlighten your mind and open your heart.

❖ Date each entry so you can go back and find it easily.

faith decision

Think about and respond to the following questions:

• How can journal writing help you learn more about yourself and deepen your faith in God? _____
_____
_____

• Would you do your daily journal writing on a computer? Why or why not?
_____
_____
_____

I will begin my journal on

_____
(day)

and I will find time each week to write in my journal.

The best time and place for me to write in my journal is _____
(time)

_____ .
(place)

229

Faith Vocabulary

Write a brief paragraph describing prayer.

Main Ideas

Choose either (a) or (b) from each set of items. Write a brief paragraph to answer each of your choices.

1. (a) Describe prayer as covenant and communion with God.

   (b) Describe the obstacles to prayer and how we could overcome them.

2. (a) Describe the prayer of Moses.

   (b) Explain how the prophets teach us the importance of prayer in our lives.

3. (a) Why do we describe Jesus' life on earth as a life of prayer?

   (b) How can our lives be lives of prayer?

Critical Thinking

Using what you have learned in this chapter explain the meaning of this statement:

"Prayer is a surge of the heart toward God." (Saint Thérèse of Lisieux)

Family Discussion

Prayer is the living relationship of the children of God with God. How can prayer strengthen our relationships with each other as family members?

Visit our
web site at
www.FaithFirst.com

The Church:
A People of Prayer

19

WE PRAY

Father,
let the gift of your life
continue to grow in us,
drawing us from death to faith,
    hope and love.
Keep us alive in Christ Jesus.
Keep us watchful in prayer
and true to his teaching till your
glory is revealed in us.

*FROM OPENING PRAYER,
SIXTEENTH SUNDAY IN
ORDINARY TIME*

Like a tree planted in rich
soil that grows strong roots,
we grow in our life in Christ
through prayer. What were
the first prayers that you
were taught? Now that you
are older, what are your
favorite prayers?

*It is good to give thanks
    to the LORD. . . .
To proclaim your love in the
    morning,
    your faithfulness in the
    night.* PSALM 92:2

In Jesus' Name We Pray

FAITH FOCUS

How does being a member of the Church help each of us become a person of prayer?

FAITH VOCABULARY

vocal prayer

meditation

lectio divina

rosary

contemplation

doxology

One major media company named Johannes Gutenberg, who printed the first Bible around 1455, the person of the millennium. The reason for choosing Gutenberg was the tremendous impact that his printing press had on the world. Gutenberg's press revolutionized our ability to communicate with one another. It responded to the human desire to discover faster and faster ways to share thoughts and information. This is why Gutenberg came out at the top of the great people of the century list.

The Praying Church

In one way, the Church is a communication community. We are the new People of God who, joined together as the one Body of Christ, constantly communicate with God through prayer. Led by the Spirit, who has been sent to us by the Father and the Son, we raise our voices as one voice in adoration, blessing, thanksgiving, intercession, petition, and praise of God.

> For those who are led by the Spirit of God are children of God. . . . [Y]ou received a spirit of adoption, through which we cry, "*Abba*, Father!" . . .
> In the same way, the Spirit too comes to the aid of our weakness; for we do not know how to pray as we ought, but the Spirit itself intercedes with inexpressible groanings.   ROMANS 8:14–15, 26

As promised by Jesus, the Spirit is always with us as our helper and our teacher. The Spirit teaches the Church how to pray, recalling to our memory Abraham and Moses, Ruth and Esther, and all the people of prayer of the Old Covenant. The same Spirit recalls to our memory Mary, Peter, and the other disciples. Most of all, the Spirit reminds us of what Jesus said and taught about prayer. The same Spirit invites and teaches us to pray and forms us into a praying community.

Describe the Church as a praying community.

and the Liturgy of the Hours. There are other rhythms as well, such as the weekly cycle centered on the Sunday Eucharist, the cycle of saints' feasts, and the seasons of the liturgical year.

The simplest, yet very powerful, prayer that we can utter is to simply speak the name of Jesus over and over again. This reminds us that every good grace that comes to us from God comes through Jesus, our Lord and Savior.

Why is being in rhythm with the praying Church important?

Having a regular rhythm to our prayer, like having a regular rhythm to our breathing, reenergizes our life. It strengthens our relationship with the Holy Trinity and with all the members of the Body of Christ. It draws us all closer to the love of God. In short, prayer transforms the way we think and act in this world.

The Christian Rhythm of Prayer

While we can and need to pray throughout each day in the midst of joy or pain, good times or bad, the Church also invites the faithful to regular prayer. The Church does this by suggesting a certain rhythm for our prayer life. This rhythm is made up of fixed times and seasons that we can mark off with regularity to insure that the time we spend in prayer flows throughout our life.

There are daily rhythms, such as morning and evening prayer, grace before and after meals, the Angelus,

WHAT DIFFERENCE DOES FAITH MAKE?

When do you usually pray? What are some other times you could pray?

_____

_____

_____

_____

233

Think of a time you saw people react to the same situation in different ways. Describe the situation and the ways people expressed themselves. The truth is that people often express themselves in many different ways. The same is true of our prayer.

The Lord wishes to draw us all into communion with himself, and he calls every Christian to be a person of prayer. The way each person responds to that call will vary from individual to individual. However, three major forms of prayer seem to mark the basic ways Christians express themselves. These expressions of prayer are vocal prayer, meditation, and contemplation.

Vocal Prayer

Vocal prayer is spoken prayer, spoken aloud or spoken within the quiet of our hearts. It consists of words that communicate our blessing and adoration, our petition and intercession, our praise and thanksgiving to the Father.

Vocal prayer is usually the first way we learn to express our prayers. Our families teach us words to pray at nighttime and at meal times. They teach us to bless ourselves, saying the words of the Sign of the Cross. Vocal prayer also plays an important role in the prayer of the Christian community. We come together lifting voices as well as hearts to God.

What is vocal prayer?

Meditation

Meditation is another type of prayer. In meditation we express what is in our heart and on our mind silently. We use our mind and heart and imagination as we seek to understand and follow what the Lord is asking of us. Meditation engages our thoughts, our imagination, our emotions, and our desires. It does so to deepen our convictions, to stimulate our conversation with the Lord, and to strengthen our will to follow Christ.

Among the most popular forms of meditation are **lectio divina** and the **rosary.** Lectio divina is the prayerful reading of Scripture that leads to thoughtful consideration of the meaning of God's word and its application to our lives. The rosary is a form of both vocal prayer and meditation that invites us to ponder the mysteries of Christ's life while

simultaneously reciting a repetitive pattern of prayers either in the silence of our heart or aloud with others.

How is meditation different from vocal prayer?

Contemplation

Contemplation is simply being with God. Saint Teresa of Avila describes contemplative prayer as "nothing else than a close sharing between friends; it means taking time frequently to be alone with him who we know loves us." Expressing our prayer this way is a gift from God.

Contemplative prayer is the simplest expression of Christian prayer. Uncluttered by words, it is a gift and a mystery that can only be accepted in humility and gratitude. It is a simple gaze of faith on the One who loves us. It is a listening to his word with an attentiveness

marked by faith and trust. Ultimately, contemplative prayer allows us to enter into the prayer of Christ himself and accept his invitation to "keep watch with me for one hour" (Matthew 26:40).

How is contemplation different from vocal prayer and meditation?

However we pray, we can pray anyplace and anytime. The choice of a place to pray is important. While we gather in our parish church for the celebration of the liturgy, it is also a favorite place for Catholics to come for prayer throughout the day. It is there that Catholics often come to visit with Christ present in the Blessed Sacrament. Our personal prayer is also enriched by setting aside a prayer corner in our homes where we can quietly read the Scriptures and listen to God's own word to us. We can also spend time with God during a walk outdoors. No matter where and when we pray, God is always there welcoming us and listening to us.

What is your favorite way of praying? How can you include different types of prayer in your life?

_____

_____

_____

WHAT DIFFERENCE DOES FAITH MAKE?

The Blessed Virgin Mary is a model of prayer for Christians. By reflecting on her life, we learn how vocal prayer, meditation, and contemplation all help us express our prayer to God.

The Prayer of Mary, the Mother of the Church

Trusting in God's promises to his people, Mary unexpectedly learned that God had chosen her to become the mother of his Son, whom she was to name Jesus. "Behold, I am the handmaid of the Lord. May it be done to me according to your word" was Mary's response (Luke 1:38).

How could Mary give her assent to God's mysterious invitation? She was a woman of prayer. Mary lived a life of faith, hope, and love. The love of God and for God filled her heart in a way that no one before had ever experienced the love of God. Mary's heart was in rhythm with the heart of God, and she said, "Yes."

Why is Mary a model of prayer for Christians?

Sources of Christian Prayer

The prayer of the Body of Christ, the Church, is nourished and strengthened through Scriptures, through the sacraments and liturgy of the Church, and through the theological virtues of faith, hope, and love. All are God's gifts to us.

Word of God. The Scriptures are the gift of God's own word present to us. Through reading and listening to the word of God, God speaks to us and we listen to God. We deepen our love for God and respond to that divine love.

Liturgy of the Church. Jesus is present with his Church in the celebration of the sacraments and other liturgical celebrations. He joins us to himself, the Father, and the Holy Spirit through the Sacraments of Initiation. He heals us and strengthens our relationship with him and with one another in the Sacraments of Healing. Through the Sacraments at the Service of

The Annunciation.
Stained glass.

Communion he consecrates both ordained ministers and also married men and women to be signs of God's saving love in the world.

Virtue of Faith. Our prayer, the surge of our heart to God, begins out of faith as Mary's did. We believe God meets us and we meet God in expected and unexpected ways. We need to be ready.

Virtue of Hope. Our prayer continues out of hope. We confidently wait, knowing that God listens and responds. He does only what is best for us. All that God does strengthens our living relationship with him and with all the children of God.

Virtue of Love. Out of love God invites us to share in the communion of the life and love of the Holy Trinity—God the Father, Son, and Holy Spirit. Out of love we respond yes to that invitation. John, the disciple who took Mary into his home after the death, Resurrection, and Ascension of Christ to his Father, came to know that love in a special way. He wrote:

> God is love, and whoever remains in love remains in God and God in him. **1 JOHN 4:16**

Describe the sources of Christian prayer.

All Glory and Honor Is Yours, Almighty Father

Like the prayer of Jesus, the prayer of Christians is addressed primarily to God the Father. We see this in the **doxologies** that conclude many of the liturgical prayers of the Church.

The word *doxology* means "praise-words." For example, at the conclusion of the eucharistic prayer we pray:

> Through him [Christ], with him, in him, in the unity of the Holy Spirit, all glory and honor is yours, almighty Father, for ever and ever. Amen.
> FROM EUCHARISTIC PRAYER, *ROMAN MISSAL*

Christians do not pray only to God the Father. We pray to God the Son and to the Father in Jesus' name. We pray to God the Holy Spirit, our helper and the Giver of Life, sent to us by the Father and Son.

To whom do Christians address their prayers?

Prayer and Christian life are inseparable. Filled with the Spirit we join with Christ, Mary, and all the saints. Together as the new People of God we offer our lives and raise our voices in praise and thanksgiving to the Father.

Mosaic representing the Sacred Heart of Jesus.

WHAT DIFFERENCE DOES FAITH MAKE?

What can you praise and thank God for right now?

_____

_____

_____

_____

WHAT DIFFERENCE
Does This Make in Our Church?

The Church is a people of prayer. We observe Jesus' command to "pray always without becoming weary" (Luke 18:1). We give expression to our prayer in many ways. These include vocal prayer, meditation, and contemplation.

Lead by the Spirit we raise our many voices as one voice in adoration, blessing, thanksgiving, intercession, petition, and praise to God. From the very first days of the Church the followers of Christ have expressed their prayers to God through music.

Christian Music

Have you ever thought what a movie would be like without music? The soundtrack subtly creates the mood for the film by carefully coloring the background with just the right music. The words and dialogue of a film will tell the story. It is the music that adds a totally new dimension to the story.

The Church uses music too. Music is part of the prayer life of Christians. Through music Christians celebrate and express the depth of their faith in and love for God—in ways they cannot express through words alone.

Psalms

From the days of the apostles, the followers of Jesus used music in their prayer life. This should come as no surprise since Jesus' first followers were Jews who regularly sang psalms in the Temple and synagogues—and in some cases, in their homes. The Gospel tells us that Jesus and his disciples sang at the Last Supper: "Then, after singing a hymn, they went out to the Mount of Olives" (Matthew 26:30). Singing psalms continues to be an integral part of the worship and prayer life of Christians today.

Hymns

Christians also express their faith through hymns. Some of the music and hymns that we sing today have lyrics that are based in early Church writings.

Gregorian chant.
Decorated manuscript.

In the third and fourth centuries, when Christians were struggling against heresies, hymns were often used to teach correct doctrine. Read the text of popular hymns that are used by your parish today. Discover how some of these hymns teach Bible stories and reinforce what Catholics believe.

During the Reformation, Martin Luther and other reformers encouraged congregational singing. The text became the most important part of a hymn, and not the music. The Council of Trent affirmed that music must serve the text.

Chant

Recently, Gregorian chant has become popular again. This simple yet melodic form of music was developed around the year 900 when the plain chant of the Romans was blended with Gallic music. Chant became the preferred musical style of the Church for a long time.

It was in the classical period of music, around 1750, that sacred music in the West reached its height with the Austrian composers Wolfgang Amadeus Mozart (1756–1791) and Franz Joseph Haydn (1732–1809). The Masses and sacred music that they composed blended text, music, and belief in God to a new level. The major parts of the Mass that the whole worshiping assembly sung—the Kyrie, Gloria, Credo, Sanctus, and Agnus Dei—would be set to grand and glorious music by almost all composers.

By the nineteenth century, sacred music used in worship became almost symphonic. Composers designed their music more to be played in a concert than to be sung as prayer during the liturgy.

Organ

Not all the sacred music created by Christian composers was intended to be sung. Many churches, especially the great cathedrals in Europe, had a resident composer as their organist. This person created brilliant new music that was meant to inspire people to lift their minds and hearts to God in silent prayer.

The tradition of creating sacred music continues in the Church today. Contemporary church music has set new standards for worship. Music is more than just something in the background to set a mood. Music invites people to actively participate in the liturgy, lifting their minds and hearts to God in song.

What type of music helps you express your love for God? How does this music help?

WHAT DIFFERENCE

Does It Make in My Life?

Like the disciples who spent time with Jesus while he was on earth, you too can spend time with Jesus. You can ask him to teach you to pray, to help you understand what it means for you to live as one of his followers. One way you can do this is through the prayer of meditation.

Meditation

Meditation is a form of prayer. We use this prayer to strengthen our desire to know God better, to love him more, and to listen to Jesus speak to us in our hearts. Taking time for meditation is a wonderful gift you can give yourself. Just to take fifteen or twenty minutes away from the noise and busyness of your day can help you relax in body and mind and deepen your relationship with God.

Meditation Steps

Here are some steps and some questions to help you get started.
1. Set aside some time to meditate. What time could you set aside and where would you find your quiet place to pray?
2. Quiet your mind and just relax. What would be the best way for you to do this?

3. Pray to the Holy Spirit, asking for help to open your mind and listen to God. If you are distracted, just relax and try to refocus your thinking on God's presence.

4. Choose what you are going to pray about. It could be a line from a poem, or a reading from your favorite Scripture story. Use your imagination and create a scene picturing yourself with Jesus. Where would you be? What would you talk about?

5. Begin your conversation with Jesus. What do you think Jesus would say to you?

6. Tell Jesus what's going on in your life right now and ask him for what you need. What do you really want Jesus to know about?

7. You may want to write some thoughts from your meditation in your journal.

faith decision

- Take some time this week to meditate. Use the seven steps on pages 240 and 241.

- Talk to someone you know who uses meditation as a way of praying. Ask this person how meditation helps them.

This week I will choose a special place to help me meditate. The place will be

_____

_____

_____

_____

_____

_____

_____

_____

_____

Faith Vocabulary

Define each of these terms:

1. vocal prayer
2. meditation
3. lectio divina
4. rosary
5. contemplation
6. doxology

Main Ideas

Choose either (a) or (b) from each set of items. Write a brief paragraph to answer each of your choices.

1. (a) Describe the Church as a praying community.
   (b) What do we mean by the rhythm of prayer?

2. (a) Describe the difference between vocal prayer and meditation.
   (b) Why do we say that contemplation is the simplest form of prayer?

3. (a) How is Mary a model of prayer for Christians?
   (b) Name and describe the sources of Christian prayer.

Critical Thinking

Using what you have learned in this chapter, explain the meaning of this statement: Every joy and suffering, every event and need can become the matter of prayer.

Family Discussion

Family members need to communicate with one another. What are some of the ways we communicate with God as a family? What can we do as a family to put a more regular rhythm to our praying together as a family?

Visit our
web site at
www.FaithFirst.com

The Lord's Prayer

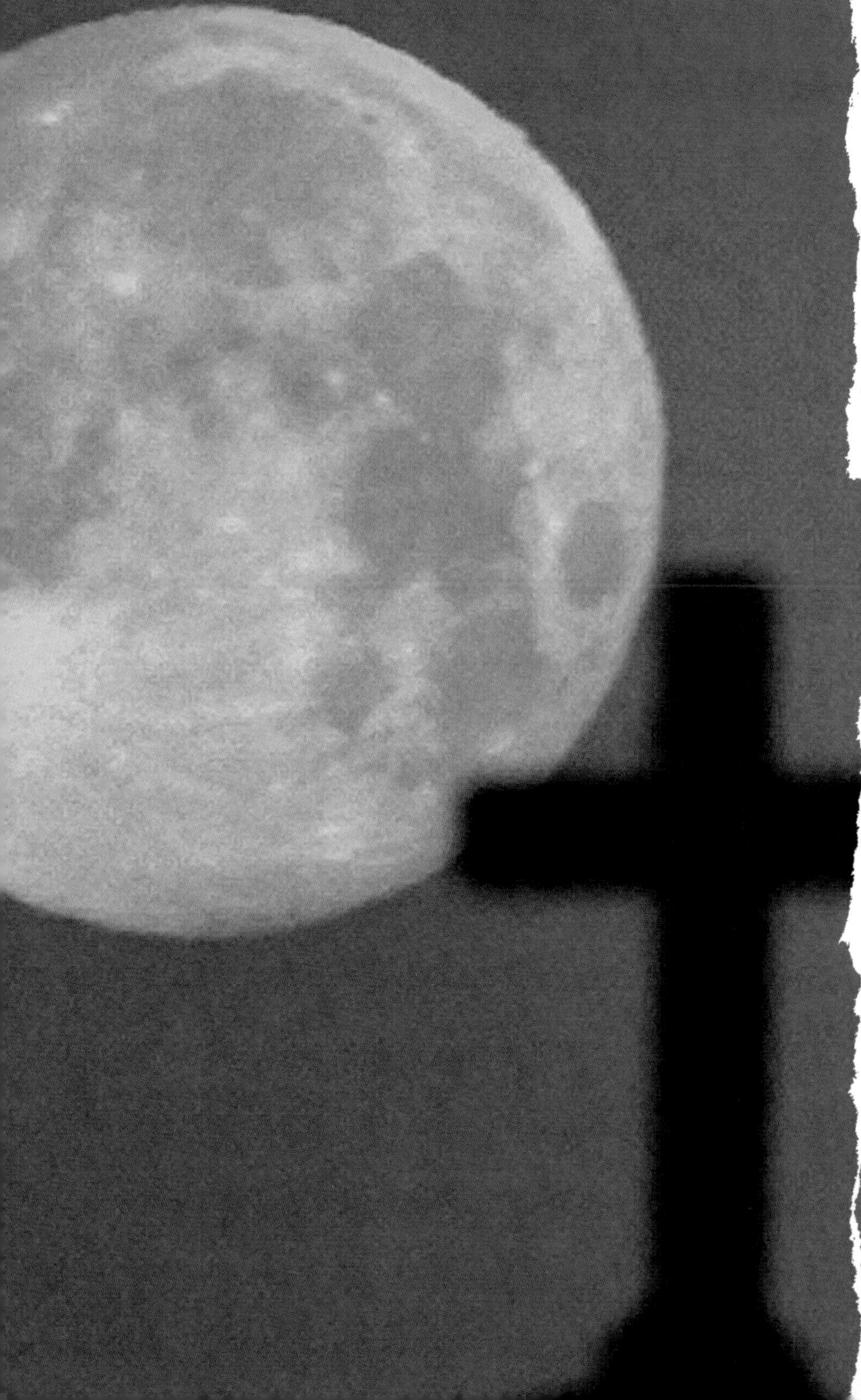

20

WE PRAY

Father,
in the rising of your Son
death gives birth to
    new life. . . .
Make us one with you always,
so that our joy may be holy,
and our love may give life.

FROM *ALTERNATIVE OPENING PRAYER,*
FOURTEENTH SUNDAY IN ORDINARY TIME

When the disciples asked Jesus to teach them to pray, he taught them the Lord's Prayer. What other name do we call the Lord's Prayer? Why do you think Christians pray the Lord's Prayer so often?

*For the kingdom, the power
and the glory are yours,
now and for ever.*

FROM *ROMAN MISSAL,*
LORD'S PRAYER, DOXOLOGY

Architects dream and imagine cathedrals and skyscrapers, monuments and court houses, bridges and tunnels. At the right moment, they begin to draw sketches of their ideas. How much stone, glass, and steel will make their dream come to life and have just the right look? Eventually blueprints are drawn up that will enable countless craftsmen to make the architect's plan come alive.

Summary of the Gospel

The **Lord's Prayer**, or the Our Father, is in some ways a blueprint for living the Gospel and making it come alive in our lives. It is the prayer that Jesus, the architect of the Gospel, gave to his followers. The Christian writer Tertullian (ca. 160–ca. 225) described the Lord's prayer as "the summary of the whole gospel." Not many years later Saint Augustine of Hippo (354–430) wrote:

> Run through all the words of the holy prayers [in Scripture] and I do not think that you will find anything in them that is not contained and included in the Lord's Prayer.

Jesus, the master and model of prayer for Christians, taught us to pray the Our Father. Flowing from Jesus' heart, this prayer expresses the intimacy between Jesus and his Father. By giving us this prayer, Jesus invites us to share in that intimacy.

The Lord's Prayer

The Lord's Prayer is part of the Sermon on the Mount in Matthew's account of the Gospel. Jesus said:

> "This is how you are to pray:
> Our Father in heaven,
>   hallowed be your name,
>   your kingdom come,
>   your will be done,
>   on earth as in heaven.
>   Give us today our daily bread;
>   and forgive us our debts,
>   as we forgive our debtors;
>   and do not subject us to the
>   final test,
>   but deliver us from the
>   evil one."   MATTHEW 6:9–13

Jesus concluded:

> "If you forgive others their transgressions, your heavenly Father will forgive you. But if you do not forgive others, neither will your Father forgive your transgressions."   MATTHEW 6:14–15

Describe the importance of the Lord's Prayer.

On the surface, the words of the Lord's Prayer are simple enough. But there is sufficient meat here to provide us food for meditation for a lifetime. The first half of the Lord's Prayer describes our belief in God and his plan for us. The second half presents our needs to God.

Why do you think it is important for Christians to pray and think about the Lord's Prayer each day?

WHAT DIFFERENCE DOES FAITH MAKE?

Instead, Jesus taught us to pray, "Our Father." He is the God of heaven and earth, the Almighty One, the Creator, who has entered into a covenant of friendship with his people.

Explain the importance of Jesus teaching us to pray, "Our Father in heaven."

Hallowed Be Thy Name

After addressing God as Father, we pray seven petitions. The first three petitions focus on God and acknowledge that God is the center of our lives. The final four petitions acknowledge our dependence on God for our every need and our very life. With the help of the Holy Spirit we do what Jesus taught us. We open our arms and our hearts to God in total trust. We surrender our lives to him as Jesus did.

In the first petition, we acknowledge the goodness and holiness of God. God is so good that we describe his very name as holy. From the first moment of creation to the saving of Noah at the time of the great flood, from the covenant with Abraham to the covenant with Moses, from the time of the prophets, up to the fullness of revelation and salvation given to us in Jesus Christ, the story is always the same. God invites us to share in his holiness. We are to live holy lives. In Jesus' final prayer for his disciples, he prayed:

"Holy Father, keep them in your name that you have given me, so that they may be one just as we are." JOHN 17:11

FAITH FOCUS

How do the first three petitions of the Our Father focus on belief in God and his loving plan for us?

The first words we speak in a conversation are always important. Our opening words set the tone for the remainder of the conversation. Think about your own experiences. Name a time you were greeted warmly. How did you feel? Think about a time you were greeted sternly or harshly. How did you feel?

Our Father in Heaven

The very first words of address in the Lord's Prayer set the tone of our meeting with God in prayer. We say, "Our Father in heaven." We call God "Abba." He is our loving, caring, faithful Father, whose love for us has no limits. He is the One who always walks by our side.

God is the Father of everyone. We do not say "My Father" or "Your Father" or even just plain "Father."

With the birth of the Church, we experience the overwhelming goodness and holiness of God in the celebration of the sacraments, in prayer, and in the example and witness of believers as they live their faith.

Thy Kingdom Come

At the heart of Jesus' preaching is the announcement of the coming of the kingdom of God (see Matthew 3:2). In the second petition, we profess our belief that God has created all people to live in communion with him and with one another and with all creation—not only on earth but forever in heaven. This is the kingdom Jesus proclaimed—the fulfillment of God's loving plan of goodness for us. At the end of time we believe that kingdom will come when Christ comes again in glory.

Thy Will Be Done on Earth as It Is in Heaven

God's will is that his loving plan of creation and salvation be brought to completion as he wills it. In the third petition, we affirm not only that God loves us, cares for us, and has a plan for us but that we will work at bringing about God's will—God's plan, God's kingdom.

Describe the meaning of our prayer "Thy will be done."

Doing God's will is not always easy. It is often a struggle. Jesus himself found it a struggle (see Luke 22:42). God has not left us alone to know and do his will. He reaches out and helps. The Son of God became human to help us know what God's will is for us. The Father and the Son have sent the Holy Spirit to guide us in discovering and understanding God's will and to strengthen us to make it the foundation of our lives.

What might you do to better prepare for the coming of the kingdom of God?

_____

_____

_____

_____

FAITH
FOCUS

How do the final four petitions of the Our Father help us focus on our needs as children of God?

The Lord's Prayer is a model for our conversation with God the Father. First, we direct our words toward God. Second, we talk about ourselves and our needs. This openness about ourselves flows from our confidence in God's love for us.

Give Us This Day Our Daily Bread

We share our needs with a Father whom we have come to know and trust and love. Jesus taught us:

> "What father among you would hand his son a snake when he asks for a fish? . . . [H]ow much more will the Father in heaven give?" LUKE 11:11, 13

It is with confidence that we place our spiritual and material needs ("our daily bread") before God. The depth of our trust is shown by the urgency of our request. We seek an immediate answer ("this day") to our prayers.

We not only talk to God about ourselves, we also pray with and for one another. We share with God the many, many needs of those who cry out in anguish and suffering around the globe. This heartfelt prayer for "our daily bread" has the power to transform our lives. We resolve to look for and work for solutions to the human problems that stand in the way of the coming of the kingdom of God.

Forgive Us Our Trespasses As We Forgive Those Who Trespass Against Us

The center of Jesus' work on earth was his reconciliation of humanity with God and with one another. In this petition we acknowledge that we sometimes turn our hearts away from God's love. We sin. We acknowledge that we hurt others and are hurt by them. Recalling the words Jesus spoke after he taught the disciples the Our Father helps us understand the meaning of what we are saying. Jesus said:

> "If you forgive others their transgressions, your heavenly Father will forgive you. But if you do not forgive others, neither will your Father forgive your transgressions." MATTHEW 6:14–15

It is a simple fact that our forgiveness must have no limits (see Matthew 18:2–22). If we close our hearts to the love of others, our hearts remain closed to the love of God. If we refuse to forgive others, our hearts remain closed to the forgiveness that God wishes to shower upon us.

Explain how forgiveness of others and openness to receive God's forgiveness are intertwined.

Lead Us Not into Temptation

There is something within us that makes doing God's will, forgiving others, and living our life in Christ a struggle. It is the struggle between choosing to do good and choosing to do evil. The struggle is complicated by the fact that evil so often misrepresents itself as good. In other words, we are faced with **temptation.** Temptation is the desire or attraction to do or say something wrong or not to do what we know we have the responsibility to do.

In this petition we ask for the guidance of the Holy Spirit to see the truth in every situation and to recognize evil for the lie that it is.

Explain what we mean when we pray, "lead us not into temptation."

But Deliver Us from Evil

At the Last Supper Jesus said:

> "I do not ask that you take them out of the world but that you keep them from the evil one."
> JOHN 17:15

It is the "evil one," Satan, from whom Jesus asks us to be delivered. He is the one whom Jesus calls "a murderer from the beginning . . . a liar and the father of lies" (John 8:44).

Why is the Lord's Prayer a prayer of trust and hope?

Filled with the Spirit we confidently share our deepest hopes with God our Father. We pray that we will share now and will share forever in the victory of his Son over evil and death in all its forms.

Did you Know...

The Gospel describes how Jesus was tempted by the devil at the beginning of his ministry. You can read about the temptation of Jesus in Matthew 4:1–11.

WHAT DIFFERENCE DOES FAITH MAKE?

How can the Lord's Prayer be a blueprint, or model, for all your prayers?

_____

_____

_____

WHAT DIFFERENCE

Does This Make in Our Church?

Bishop John Richard, president and chairman of Catholic Relief Services, feeds malnourished displaced Southern Sudanese children in Bahr-el-Gazal, Southern Sudan, November 4, 1998.

When the crowd asked Jesus to teach them to pray, he taught them the Our Father, or Lord's Prayer. In teaching them this prayer, Jesus not only taught them how to pray but he also gave them a blueprint for living the Gospel. In the Our Father, we pray, "Give us this day our daily bread." We pray for our own material and spiritual needs as well as the needs of others. The Catholic Relief Services puts those words of the Our Father into action.

Catholic Relief Services

Newspaper headlines regularly tell of sufferings and needs of people around the globe. "Earthquake Shakes Mexico." "War Ravages Eastern Europe." "Famine Spreads in Africa." "Hurricanes Pound Puerto Rico." These headlines are accompanied by vivid pictures that

bring the sufferings and needs of people into our living rooms. They also bring Catholic Relief Services into action.

Catholic Relief Services was founded in 1943 by the Catholic bishops in the United States to respond to the victims of disaster outside the United States. Catholic Relief Services provides "daily bread" to people in two ways. Short range, it reaches out to help people in times of need. Long range, it helps people develop programs that will meet their needs on their own. All the programs of Catholic Relief Services restore the dignity of people and encourage them to realize their potential.

Catholic Relief Services bases its ministry on the Scriptures and the social teachings of the Catholic Church. The ministry of Catholic Relief Services is the Gospel being lived. In the Gospel Jesus Christ calls all people to work to alleviate human suffering. He clearly tells us that when we feed or clothe or give drink to someone in need, we are doing those things for him. In fact, doing those things is a sign of a faithful and true disciple of the Lord.

The ministry of Catholic Relief Services proclaims the Gospel throughout the world. People in over eighty countries around the world benefit from Catholic Relief Services. Every time Catholic Relief Services workers reach out to others, they proclaim the moral responsibility of all people toward all people. They teach us that we are all part of one global family—the one family of God spread throughout the world. We have a responsibility to work to remove the causes of poverty and to promote social justice among all people. In this way we prepare for the coming of the kingdom of God.

Operation Rice Bowl

Operation Rice Bowl is one of the most popular programs of Catholic Relief Services. Operation Rice Bowl began in 1976 as a Lenten program inviting all Catholics to be part of the work of Catholic Relief Services. Operation Rice Bowl is designed to bring a parish community together to pray, fast, learn, and to share what they have with the poor. Through Operation Rice Bowl Catholics in the United States have donated more than 88 million dollars over the years to help alleviate poverty and hunger in the world.

Catholic relief aid worker from Caritas Albania distributes milk to ethnic Albanian refugees from Kosovo, Yugoslavia, April 10, 1999.

Catholics are called in the new millennium to work for a more just and peaceful world by proclaiming the Gospel of Jesus. Through Catholic Relief Services we are able to renew our commitment to the belief that everyone in the world is part of the one Body of Christ.

How can you live the petition "Give us this day our daily bread," which you pray in the Our Father?

251

WHAT DIFFERENCE

Does It Make in My Life?

In the Our Father we pray, "Give us this day our daily bread." We ask God to give us what we need to live caring, happy lives. It is easy sometimes to confuse what we really need with what we want. Much of that confusion stems from what we refer to as consumerism. Put yourself in this familiar scene.

As the music grows louder and louder, you are told you cannot possibly live without eating this certain food. The super action and special effects lure you to stay glued to the TV. You are labeled a loser or not cool unless you own these brand name shoes or jeans. You absolutely cannot function unless you have this particular CD, DVD, or the latest big screen TV.

You are constantly bombarded on the radio, TV, and billboards by thousands of advertisements that promise to enhance your life.

Consumerism

Consumerism can be defined as the strong promotion of products that interest potential customers to buy certain things that will satisfy their wishes and wants.

The youth of today have been labeled "consumers in training." According to marketers in big businesses, young people have tremendous spending power and great economic clout. Companies want to convince you while you are young and impressionable to buy their products and be loyal to their name brand. Advertisements target teenagers to persuade them to buy a particular, usually more expensive item, and convince them that they really need it and must have it.

The Pope's Challenge

Pope John Paul II has asked the youth of today to fight against consumerism, to stop instant self-gratification, and to grow in the gift of service and compassion. The challenge is not to be tricked or fooled by some half-truths or misleading suggestions that encourage you to buy things you do not even need. The virtue of temperance reminds you to understand the difference between needs and wants. Yes, you like to own a lot of possessions—things that give you pleasure and make you feel good—but these are usually "wants." How can you resist the temptation to buy or own the latest and greatest "thing" and maintain control and balance over your choices? Remember that you are in charge of your possessions; you are not a slave to them.

What Can You Do?

Here are some skills to help you answer the pope's challenge to avoid consumerism.

◆ **Be an informed customer.** Look at the facts about a product. If you don't need it, don't let someone convince you to buy it.

◆ **Respect yourself.** Your self-esteem does not depend on brand name possessions.

◆ **Analyze the advertisement.** Talk about it with your family and friends. What hook or gimmick is the company using to convince you to buy their product?

◆ **Be a comparison shopper.** Evaluate the product for quality, price, and actual need.

◆ **Be generous and compassionate.** Hold back on your desire for instant gratification and set aside that money to donate to a good cause. Create a handmade gift or card to give to someone you love or to someone who is lonely.

faith decision

Discuss these questions in class and also with family members at home.

- In a small group talk about some of the advertisements that influence you the most.

- Think about how each advertisement attracts you to a certain product.

- How does each advertisement try to convince you that this product is something you really need?

- How can you support one another in recognizing the difference between what you really need and what you want?

- How can practicing the virtue of temperance help you grow in love and service of others?

This week I will accept the pope's challenge to fight consumerism and instant gratification by

_____

_____

_____.

Faith Vocabulary

Use each of these terms correctly in a sentence.

1. Lord's Prayer

2. temptation

Main Ideas

Choose either (a) or (b) from each set of items. Write a brief paragraph to answer each of your choices.

1. (a) Describe the Lord's Prayer as a blueprint for living the Gospel.

   (b) Explain how the Lord's Prayer provides us with "food for meditation for a lifetime."

2. (a) Describe the focus of the the first three petitions of the Lord's Prayer.

   (b) Name the first three petitions of the Lord's Prayer. Choose one and explain its meaning.

3. (a) Describe the focus of the final four petitions of the Lord's Prayer.

   (b) Name the final four petitions of the Lord's Prayer. Choose one and explain its meaning.

Critical Thinking

Using what you have learned in this chapter, explain the meaning of this statement: "You cannot call the God of all kindness your Father if you preserve a cruel and inhuman heart." (Saint John Chyrsostom)

Family Discussion

Since we ask God to "give us this day our daily bread," we too must do the same for one another. What is the "daily bread" we need to share with one another?

Visit our web site at www.FaithFirst.com

CHURCH HISTORY
UNIT 5

PARENT PAGE—UNIT 5

FAITH

A unique feature of the **Faith First Junior High** series is the opportunity for your child to learn about the history of the Church. As your child studies four major time periods, he or she will be introduced to the major themes, events, and people that helped build the Church during each of these time periods.

Your child will learn about some of the great councils of the Church and the issues these councils addressed. They will study about the Church's commitment to learning, the development and spread of monasticism, and the role of the popes and other church leaders throughout history. They will explore the growth of the Church from a small group

of disciples into a worldwide community of believers.

Central to the story of the Church are the many heroes of the faith. Among the people your child will learn about are Saint Ignatius of Antioch and the other early martyrs; Saints Augustine and Bernard of Clairvaux; Saints Hildegard of Bingen, Thomas Aquinas, and Francis of Assisi; Saints Charles Borremeo, Rose of Lima, and Elizabeth Ann Seton. Pope John XXIII, Pope Paul VI, and Pope John Paul II will also be studied. Of special interest will be the presentation of World Youth Day, when Catholic youth from around the world gather with one another and the pope to celebrate their faith in Christ.

WHAT DIFFERENCE
DOES IT MAKE?

Church history is the story of God's people, guided by the Holy Spirit, as they live out their commitment to prepare for the coming of the kingdom of God. Like the Church, the Christian family also has its faith story to tell. Like the Church, the family experiences moments of great joy as well as times of great pain. Like the story of the Church, a family's faith story is centered around people—the generations of family members who had the courage and wisdom to live out their baptism, both when it was easy and when it was difficult. Family histories too are filled with stories of the people of faith who helped shape and build a family, who may have brought the family to a new land or to a new home, or who made a great personal sacrifice for the good of others.

Read with your child about some of the important people and leaders of the Church who are highlighted in the unit. They can be role models for your family to live out your baptism in your own time and place. Talk about important people and events in your family's history. Together you might enjoy beginning a genealogy search for past leaders of your family. As a family you are part of the Church's present and future.

Studying the history of the Church is an important aid in remembering not only the great heritage we have inherited but also the role we have today in shaping and writing the Church's story for future generations. As your family prays, worships, and witnesses your faith, you are cooperating with the work of the Holy Spirit in preparing for the kingdom announced and promised by Christ.

This unit offers several ideas for you and your child to assist in building up the Body of Christ. Like the Church, all families experience times of distress and stress. Change is often stressful, yet it is an inescapable part of all life. Likewise, conflict between people is also part of all of our lives. Pages 267 and 291 offer methods for handling this stress and conflict in a positive manner. Consider sitting down with your family and making your own plan for handling stress and conflict as they arise in your daily lives. Be sure to incorporate prayer in your discussions. Faith in God cannot guarantee a stress-free and conflict-free life. However, faith, prayer, and a strong relationship with God and the larger church community offer support, encouragement, and hope to your family as you contribute to telling the future story of the Family of God.

Apostolic Age to A.D. 325

21

WE PRAY

Lord,
protector and ruler of your
    Church,
fill your servants with a
    spirit of understanding,
    truth and peace.
Help them to strive
    with all their hearts
to learn what is pleasing to you,
and to follow it with all their
    strength.

FROM ROMAN MISSAL, OPENING PRAYER
MASS FOR A COUNCIL OR SYNOD

The history of the Church, like the history of any nation or people, is made up of events and people. Tell what you know about the significant events and people that are part of the story of the Church in the first three centuries of its existence.

*My heart is steadfast, God;
    my heart is steadfast. . . .
I will praise you among the
        peoples, LORD;
    I will chant your praise
        among the nations.*

PSALM 108:2, 4

FAITH FOCUS

What were some of the major challenges confronting the Church in its first few centuries of existence?

In the next four chapters we will survey two thousand years of church history. Imagine these twenty centuries as four periods of time. In each period we will focus on ecumenical councils. These councils are called ecumenical because they address concerns of the whole Church. Each of these gatherings, in its own unique way, helped address the issues that would shape the life of the Church for generations to come.

Paul and Barnabas. Contemporary stained-glass window.

In looking at each period of the Church's history, we will consider three topics. First, we will take an overview of the main characteristics of that period. Second, we will capture that era's flavor by telling the stories of some of the Church's heroes. Finally, we will look at what the relationship was between the Church and the larger world in which it existed.

The Council of Jerusalem

Chapter fifteen of the Acts of the Apostles describes a gathering of the apostles and other leaders of the Church in Jerusalem. Scholars suggest a date for that gathering around the year 51, early in the ministry of Paul to the Gentiles, or non-Jews. This "council" of Jerusalem, as it is sometimes called, was an important turning point for the first followers of Jesus. Most of these followers still considered themselves to be faithful Jews who were following the way of Jesus.

At this gathering Peter, James, and other leaders of the Church in Jerusalem discussed with Paul and Barnabas the implications of the decision to allow Gentile converts into the community of believers in Jesus Christ. This decision, which occurred at that gathering, opened the door to the vast growth of Christianity in the years to come. Up to this time most of the followers of Jesus were Jews. They wondered if people had to become Jews first before becoming Christians.

Explain the importance of the gathering of the leaders of the Church in Jerusalem.

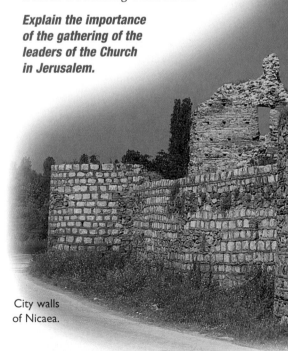

City walls of Nicaea.

Council of Nicaea, 325. Cesare Nebbia (1534–1614), Italian painter.

The Council of Nicaea

Within the next three hundred years, Christianity became a primarily Gentile religion. Small communities of Christians were founded throughout the entire Roman Empire and embraced every segment of society.

Despite sporadic, sometimes savage persecutions, the followers of Jesus eventually won the day with the conversion of the Roman emperor Constantine to Christianity. With the official support of the emperor, a council of the Church was held at Nicaea in 325. At Nicaea, Church doctrinal matters were discussed and officially explained and taught.

One of the most important teachings of Nicaea is preserved in the Nicene Creed. To correct the mistaken views of those who questioned the divinity of Jesus, the bishops at Nicaea declared that Jesus is "one in being with the Father." Jesus is truly God and truly man.

Explain the importance of the Council of Nicaea.

51	Council of Jerusalem
ca. 64–67	Martyrdom of Peter and Paul in Rome
95	Persecutions under Domitian
ca. 100	Death of the last apostle, John, and end of the apostolic age
ca. 107	St. Ignatius of Antioch martyred
117–38	Persecutions under Hadrian
ca. 155	St. Polycarp martyred
165	St. Justin martyred
249–51	Persecutions under Decius
ca. 251	St. Agatha martyred
257	Persecution under Valerian
258	St. Cyprian martyred
292	Roman Empire divided into East and West
ca. 304	St. Agnes martyred

WHAT DIFFERENCE DOES FAITH MAKE?

What are the beliefs expressed in the Nicene Creed about the divinity of Jesus Christ?

_____

_____

259

Witnessing to the Faith

The Acts of the Apostles details the missionary efforts of Peter and Paul and other apostles. After the death of the first apostles, countless others who felt called by God to spread the Gospel paid whatever price was necessary—including the sacrifice of their lives. These witnesses to the faith are still honored by the Church as martyrs.

The Colosseum in Rome: Arena. Gaspar van Wittel, also known as Van Vitelli in Italy, (1652–1736), Dutch painter and craftsman.

Christian witnesses won over their spouses by their example of virtuous living. Many other people asked for baptism because of the way that Christians loved one another and cared for the poor and suffering. The courage of martyrs testified to the faith of Christians in the resurrection of Jesus and their hope in the eternal life that awaited them.

Persecutions

Throughout the ancient Roman Empire, there was a very high degree of religious tolerance. The Romans had a "live and let live" approach to those people living in the territories they had conquered. The four accounts of the Gospel document how the Jewish religious leaders cooperated with the Roman authorities. In turn, they were allowed to conduct their religious practices unhampered. As long as the Jews and other conquered peoples paid taxes, observed Roman rule, and did not engage in any rebellious activity, the Romans let them be.

Initially, the Roman authorities did not perceive the followers of Jesus as anything more than a Jewish sect. Eventually, though, Christians became identified as members of a separate religion. Even then they were mostly tolerated and left undisturbed to practice their faith. In some places, however, Christians did arouse the anger of the emperor and other local officials. This led to periodic persecutions. Most of these were localized and of relatively short duration.

However, under several of the emperors there were extensive persecutions throughout the Roman Empire. The most notable of these occurred during the reigns of the emperors Decius (d. 251), Valerian (d. 260), and Diocletian (d. 316).

303 • Persecutions under
• Diocletian begin

ca. 304 • St. Lucy martyred

311 • Edict of toleration
• ending persecution
• of Christians

313 • Edict of Milan issued;
• Christianity
• recognized as a
• lawful religion

325 • Council of Nicaea

Public Life in the Forum in Rome. Third century. Artist unknown.

Roman Emperor Diocletian.

By the fourth century, Christianity was well established in virtually every major region of the empire. Many believers were prominent people of wealth and influence. This obviously helped achieve a wider public acceptance of Christianity.

Discuss why the early Church was persecuted by the Roman emperors.

Paganism

In this first era of the Church, many believers perceived the greatest threat to the Church to be the culture of paganism that surrounded them. In those times of peace between the Church and the Roman state, pagan values and customs were still considered a deadly threat to the spiritual welfare of the Christian community.

The value of life was minimal in the ancient world. This is seen in the widespread practice of infanticide, or the killing of infants. Concern for the poor was also not considered a civic virtue or an important part of any pagan religious ethic. Undisciplined and immoral behavior was looked upon as acceptable behavior. Pagan religious values were often mixed with views strongly opposed to the Christian faith.

Discuss how pagan values were a threat to Christianity.

How does the story of the early Christians help you witness to your faith in God?

_____

_____

_____

Trial of Saint Lucy. Altichiero da Zevio (1320–1385), Italian painter, especially of frescos.

When Emperor Trajan ordered the persecution of Christians who refused to worship the pagan gods of the Roman state, Ignatius was targeted for death because of his prominence. When he steadfastly witnessed to his faith in Jesus, Ignatius was taken prisoner and sent to Rome. He knew a death sentence awaited him.

During the long trip to Rome, he wrote seven letters. In his letters he urged various local churches to remain strong in their faith and to preserve the unity of the Church. When his friends offered to intercede with the Roman authorities on his behalf, Ignatius declined their offer, lest he be deprived of the crown of martyrdom. Tradition has it that he was eaten by lions in Rome's amphitheater.

Agatha (d. ca. 251), Lucy (d. ca. 304), and Agnes (d. ca. 258), saints and martyrs, are mentioned by name in the first eucharistic prayer, also known as the Roman Canon, which we use today. Very little historical detail is known about their lives, although there are many legends that have come down to us with inspiring stories of their holiness. What we do know is that all three were young women who died during the persecutions of Diocletian.

Agatha, Lucy, and Agnes chose to profess their loyalty to Christ rather than give in to those who sought to lead them away from Christ. Agatha and Lucy are associated with the island of Sicily, while Agnes lived in or near the city of Rome. Devotion to these virgin martyrs spread

FAITH FOCUS

What roles did Ignatius of Antioch, Agatha, Lucy, Agnes, and the Emperor Constantine play in the early Church?

Martyrs

History has shown that persecution has always strengthened the Church. The blood of the martyrs was the seed of the faith then as it is even in our day.

In the first centuries of the Church, the martyrs inspired countless numbers of the faithful with their dedication and acts of courage. Saint Ignatius of Antioch exemplifies the importance of the early martyrs for the faith of the entire Church. As bishop of Antioch for nearly forty years, Ignatius had become both beloved and influential.

rapidly. Christians were inspired by how those whom the world considered weak and helpless were made strong and brave by the power of the Lord.

Discuss how the martyrs helped the spread of Christianity.

Emperor Constantine

Emperor Constantine is not considered a saint but he was certainly a hero for many Christians. During the course of a fierce war, Constantine fought a decisive battle at the Milvian Bridge outside of Rome on October 28, 312. Prior to the battle, Constantine reported seeing a sign of the cross in the sky with the words *in hoc signo vinces*, which means "By this sign you shall conquer."

On the night before the battle, Constantine believed Christ himself appeared to him in a vision, telling him to place a cross on his army's flags, or standards. Constantine attributed his overwhelming victory the next day to the power of Christ.

As Constantine entered Rome in triumph, he was acclaimed emperor by all who had hated his opponent, the tyrant Maxentius. The following year (313), Constantine proclaimed the Edict of Milan. This established Christianity as a legitimate religion within the Roman Empire.

The Arch of Constantine, The Roman Forum, Rome, Italy.

This began a whole new era in the growth of the Church. The emperor and his mother, Saint Helena, erected numerous churches throughout the empire to encourage Christians to worship in public. The Church was changing from a persecuted enemy of the state to its status as the established religion of the empire.

Discuss how Constantine helped the spread of Christianity.

WHAT DIFFERENCE DOES FAITH MAKE?

How does being free to worship God contribute toward your living the Catholic faith?

_____

_____

_____

WHAT
DIFFERENCE
Does This Make in Our Church?

As in the first three centuries, the Church today often finds itself at odds with contemporary culture. Members of the Church find themselves being called by the leaders of the Church to take a stand against the injustices in our world.

The Voice of Pope John Paul II

On a world stage crowded with huge divisions—rich oppressing the poor, nations warring against nations—Pope John Paul II speaks out for universal values. From the time he was elected pope in 1978, John Paul II has been a voice crying out in the wilderness of world misery and division. His voice has always proclaimed Jesus' gospel of hope and salvation.

During the first three centuries of the Church's history Christians found themselves at odds with the Roman culture. Sometimes this resulted in Christians being persecuted by the Roman government. The first three centuries were also a period of transition and change for the Church. The Church grew from being a tolerated small Jewish sect, to a persecuted group of enemies of the state, to a legally recognized religion. Differences also arose within the Church about the meaning of the teachings of Jesus and about the identity of Jesus himself.

Encyclicals of John Paul II

Encyclicals are the letters written by popes to teach about matters of faith and morals. Encyclicals get their names from the first several words in the letter, once it is translated into Latin. John Paul's encyclicals have been punctuated with poetry and impassioned prose to promote Christ's message to today's world.

The 100th year

Not one to shy away from thorny issues, Pope John Paul II has taken on this era's new idols: selfishness, nationalism, indifference to the sacredness of human life, profits over people, and the scandal of worldwide starvation. "Something is owed to human beings, because

they are human beings," he declares in his encyclical *The 100th Year* (1991). Throughout this encyclical, John Paul II proclaims the dignity of the human person, which is often endangered by economic

policies. To John Paul II, the message of the Gospel is not just a theory, "but above all else a basis and motivation for action."

On the Social Concerns of the Church

In his 1988 encyclical *On the Social Concerns of the Church*, John Paul II laments that the gap between the rich and poor is widening. John Paul II places some of the blame at the feet of superpowers whose rivalry has diverted human energy and resources from meeting basic human needs. Like a loving father, John Paul II points to his poor children and declares that the goods of the world are intended for all. For Pope John Paul II, wealthy nations and people blessed with abundance must actively make impoverished people and nations their top priority.

How can you make the teachings of Pope John Paul II part of your life?

WHAT DIFFERENCE

Does It Make in My Life?

The early days of the Church were times of great change and transition. The disciples were confused and afraid until the Holy Spirit filled them with peace. They spread the Gospel far and wide. The early believers made the transition from their Jewish roots to Christianity.

Change Brings Stress

Any change or transition brings with it a time of distress. It is an uncomfortable time because it stirs up uneasy feelings and it is new and unknown. Many people do not like change, yet it is one of the certainties of life. We are ever growing and constantly changing throughout our lives.

Stress Versus Distress

Many researchers claim that stress is neutral, neither negative nor positive. Stress is needed in our lives. It stimulates the athlete into motion and it is the thing that gets us moving to do what we need to do. It is the way our body automatically responds to whatever happens. For example, you hear a loud noise overhead. You are startled, your body responds, your heart rate quickens, and your blood pressure rises. This is stress. Or, it is your birthday and people say "surprise" and sing to you. This is also stress and your body will respond in the same way. Hopefully one situation is more pleasant than the other. Your body responds the same way whether the situation is pleasant or not.

Distress

The culprit is called distress. A research doctor found that prolonged distress can make you sick. Distress is the negative stress that we cause within ourselves. It is caused by tension that results from the way we are handling a situation. We may overreact, get angry at times, and show our temper. Most doctors agree that it is our attitude, our reaction, and our response to something that causes this distress.

Attitude Is Your Paintbrush

There is a poster that states your attitude is your paintbrush that colors every situation.

There are many situations over which you have no control. Think about the following and write how you would typically respond.

- Someone bumps into you in the movie line. Your popcorn and soda spill all over you.
- The cable goes off in the last ten minutes of your favorite TV show.

You are ready to go out with your friends when your mom calls and says she has to work late so you will have to stay home and babysit your younger brother.

How would you respond? Could you respond differently?

When things happen, or things don't go your way, you have a choice about the way you handle it. You can choose to act or to react to what happened. This does not mean to push down your feelings or pretend that what happened didn't bother you. It is your attitude, your choice that determines whether it is stress or distress. It's usually the little everyday stuff that gets us so upset. How we choose to respond to these everyday situations will have an influence on how we respond to the more serious tragedies that are sometimes part of life.

Steps to Handle Stress

State what just happened.

Take a look at your attitude.
    Did you . . .

Rant and rave, or stay calm?

Express your feelings—
    "I feel mad or upset."

Stop and calm down.

Strive for positive self-talk
    and self-control.

You cannot always control what happens. But you can control your attitude toward it. Change your attitude when little annoying things happen. You will be a better person and your body will thank you.

faith decision

- Discuss with a partner a stressful situation in your life. Share how you could choose to handle the situation.

- Since you cannot avoid change, explain what you can do to make it easier to deal with change.

This week I will look at my attitude and choose to deal with situations by

_____

_____

_____

_____

_____

_____.

REVIEWREVIEW

People and Places and Events

Identify these people, places, and events:

1. Council of Jerusalem
2. Council of Nicaea
3. Saint Ignatius of Antioch
4. Emperor Constantine

Main Ideas

Choose either (a) or (b) from each set of items. Write a brief paragraph to answer each of your choices.

1. (a) Explain the importance of the Council of Jerusalem.

   (b) Explain what happened at the Council of Nicaea.

2. (a) Describe the role of persecutions in the growth of the Church.

   (b) How did pagan values affect the lives of Christians in the first three centuries?

3. (a) Explain the effect of the lives of martyrs on the growth of the Church.

   (b) Describe the importance of Emperor Constantine's conversion to Christianity.

Critical Thinking

Using what you have learned in this chapter, briefly explain this statement:
   The blood of martyrs is the seed of faith.

Family Discussion

What attitudes and beliefs in our society support Catholics in living our faith as a family? What attitudes and beliefs make it more difficult to live our faith?

Visit our
web site at
www.FaithFirst.com

A.D. 325 to the Fourth Lateran Council 1215

22

WE PRAY

Father of providence,
look with love on our Pope,
your appointed successor to
    St. Peter
on whom you built your Church.
May he be the visible center
    and foundation
of our unity in faith and love.

FROM *ROMAN MISSAL, MASSES AND PRAYERS
FOR VARIOUS NEEDS AND OCCASIONS, OPENING
PRAYER OF THE MASS FOR THE POPE*

What factors contributed to
the Church's phenomenal
growth from A.D. 325 to 1215?
Who were some of the
champions of the faith during
these centuries?

*"He that rules over men in
    justice,
    that rules in the fear of God,
Is like the morning light at
    sunrise
    on a cloudless morning,
    making the greensward
    sparkle after rain."*

2 SAMUEL 23:3–4

269

FAITH
FOCUS

In what ways did the Church grow in the nine hundred years after Constantine?

As we look at this second period of the history of the Church, we will learn about the privileged status of the Church that began under Constantine and grew even as the Roman Empire declined. The term **Christendom** refers to the eventual outcome of that process. Christendom is the time when the pope's authority in the West surpasses that of the emperor's in the West, and eventually that of kings.

Describe the term Christendom.

The Lamp of Learning

The first three hundred years following the Council of Nicaea are known as the Patristic Era. This was a period of brilliant learning and theological development led by writers known as the Fathers of the Church. Among the most famous Fathers of the Church in the West are Saint Ambrose (d. 397), Saint Jerome (d. 419), Saint Augustine (d. 430) and Pope Saint Gregory (d. 604). Among the Fathers of the Church in the East are Saint Basil (d. 379), Saint Gregory Nazianzus (d. 390), Saint Gregory of Nyssa (d. 394), Saint John Chrysostom (d. 407), and Saint Cyril of Alexandria (d. 444).

After the close of the Patristic Era (ca. A.D. 100–ca. 750), the lamp of learning dimmed for more than four hundred years. It was not until the early centuries of the second millennium that a revival of learning occurred. This was sparked by a rediscovery of Plato, Socrates, Aristotle, and other Greek philosophers.

Describe the Patristic Era.

The Golden Age of Christianity

The newly favorable status of the Christian Church also opened the door for people to accept the Christian faith without fear of persecution. During the fourth through sixth centuries, the Roman Empire became thoroughly Christian. So many people sought Baptism that this period became known as the Golden Age of the Catechumenate. The **catechumenate** is the process by which a person is initiated into the Church. As the Church grew and lived in freedom, elaborate churches were

Saint Gregory. Titian, Tiziano Vecellio, (ca. 1477–1576), Italian painter, chief master of the Venetian school.

Saint Augustine. Sandro Botticelli (ca. 1444–1510), Italian painter.

FAITH
VOCABULARY

Christendom

catechumenate

monasticism

papacy

abbot

schism

constructed. The liturgy of the Church took on a splendor appropriate to the massive basilicas being built throughout the Roman Empire.

From the seventh through the ninth centuries, the spread of Christianity in various parts of the Western world continued. By the turn of the first millennium the Gospel had been preached virtually throughout all of Western Europe.

The Spread of Monasticism

All of this visible growth of the Church was a sign of the inner, spiritual growth of the Church that was also taking place. This was centered in **monasticism.** Monasticism is a way of living the Gospel. Either men or women live in community and devote themselves to live out the Gospel in prayer, work, and learning.

The Monk Copyist. Edward Laning (1906–1981), American painter.

The origins of the monastic movement are in Egypt and are tied to the names of Saint Anthony (d. 356) and Pachomius (d. 346), called the Desert Fathers. This movement spread to the West in the fifth century, but it is Saint Benedict (d. ca. 543) who is considered the Father of Western Monasticism. The *Rule of Saint Benedict* became a model for future ages.

Who were some of the leaders of the monastic movement?

The Papacy

The **papacy** underwent enormous changes during this period. The papacy is the name of the position of leadership of the pope. From the Council of Nicaea through the pontificate of Gregory the Great (d. 604), the role of the bishop of Rome, the pope, grew stronger. By the twelfth century the papacy once again became the dominant force that guides the shape of the West. The councils at the Lateran in Rome (1123, 1139, 1179, and 1215) are the most visible sign of the resurgence of the papacy during this period. The work of the Fourth Lateran Council in 1215 still shapes our Catholic teaching today. At this council the teaching of the Church on the real presence of Jesus in the Eucharist was affirmed.

313	Edict of Milan
325	Council of Nicaea
331	St. Monica, mother of St. Augustine (d. 387)
354	St. Augustine (d. 430)
374	St. Ambrose becomes bishop of Milan
431	Council of Ephesus
451	Council of Chalcedon
476	Vandals depose last Roman emperor in West
480	St. Benedict of Nursia, founder of Benedictine Order (d. 543)
521	St. Columba (d. 597)
540	St. Gregory the Great, pope 590–604
570	Mohammad, founder of Islam (d. 632)
742	Charlemagne, first Holy Roman emperor (d. 814)
1054	East/West Schism
1091	St. Bernard of Clairvaux (d. 1153)
1198	Innocent III elected Pope

WHAT DIFFERENCE DOES FAITH MAKE?

How can you incorporate the monastic ideal of prayerful simplicity into your daily life?

_____

_____

_____

271

FAITH
FOCUS

How do the lives of Augustine and Monica, Bernard of Clairvaux, and Hildegard illustrate the Church's growth during this period?

Many Christians who lived the Gospel during this period of the history of the Church are honored by the Church as saints. By learning about these holy people we can see how the Gospel shaped their lives and the life of the world in which they lived.

Saint Augustine of Hippo

Saint Augustine (354–430) is the greatest and most influential of the Fathers of the Church. As a young man he searched for meaning in various ways, generally living a life apart from Christian values. After meeting Saint Ambrose in Milan, he gave himself over to God completely. Ambrose baptized him in 387; four years later he was ordained a priest. Four years after that he was consecrated bishop of Hippo. The brilliance of Augustine's writings and the energy he brought to the care of the faithful in his diocese have earned Augustine the highest regard as a bishop and Doctor of the Church. His thought continues to influence Catholic theology to this very day.

Saint Monica. Stained glass.

Saint Monica

Monica (332–387), the mother of Augustine, is honored as a saint for her example of devotion to God and care for her family. A dedicated believer herself, she prayed for the conversion of her pagan husband, who eventually converted on his deathbed.

Monica instructed Augustine in the Christian faith when he was a child, but he was never baptized as a child. Her prayers for his conversion were tireless, and she eventually had the joy of seeing him baptized only a few months before her own death.

How did Monica and Augustine influence the Church?

Saint Columba

Also known as Colm, Columcille, and Colum, Columba (521–597) possessed a striking figure of great stature and athletic build. Columba spent fifteen years traveling about Ireland, preaching and establishing monasteries. In 563 Columba embarked in a wicker boat for the island of Iona, off the west coast of Scotland. Iona soon became the center of Irish missionary activity in Scotland and northern England. During a time of darkness and decline on the European continent, Saint Columba and his monks created a haven of culture and learning and preserved manuscripts that continue to influence us today.

What did Saint Columba achieve?

Saint Bernard of Clairvaux

Bernard (ca. 1090–1153) was born into a noble French family. In his youth he enjoyed being alone and stayed pretty much to himself. When he learned about the newly formed Benedictine monastery at Citeaux, it drew his attention and he eventually asked to become a member.

Island of Iona, Scotland.

During his three years at Citeaux, his leadership qualities were noticed. He was asked to found a new monastery at Clairvaux and become its first **abbot.** An abbot is a monk who is the head of a monastery. Under the leadership of Bernard this one monastery at Clairvaux eventually became the center for sixty-eight other monasteries. The work of this quiet, shy young boy who became a great church leader in the twelfth century still renews the Church in the twenty-first century. His work was so important in his own times that it was said that Bernard carried the twelfth century on his shoulders.

How was Saint Bernard a light in a time of darkness?

Saint Hildegard of Bingen

Hildegard lived her life according to the Rule of Saint Benedict. She was a woman of remarkable intelligence and dazzling spiritual gifts. She was the first of the great German mystics, as well as a poet, prophet, physician, and composer. A mystic is one who experiences a close union or communication with God. Famous for her visions and advice, Hildegard was much in demand by all kinds of people.

In her first seventeen years as a Benedictine sister, her life was uneventful. Eventually her visions pressed upon her and compelled her to write what she saw. Hildegard's writings detail her conversations with God as well as her insights into natural history and medicine. What Hildegard had to say remains as fresh today as it was in her time. The evidence for this is the many Christians who read the writings of this saint and apply her spirituality and insights to their own lives.

Who was Hildegard of Bingen?

Time LINE

1096	Start of First Crusade
1098	St. Hildegard of Bingen (d. 1179)
1125	First Lateran Council
1155	Carmelite Order founded
1215	Fourth Lateran Council
1216	Dominican Order founded
1223	Franciscan Order founded

Scivias (Know the Ways of the Lord). Saint Hildegard of Bingen. Illuminated page.

Which of these four saints affects you most? What quality from this saint would you choose to imitate?

_____

_____

_____

273

At the time of the Council of Nicaea, Constantine was the Roman emperor and Sylvester I was pope. The Church was just emerging from three centuries of on-and-off persecution by a hostile Roman state. The freedom enjoyed by Christians brought a rush of energy and a rash of changes.

Coronation of Charlemagne by Pope Leo III. Miniature from *History of the Emperors.* Artist unknown.

Pope Saint Sylvester I and Emperor Constantine

Pope Sylvester I, who was pope from 314 to 335, is a symbol of the Church living in its new-found freedom. Now that Christians could worship out in the open without fear of persecution, he oversaw the beginning of the building of two important churches, Saint Peter's Basilica and Saint John Lateran Basilica in Rome.

In the centuries that followed the leadership of Sylvester I and Constantine, a strange change in leadership within the empire occurred. As the military and political power of Imperial Rome declined, the spiritual authority of the pope and the Church increased in the West. Divergent political and religious views separated the Church in the West and the Church in the East. The gap eventually grew so wide that it resulted in the Great East-West Schism in 1054. A **schism** is a formal separation of groups within the Church.

Describe the authority of the pope in the West from the time of Pope Saint Sylvester I to 1054.

Charlemagne and Pope Saint Leo III

Out of the ruins and the chaos of the old Roman Empire Charlemagne emerged. *Charlemagne* means "Charles the Great." Charlemagne (742–814) was the greatest ruler in the West during the Middle Ages (500–ca. 1500). He was so powerful and charismatic that he built an empire in the West that rivaled in geographical size the former glory of ancient Rome.

On Christmas night in the year 800, Pope Leo III (750–816) crowned Charlemagne as the Holy Roman emperor. The pope crowning a king symbolized the dawn of a new era in the relationship of the Church with the world. The temporal power of the papacy was established side by side with the power of the king. Leo III, the pope, and Charlemagne, the Holy Roman emperor, became partners. Together they forged an alliance that reestablished stability and unity throughout the lands ruled by Charlemagne.

Describe the significance of the coronation of Charlemagne.

Pope Innocent III

By the time of Pope Innocent III (1161–1216), the Church and the world, the secular and the sacred dimensions of society, were joined. The pope himself became increasingly seen as both a temporal as well as a spiritual leader. Innocent III was intensely involved not only in the spiritual reform of the Church, but also in the world's political situation. His time in office marks the climax of the power of the pope during the medieval period of Western history.

The era of the Crusades (1096–1270) points out how the spiritual and temporal leadership of people merged in the pope. The Crusades were a spiritual quest under the military and temporal leadership of the pope. The aim of the Crusades was to free Jerusalem and the Holy Land from Muslim rule.

To see how greatly this relationship changes over the centuries, one has only to compare the actions of Pope Innocent III with those of Pope Leo I. In 452 Leo I met Attila the Hun. Leo used no display of force and persuaded Attila to stop his campaign of terror in Italy. In 1215 Innocent III presided over the Fourth Lateran Council (November 11, 1215 to November 30, 1215) and laid the groundwork for the Fifth Crusade (1217–1221). As Vicar of Christ, Innocent III asserted that he had been given the whole world to govern. He claimed the right to intervene in affairs between secular rulers.

This merging of leadership in the pope has had a great effect on the development of Western history— its effects are still felt in the world today. We see the opposition to such a close connection at work in the United States of America in the great efforts people make to maintain the separation between Church and state.

Describe how Innocent III was both a spiritual and a temporal leader.

Saint Louis before Damietta, Egyptian Crusade. Gustave Paul Doré (1832–1883), French painter.

WHAT DIFFERENCE DOES FAITH MAKE?

If you were pope today, how would you serve the Church?

_____

_____

_____

WHAT DIFFERENCE

Does This Make in Our Church?

The pope and bishops continue to have an important role as leaders both of the world and of the Church. Today the bishops throughout the world proclaim the Gospel and remind the people of the Church, and society in general, of its responsibility to live according to God's Law. In the United States of America the bishops do this together through the National Conference of Catholic Bishops and the United States Catholic Conference.

National Conference of Catholic Bishops

The National Conference of Catholic Bishops (NCCB) and the United States Catholic Conference (USCC) are the organizations of the Catholic hierarchy in the United States of America. Through these organizations, the bishops fulfill

Bishop Ricardo Ramirez, Bishop of Las Cruces, New Mexico. Meeting of National Conference of Catholic Bishops, Washington, D.C., November 16–19, 1998.

their responsibilities of leadership and service to Church and nation.

The creation of a council of bishops started because of World War I. When the United States entered World War I in 1917, the bishops saw a need for a national group that would enable Catholics to contribute funds and commit personnel to meet the spiritual and other needs of those serving in the armed forces. Under the leadership of James Cardinal Gibbons of Baltimore, the National Catholic War Council was formed.

This council demonstrated the value of the national collaboration of bishops. Further encouragement arrived from the pope at that time, Benedict XV. In a 1919 letter, Pope Benedict XV urged the hierarchy to join him in working for peace and social justice. The bishops responded by deciding to meet annually and set up several committees to organize their work. Over the years the bishops addressed many national concerns. In 1966 the hierarchy voted to establish the NCCB and the USCC. These two organizations of the Catholic Church in America continue the work of the bishops begun in 1917.

In the NCCB the bishops attend to the Church's own affairs in this country. Like other conferences of bishops around the world, the organization fulfills the Vatican

Bishop Paul Zipfel, Bishop of Bismarck, North Dakota, prays with fellow bishops. Annual fall meeting of NCCB, November 16–17, 1998.

Council's mandate that bishops "exercise their pastoral office jointly" (*Decree on the Bishops' Pastoral Office in the Church*, 38).

To get an idea of the scope of concerns addressed by the national bishops, here is a sample of the departments of the NCCB/USSC: Communications, Education, African American Catholics, Campaign for Human Development, Catholic News Service, Film and Broadcasting, Liturgy, Hispanic Affairs, Migration and Refugee Services, Social Development and World Peace, and the New American Bible.

Pretend you are an advisor to a bishop. What national issues would you want to address with your fellow bishops?

Headquarters for National Conference of Catholic Bishops/ United States Catholic Conference, Washington, D.C.

NATIONAL CONFERENCE OF CATHOLIC BISHOPS
UNITED STATES CATHOLIC CONFERENCE

WHAT DIFFERENCE

Does It Make in My Life?

In this chapter on church history you learned about some of the great leaders of our Church who continued to build up the faithful and keep the Church alive and flourishing.

You Are the Church

While churches, cathedrals, and other places of worship have been built over the centuries, we must always remember that the Church is not simply a building. The Church is the new People of God. You are the Church. The Church needs you to be fully active and to participate in preparing for the coming of the kingdom of God. There are many different ministries in which you can offer your services. The Church, as in any organization, is always looking for new leaders and vibrant, active members.

Who Can Be a Leader?

Some people are said to be born leaders. Others are recognized for their charisma. With sufficient motivation and a certain amount of work, most of us can develop the qualities needed to be a good leader. One broad definition of a leader is one who influences the behavior of others. Naturally that influence can be positive or negative. Every day you are influenced by others and at the same time you are an influence on others—more than you may even know. Recognizing and building good leadership qualities is important for all of us.

Leadership Qualities

Here are a few qualities that characterize a good leader.

✳ They have a positive influence on people. They encourage people to use their gifts and reach their potential.

✳ They use effective communication skills. They can communicate ideas and listen as other people express their opinions.

✳ They are patient. They know it takes time to do things correctly. Remember becoming a good leader takes time and energy.

✳ They are persistent. They are determined to do whatever it takes to get the job done. They are compassionate and concerned for the welfare of others.

✳ They are people of integrity. They are honest, genuine, and trustworthy. They are dependable and can lead others in the right direction, even if it is unpopular.

✳ They are positive thinkers with a sense of humor. They recognize their own limitations and view potential problems as opportunities and challenges. They are able to see the humor in situations.

faith decision

Take a few moments to think about what it takes to be a leader.

• What qualities do you believe are essential for good leaders?

• Do you believe that someone who is shy or quiet can be a good leader?

• What leadership qualities do you already have?

• What qualities would you like to enhance?

• In what situations at home and in school have you been called upon to be a leader?

This week I will be a better leader by

_____

_____

_____

_____

_____.

Faith Vocabulary

Define each of these terms:

1. Christendom
2. monasticism
3. papacy
4. abbot
5. schism

Main Ideas

Choose either (a) or (b) from each set of items. Write a brief paragraph to answer each of your choices.

1. (a) Discuss the effect of the Patristic Era on the Church.

   (b) Explain the changes in the papacy during this period.

2. (a) Discuss Saint Augustine's and Saint Hildegard's contributions to the Church.

   (b) Discuss the contributions of Saint Columba and Saint Bernard of Clairvaux to the Church.

3. (a) Describe the relationship between the Church and the world from 314 to 1054.

   (b) Explain why the papacy of Innocent III was the climax of the medieval papacy.

Critical Thinking

Using what you have learned in this chapter, briefly explain this statement: The Church was gradually becoming more at home in a world that was increasingly Christian in its outlook, laws, and culture.

Family Discussion

How can we as a family contribute to the growth of the Church on earth?

Visit our web site at www.FaithFirst.com

A.D. 1215 to the Second Vatican Council

23

WE PRAY

Almighty and ever-living God,
I approach the sacrament of
    your only-begotten Son,
our Lord Jesus Christ.
I come sick to the doctor of life,
unclean to the fountain of
    mercy,
blind to the radiance of eternal
    light,
and poor and needy to the Lord
of heaven and earth.

FROM *A PRAYER OF SAINT THOMAS AQUINAS*

What do you know about what
the Church was like just before
the Protestant Reformation?
Can you describe some of
the things that needed to be
reformed?

*[The] holiness of the Church
is constantly shown forth
in the fruits of grace which
the Spirit produces in the
faithful and so it must be.*

VATICAN II,
CONSTITUTION ON THE CHURCH, 39

Reformation and Renewal

FAITH FOCUS

Why are the Protestant Reformation and the Council of Trent such important events in the history of the Church?

Our survey of the history of the Church has been more like looking at a photo album than reading volumes of history books. We have been examining snapshots of the people and events that make up the history of the Church. That album has been made up mostly of snapshots of that part of the Church that developed in what is today Western Europe. But we know that people of the Church live far beyond the boundaries of this small part of the world.

Council of Trent. Fresco detail. Taddeo Zuccaro (1529–1566), Italian painter, especially of decorative frescoes.

Lateran IV to Trent

The three hundred fifty years between the Fourth Lateran Council (1215) and the Council of Trent (1545–1563) were troubled times for the Church. As Lateran IV closed, the papacy was growing in influence, and theology was experiencing renewed vigor under the leadership of Thomas Aquinas and the other scholastics. The mendicant orders also emerged under the inspiration of Saint Francis of Assisi (Order of Friars Minor, or Franciscans) and Saint Dominic (Order of Preachers, or Dominicans). Committed to rebuilding the Church by living the Gospel with simplicity, the followers of Francis and Dominic spearheaded a spiritual renewal within the Church.

Rebuilding the Church is always a long and difficult task. The involvement of the papacy and other church leaders in the affairs of government during this period of the history of the Church led to corruption at the highest levels of the hierarchy. Neglect of the spiritual and other needs of the faithful by bishops and priests led to ignorance and superstition. The Protestant Reformation, which started in 1517 as an authentic call for much-needed reform of the Church, tragically ended in the splintering and division of Christianity into many different denominations.

Describe the story of the Church from Lateran Council IV to Trent.

Trent to Vatican I

The issues raised by Martin Luther (1483–1546) and the other Reformers were formally addressed by a call for reform in the Catholic Church. This is known as the Catholic Counter-Reformation. The highpoint of the Catholic efforts at reform during this period of Church history was the ecumenical council that was held in the city of Trent in Northern Italy from 1545 to 1563. At Trent the teachings of the Church on the sacraments and other matters were clarified. A plan for a renewal of the education of the clergy was set in motion with the establishment of seminaries.

In the three hundred years following Trent, the Catholic Counter-Reformation was largely successful. Many Christians renewed their efforts to live the Gospel. The lives of these people, such as Ignatius of Loyola (1491–1556), inspired others to join with them. Many religious communities were established, each with its own special charism aimed at furthering the renewal of the Church. These included the Jesuits, Redemptorists, Salesians, Brothers of the Christian Schools, Daughters of Charity, White Fathers, Oratorians, Sulpicians, Oblates of Mary, Vincentians, and many more.

As you know from your study of social studies, this was also a period of the expansion of trade between Europe and the rest of the world. It was the time of Christopher Columbus and the search for trade routes, new lands, and new sources of wealth for England, Spain, France, and the other powers of Europe. Missionaries from the many religious orders accompanied these explorers and their crews and brought the Gospel to the New World and other lands.

What were some of the accomplishments of the Church following the Council of Trent?

Vatican I to Vatican II

As we turn the page of the photo album of our church family, we now come upon Vatican Council I (1869–1870). Called together by Pius IX (1792–1878), over eight

hundred bishops and other leaders of the Church gathered in Rome. They met ninety-three times between December 8, 1869 and September 1, 1870. Their primary concerns were clarifying the relationship between faith and reason, and the teaching authority of the pope and the bishops.

Not quite a century would pass before Pope John XXIII (1958–1963) called the twenty-first and latest ecumenical council of the Church, Vatican Council II. Nonetheless, this period between the two councils was packed with numerous developments that significantly affected the life of the Church and the world.

The challenge of making the Christian message meaningful in the secular, industrialized, and technological world of the twentieth century became something the Church became more and more aware of. The two World Wars among nations—nations that were mostly Christian—served as a wake-up call to all Christian churches to renew their commitment to living the Gospel and proclaiming its significance for the people of the twentieth century.

Describe some of the challenges faced by the Church between Vatican Council I and Vatican Council II.

How can you better live the Gospel each day?

1225	**Thomas Aquinas (d. 1274)**
1308	**Papacy moves to Avignon**
1377	**Papacy returns to Rome**
1378	**The Great Schism**
1417	**End of the Great Schism**
1455	**Gutenberg Bible**
1491	**Ignatius of Loyola, founder of the Jesuits (d. 1556)**
1492	**Columbus discovers America**
1517	**Protestant Reformation begins**
1538	**Charles Borromeo (d. 1584)**
1545	**Council of Trent (1545–63)**
1626	**St. Peter's Basilica in Rome is consecrated**
1633	**Galileo imprisoned**
1774	**Elizabeth Ann Seton (d. 1821)**
1776	**American Declaration of Independence**
1789	**French Revolution**
1790	**John Carroll consecrated first bishop in U.S.A.**

WHAT DIFFERENCE DOES FAITH MAKE?

How did the work of Thomas Aquinas, Charles Borromeo, and Elizabeth Ann Seton influence the Church?

You have already learned about many of the heroes of the Church who lived during these centuries of the Church's story. Can you remember who they are? Here are three for you to become better acquainted with.

Saint Thomas Aquinas

Thomas Aquinas (1225–1274) was born to a noble family near Monte Cassino, the famous Benedictine monastery in Italy, where he was sent to receive his early schooling.

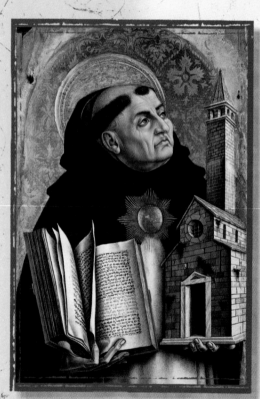

As a young man he continued his studies in Naples, Italy, where he met and became friends with members of the Dominican Order. When Thomas decided to join the Dominicans, his family was outraged because of the vow of poverty that he would be required to take. His parents forcibly brought him back to the family home, where Thomas was kept against his will for more than a year.

"Saint Thomas Aquinas" from *The Demidoff Altarpiece.* Carlo Crivelli (1430–ca. 1493), Italian painter.

However, when his parents saw the strength of his determination, they eventually relented and allowed Thomas to join the Dominicans.

Thomas pursued his theological studies and won recognition for the brilliance of both his preaching and his teaching. His works fill twenty volumes. The most famous of these writings, the *Summa Theologica,* is still considered an unsurpassed summary of scholastic Catholic theology. Thomas's personal qualities included great humility and gentleness, as well as a deep life of prayer.

The year before he died at the age of fifty, Thomas had a divine inspiration while he was celebrating Mass. This affected him so deeply that Thomas never wrote again. To those who asked him why he was no longer writing, Thomas explained that after what God had shown him, all of his writings seemed as worthless as straw.

What did Thomas Aquinas contribute to the Church?

Saint Charles Borromeo

Charles Borromeo (1538–1584) rejected the opportunity to inherit the leadership and the wealth of his family and chose to enter religious life. By the age of twenty-two Charles had already received the highest religious and secular honors and responsibilities. He was ordained to the priesthood at the age of twenty-five and only two months later was consecrated the bishop of Milan, in northern Italy. In the years after the Council of Trent, he supervised the composition of the Roman Catechism and the reform of the Church's liturgical books.

Saint Charles Borromeo.
Carol Dolci (1616–1686),
Italian painter.

As bishop of Milan, Charles was tireless in implementing the reforms of the Council of Trent. He established seminaries for the training of priests and worked to improve how priests celebrated the sacraments and how they instructed the people in the faith. He directed his considerable wealth to the care of the poor, and often personally tended to many people who suffered from starvation and diseases. His death at the age of forty-six was caused in no small measure by the way he gave of himself—often to the point of exhaustion—in the service of his people.

How does Charles Borromeo exemplify the spirit of the Council of Trent?

Saint Elizabeth Ann Seton

Born in New York City into an Episcopalian family, Elizabeth Ann Seton (1774–1821) married and had five children. Widowed and a single mother by the time she was thirty, Elizabeth decided to become a Catholic. This decision resulted in Elizabeth being estranged from her family and from her financial security. She accepted the invitation of a Baltimore priest to start a girls' school. Shortly thereafter Elizabeth established the Sisters of Charity, the first religious congregation of women founded in the United States of America. The Sisters of Charity devoted themselves primarily to education and to working in orphanages and hospitals.

From the community's headquarters in Emmitsburg, Maryland, Mother Seton oversaw the spread of her sisters' works of charity in twenty communities throughout the United States. She is the first native-born North American to be canonized a saint.

What is unique about Elizabeth Ann Seton?

Time LINE

1861	American Civil War begins
1869	Vatican Council I (ends 1870)
1914	First World War (ends 1918)
1939	Second World War (ends 1945)
1962	Vatican Council II (ends 1965)

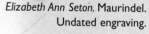

Elizabeth Ann Seton. Maurindel.
Undated engraving.

WHAT DIFFERENCE DOES FAITH MAKE?

What do you find most appealing about these three saints?

_____

_____

_____

_____

285

Green World #1. Diana Ong (1940–), Chinese/USA artist.

clashed with civil law, church law prevailed. In 1215 the Church enjoyed special privileges and considerable power. It was sometimes respected. At other times, the Church was feared.

Explain the place of the Church in the vision of the world as a sacred universe.

The Global Village

What a difference 750 years make! In the centuries following the Fourth Lateran Council, the world underwent incredible transformation. The sacred universe of Western Europe gave birth to the global village in the twentieth century. Communication evolved from handwritten letters to the printing press to the telegraph and the telephone to radio and television to the Internet. Communication that once took days, weeks, and months now unites people as quickly as you can hit a key stroke on a keyboard and speak a single syllable of a word.

Science and technology discovered secrets of creation never known and never even imagined. The Age of Exploration opened new worlds and new ways to the universe. Individuals such as the Italian painter, sculptor, architect, and engineer Leonardo da Vinci (1452–1519); the Polish-born French chemist Marie Curie (1867–1934); and the German-born American physicist Albert Einstein (1879–1955) provided ideas that challenged traditional ways of looking at the world. The Church responded to all these new insights cautiously, defending long-held truths and integrating scientific discoveries into the Church's understanding of revelation.

As you can imagine, the world of the Fourth Lateran Council in 1215 was vastly different from the world of Vatican Council II in 1962. Likewise, the Church's relationship to these two worlds is remarkably different.

A Sacred Universe

At the time of the Fourth Lateran Council, people had a view of the world and society that might be called a sacred universe. Church authority rather than civil authority was at its center. There was little doubt that the pope stood not only over the Church but over kings and princes as well. If church law

By the time of Vatican Council II, legitimate scientific research had come to be an ally of the Church. Reason and faith joined together in the search for truth. No longer were the results of human reason and scientific inquiry a threat to traditional faith. No longer did the Church feel that it needed political dominance to protect its legitimate concerns for religious matters.

In a global village respect for diversity prevails. No longer is it demanded that everyone share the same religious worldview. The Church lives together in the global village with people whose faith journey is different than its own. The Church speaks but does not force its teachings on world leaders and governments.

Describe the role of the Church in today's global village.

Galileo, in 1613, published his beliefs that the sun was the center of the universe with the earth revolving around it. The Church felt that the earth was immovable and the stars, sun, and planets revolved around it. In 1633 the Church forced Galileo to recant. He lived the rest of his life under house arrest. In 1979 Pope John Paul II conceded that the Church had erred in its treatment of Galileo.

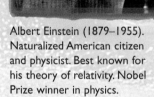

Albert Einstein (1879–1955). Naturalized American citizen and physicist. Best known for his theory of relativity. Nobel Prize winner in physics.

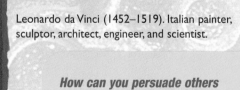

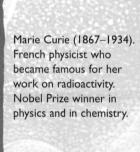

Marie Curie (1867–1934). French physicist who became famous for her work on radioactivity. Nobel Prize winner in physics and in chemistry.

Leonardo da Vinci (1452–1519). Italian painter, sculptor, architect, engineer, and scientist.

WHAT DIFFERENCE DOES FAITH MAKE?

How can you persuade others to listen to Christ's message?

_____

_____

_____

WHAT DIFFERENCE

Does This Make in Our Church?

The Church grew and changed radically during the period of reformation and renewal. Ideas were developed, religious communities were formed, and individual people made an impact on the Church. In every age and in every part of the world, dynamic people rose to influence the faith of all Christians. Here are the stories of three of those heroes of our faith.

Saint Rose of Lima. Stained glass.

Saint Rose of Lima

Saint Rose of Lima (1586–1617) is the first canonized saint of the Americas. She is the patron saint of South America and the Philippines. So, what did she do to merit such honors?

Rose was born in Lima, the capital of Peru, in 1586. Her parents were decent folks of moderate means. Yet at an early age, Rose chose a life of penance and austerity. With practice of extraordinary prayer and fasting, she gave herself to God, who responded to her sacrifices with many graces. Throughout her life, she suffered greatly from the criticism and misunderstanding of family and friends. However, in 1617, when she died after a long illness at the age of thirty-one, the leaders of the city took turns carrying her body to the grave.

Saint Frances Xavier Cabrini

Saint Frances Xavier Cabrini (1850–1917) is the first American citizen to be canonized a saint. She was born into a prosperous farm family in northern Italy in 1850. Despite poor health throughout her life, Frances was a gifted student. In 1868 she became a licensed schoolteacher, but her dream was to become a religious missionary sister in the Orient.

In 1880 part of her dream was fulfilled. Frances established the first community of missionary sisters, the Missionary Sisters of the Sacred Heart. However, instead of doing missionary work in the East, her bishop advised her to serve Italian families in the United States of America.

Saint Frances Cabrini. Stained glass.

Suffering from malaria, Mother Cabrini died on December 22, 1917, in a wicker chair in her room at Columbus Hospital in Chicago. She was canonized a saint on July 7, 1946, and is the patron of immigrants.

Saint Thérèse of Lisieux

This remarkable woman lived only twenty-four years, from 1873 to 1897. The youngest of five sisters who became nuns, Thérèse Martin entered the Carmelite monastery in Lisieux, France, at age fifteen. She received the name Thérèse of the Child Jesus.

Told to write the story of her life, Thérèse composed an autobiography that focused not on her life's work but rather on God's grace working within her. Who would have guessed that this writing assignment by an obscure nun would produce a spiritual masterpiece? In fact, *The Story of a Soul* has been recently rated one of the top ten spiritual books of the twentieth century. Her words of simplicity, gratitude, and hope have been translated into all major languages and are as fresh today as when she wrote them. Thérèse died of tuberculosis in 1897.

Saint Thérèse of Lisieux. Stained glass.

Mother Cabrini and six other Missionary Sisters arrived in New York City in 1898. This small band of seven women cared for orphans, was involved in religious education for adults and children, visited the sick, and worked with the poor.

As a child, Mother Cabrini was captivated by stories about missionaries in foreign lands. In many ways her accomplishments reach far beyond her childhood dreams of being a missionary sister in the Orient. During her lifetime she founded over seventy schools, hospitals, and orphanages in the United States of America, Europe, and South America. Ironically, she never visited the Orient.

What can you learn from each of these courageous women to help you live as a more committed Christian?

WHAT DIFFERENCE

Does It Make in My Life?

During this period of church history there was internal conflict and disagreement. There was a strong movement to reform the Church and to resolve these differences so renewal could take place. The members of the early Church of the thirteenth through sixteenth centuries certainly knew what conflict was all about.

Dealing with Conflict

She says, "No way!" Check what you would do:

____ Get really mad.

____ Beg her, plead with her, promise her stuff, make a deal.

____ Tell your mother or father.

____ Scream at her to get off the computer, call her awful names.

____ Ask her to please let you use it and she can e-mail her friends later.

____ Try to physically move her away from the computer.

Think about how you would deal with the following conflict.

Your family has one computer. You have to finish your history report. Your sister seems to be e-mailing **all** her friends. You ask her if you could please use the computer.

____ Walk away visibly very angry and upset.

____ Negotiate a compromise where you both will win.

____ Other _____

_____

Dealing with conflict is a normal and natural part of life. Most people do not like conflict and they try to avoid it at any cost. The truth is conflict cannot be avoided.

What Is It?

Conflicts occur when people have different opinions or opposing points of view or different needs. It can also occur when people are being selfish and disregard the needs of others. For example, if I want what I want when I want it, and I don't care about your wants, there is a conflict. Most conflicts can be resolved peacefully if those involved are willing to work at it.

How Can You Resolve It?

Here are some suggestions to help you resolve conflicts peacefully.

1. **Share your opinion, state your need, make "I" statements.** For example: "I need to use the computer for about an hour to finish my report. Could you please e-mail your friends later?"

2. **Avoid being judgmental, sarcastic, or offensive.** Statements like "You're so stupid. No one in their right mind would spend hours e-mailing everyone in the universe" invite conflict.

3. **Focus on the specific problem or disagreement.** Do not bring up stuff from the past like "Six months ago I let you play my video games all night."

4. **Listen to the other person's point of view.** Hear what they are saying. Keep your mind open and be flexible.

5. **Focus on the facts.** Focus on the needs that are expressed, not just your wants.

6. **Be respectful.** Use good manners and common courtesy. Name-calling, being stubborn, or being offensive only increases conflict.

7. **Try to avoid win/lose situations.** Find the best possible solution to the problem. Bring it to a win/win situation so that both your needs can be met.

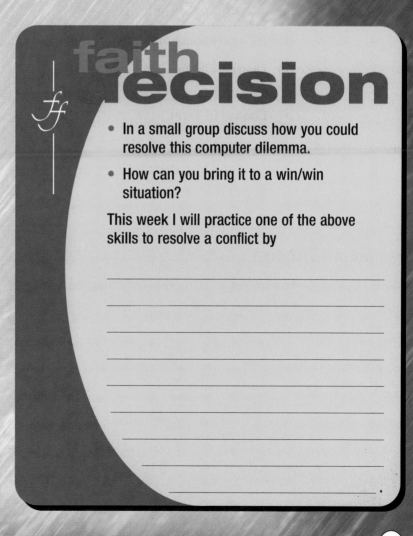

faith decision

- In a small group discuss how you could resolve this computer dilemma.

- How can you bring it to a win/win situation?

This week I will practice one of the above skills to resolve a conflict by

_____

_____

_____

_____

_____

_____

_____

_____

_____ .

People and Places and Events

Identify these people and events.

1. Protestant Reformation

2. Catholic Counter-Reformation

3. Council of Trent

4. Vatican Council I

5. Saint Elizabeth Ann Seton

Main Ideas

Choose either (a) or (b) from each set of items. Write a brief paragraph to answer each of your choices.

1. (a) Discuss the situation in the Church before the Council of Trent and how Trent changed the Church.

   (b) Describe some of the developments in the Church of the twentieth century.

2. (a) Discuss Thomas Aquinas's contributions to the Church.

   (b) Explain how Charles Borromeo implemented the reforms of the Council of Trent.

3. (a) Explain the idea of a "sacred universe."

   (b) Describe how the Church changed between Lateran Council IV and Vatican II.

Critical Thinking

Using what you have learned in this chapter, briefly explain this statement: The Church can no longer assume that everyone, everywhere, shares a religious worldview.

Family Discussion

What can we do to make our family a stronger faith community?

Visit our
web site at
www.FaithFirst.com

The Second Vatican Council (1962–1965) to the present

24

WE PRAY

Renew your wonders in our time,
as though for a new Pentecost,
and grant that the holy Church,
preserving unanimous and
    continuous prayer,
together with Mary the mother
    of Jesus,
and also under the guidance of
    Saint Peter,
may increase the reign of the
    Divine Savior,
the reign of truth and justice,
the reign of love and peace.
    Amen.

POPE JOHN XXIII'S OPENING ADDRESS
TO THE SECOND VATICAN COUNCIL

What do you know about the
Second Vatican Council?
What have you heard from
Catholics who were alive at
that time about how they felt
during the Council? Can you
describe what the Catholic
Church was like at the time
that the Council opened?

*The sacred Council has
set out to impart an
ever-increasing vigor to the
Christian life of the faithful.*
VATICAN COUNCIL II.
CONSTITUTION ON THE SACRED LITURGY, 1

We turn now to the latest period of the story of our church family. The center of this period is Vatican Council II, or the Second Vatican Council. This event had and continues to have great impact on the life of the People of God.

Announcement and Preparations

On January 25, 1959, just three months after having been elected Pope, John XXIII announced to a small group of cardinals gathered in Rome that he had decided to call an ecumenical council of the Church. His announcement stunned not only the cardinals present but eventually the entire religious world. Everyone had expected the early actions of the elderly pope to be minor and transitional in nature.

Yet, during the next three and a half years before the council opened,

Pope John XXIII made it clear that he intended Vatican II to be a major council of reform and renewal for the universal Church. He oversaw the massive work of preparation. He consulted bishops throughout the world about what they thought the agenda of the council should include. He coordinated what was to be a global gathering of more than two thousand bishops from every corner of the world. The Church was on the verge of another major renewal.

What did Pope John XXIII want Vatican II to accomplish?

The Four Sessions

The actual work of the council took place over a period of four years. During this time there were working sessions held in the fall of each of the four years

Vatican Council II. Basilica of Saint Peter. Vatican City, Rome, Italy, 1962.

the council was held. The dates of the sessions were: October 11–December 8, 1962; September 29–December 4, 1963; September 14–November 21, 1964; September 14–December 8, 1965.

The council's work, as Pope John spelled it out, primarily addressed the pastoral renewal of the Church. John XXIII repeatedly urged Catholics to pray that the council would be a "new Pentecost." He hoped the council would foster the internal reform and renewal of the Church as well as the unity of all Christians.

When Pope John died in the summer between the first and second sessions of the council, many thought the council would die with him. However, his successor, Paul VI, proved to be a staunch promoter of the vision of John XXIII. The new pope immediately announced his intention to continue the work of the council.

In his opening address at the second session of the council, Paul VI listed four goals that he saw for the Council: (1) to deepen people's understanding of the nature of the Church, especially the collaboration between the bishops and the pope; (2) to promote reform of the Church, especially in the Church's liturgy; (3) to promote the cause of Christian unity; (4) to enter into dialogue with the modern world.

Discuss the goals of the Second Vatican Council.

The Documents

It soon became clear that there were many differences of opinion at the council. Nonetheless, the climate of dialogue and debate that characterized Vatican Council II was extraordinarily invigorating. While a small but powerful minority resisted change throughout the council, the majority of bishops were able to come to agreement as the work of the council proceeded.

Eventually, four major documents, called Constitutions, were promulgated, or officially adopted. These were: (1) *Sacrosanctum Concilium* (Constitution on the Sacred Liturgy) approved December 4, 1963, by a vote of 2,147 to 4; (2) *Lumen Gentium* (Dogmatic Constitution on the Church) approved on November 21, 1964, by a vote of 2,151 to 5; (3) *Dei Verbum* (Dogmatic Constitution on Divine Revelation) approved on November 18, 1965, by a vote of 2,344 to 6; and (4) *Gaudium et Spes* (Pastoral Constitution on the Church in the Modern World) approved on December 7, 1965, by a vote of 2,309 to 75. In addition, the council approved twelve other documents: nine Decrees and three Declarations.

What issues did the four major documents of Vatican II address?

Time LINE

1881	Angelo Roncalli, future Pope John XXIII, born
1897	Giovanni Montini, future Pope Paul VI, born
1920	Karol Wojtyla, future Pope John Paul II, born
1939	Eugenio Pacelli, Pope Pius XII, elected
1958	Angelo Roncalli, Pope John XXIII, elected
1959	John XXIII announces Second Vatican Council
1962	Council opens
1963	Pope John XXIII dies and is succeeded by Giovanni Montini, Pope Paul VI
1965	Council ends
1975	Elizabeth Ann Seton canonized
1978	Pope Paul VI dies
	Albino Luciani, Pope John Paul I, elected and dies
	Karol Wojtyla, Pope John Paul II, elected
1989	Communism collapses
1992	*Catechism of the Catholic Church* published

WHAT DIFFERENCE DOES FAITH MAKE?

How can you learn more about the Second Vatican Council?

Key to the story of the Church in the second half of the twentieth century are the popes whom the Spirit called to guide the People of God and proclaim the Gospel to all nations. Let's take the time to come to know a little more about three of these popes.

Pope John XXIII (Angelo Giuseppe Roncalli)

Angelo Roncalli was born in 1881 into a large peasant family in Sotto il Monte, Italy. Following his ordination to the priesthood, he served in a wide variety of assignments in the Vatican Diplomatic Corps. His success in that role led to his being named a cardinal of the Church in 1953. Shortly thereafter he was made Patriarch of Venice where he became known for his fatherly style of pastoral leadership.

Pope John XXIII.

Upon the death of Pope Pius XII in 1958, Cardinal Roncalli was elected pope just short of his 77th birthday. "Good Pope John," as he came to be called, was beloved by people throughout the world. His vision of the need for an ecumenical council of the Church was matched by his determined and decisive leadership style. He succeeded in establishing in the Church an atmosphere of openness to other religions and to all people of good will.

Describe the contributions of Pope John XXIII to the Church.

Pope Paul VI (Giovanni Battista Montini)

From the very beginning of his priesthood, Giovanni Battista Montini seemed destined to serve the Church in important positions. By the age of forty, he had become assistant to Cardinal Eugenio Pacelli, who became Pius XII. After his election to the papacy in 1939, Pius XII promoted Montini to be one of the closest advisors to the pope, a member of the Roman Curia.

From 1954 until his own election as pope in 1963, Cardinal Montini distinguished himself as Archbishop of Milan, Italy. While archbishop of Milan, he was one of Pope John XXIII's most trusted advisors and

Pope Paul VI.

helpers in the work of the Vatican Council. His own election as Pope John XXIII's successor took place in one of the shortest conclaves in history, since he was clearly dedicated to carrying on the work of the council.

Pope Paul VI oversaw the second, third, and fourth sessions of Vatican II. After the close of the council, Paul VI set up many of the structures within the Church to implement the reforms mandated by the council. Pope Paul VI was a strong promoter of the reform of the liturgy of the Church. He worked tirelessly to keep in balance the enthusiasm of those eager to reform the liturgy and those who resisted the changes recommended by the council. The establishment of the Synod of Bishops was his most important contribution to the implementation of the council's teaching on the relationship between the working bishops and the pope. Pope Paul VI died on August 6, 1978.

Explain some of the contributions of Pope Paul VI to the Church.

Pope John Paul II (Karol Wojtyla)

Karol Wojtyla chose the name John Paul II when he was elected pope in 1978. This indicated that he wished to carry on the work of the council begun under Pope John XXIII and Pope Paul VI. As cardinal archbishop of Krakow, Poland, he participated in all four sessions of the council and made significant contributions to the debate on religious freedom. Pope John Paul II will be especially remembered for his traveling the globe, meeting with Catholics on all continents.

In addition to writing many encyclicals, Pope John Paul II oversaw the completion of the revision of the *Code of Canon Law* in 1983, which was initiated by John XXIII, and the publication of the *Catechism of the Catholic Church* in 1992. By his appointments to the College of Cardinals and his involvement in political, economic, social, and moral issues, Pope John Paul II has given the papacy an international dimension and vision that will unfold in the years to come.

Discuss some of the contributions of Pope John Paul II to the Church.

Pope John Paul II. Guatemala City, Guatemala, February 5, 1996.

Pope John Paul II. Saint Andrew Avellino Parish, Rome, Italy, February 6, 1997.

WHAT DIFFERENCE DOES FAITH MAKE?

How can these three heroes of faith help you grow in faith?

effectively to the men and women of the modern world.

In a famous address on the opening day of the council, Pope John XXIII referred to the "prophets of doom" who "see in modern times nothing but prevarication and ruin." He made it clear that he rejected such a pessimistic attitude, saying, "We must disagree with these prophets of doom, who are always forecasting disaster, as though the end of the world were imminent."

Describe the vision that Pope John XXIII had for the council.

FAITH FOCUS

How has the modern Church changed its relationship with the world at large?

Aggiornamento

By his use of the Italian word **aggiornamento** (which means "bringing up to date") to describe the work of Vatican Council II, Pope John XXIII captured a whole new spirit of the Church's relationship to the world. Pope John XXIII exhibited a spirit of openness and welcome toward the world. He said that the Church must "open the windows" and let in the fresh air of renewal if it is to preach the Gospel

The Church in the Modern World

Much of the work of the council followed the pastoral agenda of Pope John XXIII. The most striking fruit of this pastoral focus was the *Pastoral Constitution on the Church in the Modern World*. This visionary document is the first document of any ecumenical council to be addressed to the whole world. It specifically associates with the

followers of Christ "the joy and hope, the grief and anguish of the men of our time, especially those who are poor or afflicted in any way" (1).

Explain what the council said was the place of the Church in the modern world.

Catholic Social Teaching after the Council

In the decades since Vatican II, the Catholic Church has engaged the world through a remarkable body of official social teachings written both by popes and bishops. These teachings apply the Gospel to the changing situations of modern life. Especially under Pope Paul VI and Pope John Paul II, the Church has led the way in opening up the dialogue between the Church and various sectors of contemporary society. In his work promoting the Great Jubilee opening the third millennium, Pope John Paul II made explicit efforts to continue and deepen the dialogue between the Church and the entire human family.

The bishops of the United States of America are prominent among the world's bishops in promoting social justice. They have written important pastoral letters that both proclaim gospel values and guide Catholics in implementing these values into their personal lives and the life of the nation. These pastoral letters include *The Challenge of Peace: God's Promise and Our Response* (1983) and *Economic Justice for All: Catholic Social Teaching and the U.S. Economy* (1986).

The work of Vatican Council II is historic and decisive. The Church continues to critique both the positive and the negative elements of our modern world in light of the Gospel. But the overall relationship between the Church and the world is changing dramatically and irreversibly from that of previous generations. There is simply no question about the goodness of God's creation and the role of the Church in promoting human development.

Explain how the relationship between the Church and the world has changed dramatically since Vatican Council II.

How can you participate in the Church in the modern world?

WHAT DIFFERENCE DOES FAITH MAKE?

_____

_____

_____

WHAT
DIFFERENCE
Does This Make in Our Church?

World Youth Day,
Denver, Colorado, 1993.

The Church constantly calls the People of God to renewal. In the twentieth century Vatican Council II outlined a plan for renewing the life of the Church. Central to that plan is the call of all the People of God to participate actively in the life of the Church. Pope John Paul II extended this challenge to the youth of the world by meeting with Catholic youth from around the world on World Youth Day.

World Youth Days

In 1984 the Church gathered to celebrate the 1,950th anniversary of the death of Christ. A year later the Church again gathered to celebrate the International Year of Youth, which was declared by the United Nations in 1985. On both occasions about 300,000 young people gathered to celebrate with the Holy Father, Pope John Paul II.

Recognizing the significant needs and the spirit of Catholic young people of the world, John Paul II created World Youth Day. World Youth Days are celebrated each year in every diocese in the world. Every two years, the pope calls the youth of the world to gather together at an international meeting place.

The international celebration of World Youth Day has been held in many different locations throughout the world including Buenos Aires, Santiago de Compostella, Czestochowa, Denver, Manila, and Paris.

The Experience

World Youth Day is very much a pilgrimage, the journey of a pilgrim to a sacred place. It should not be considered a vacation, although sightseeing is often part of the journey. Most groups of young people meet weeks before to build their own community, plan the trip, and pray together. Throughout the week leading up to World Youth Day, the youth are gathered in regions for sessions that help them grow in the faith. These sessions are filled with speakers, prayer, and discussions.

World Youth Day, Paris, France, 1997.

Young people made a pilgrimage to Rome for the thirteenth World Youth Day to celebrate the Jubilee Year 2000. The smallest gathering at World Youth Day was 400,000. One year, over 4,000,000 youth attended.

How can gathering with the pope and the youth of the world enrich our faith?

301

WHAT DIFFERENCE

Does It Make in My Life?

heritage of all Catholic Christians today.

We study the history of the Church to learn about our roots and to recognize that the work of the Holy Spirit has always been present within our Church. We take from the past that which will help us continue to know, love, and serve God and his people today.

Present

You are the Church of today. The virtues and qualities that our Catholic ancestors needed in order to keep their faith alive even in times of great conflict are the same virtues you need today. You are living in a world where certain teachings, values, and beliefs stand in contradiction to the Gospel and the teachings of the Church. This may at times make it difficult for you to practice your faith. What will help you continue to face and overcome the challenges of keeping your faith alive each day?

The history of the Catholic Church that you have been exploring in this last unit has highlighted some of the key events, issues, and people who have shaped the Church as we know it today.

Past, Present, and Future

The Church, the new People of God, has a past, a present and a future. The two-thousand-year history of the Church, beginning with the first Pentecost, tells us where we have been. The struggles, challenges, reforms, accomplishments, joys, and sorrows of the new People of God throughout history make up the

Virtues, Past and Present

You may have heard the expression "Carpe diem," which means "Seize the day." You may also have heard the expression "Live today as if it were the first day of the rest of your life." You are asked to live in the present and not dwell in the past or hold on to hurts, grudges, or revenge. How can you do that? A few of the most important virtues that will help you are faith, courage, perseverance, and wisdom.

Faith

Your faith can sustain and help you through any challenge. Faith is a gift. It is trust in God, who promised to be with you forever. Faith is your belief that God loves and cherishes you and is with you as you live one day at a time. Affirm your belief in that good news. How can you increase your faith each day?

Courage

You need courage to really live your faith. Courage is the moral and mental strength to choose what is right. It is the virtue that strengthens you to live your values and beliefs even when they are unpopular. With the virtue of courage you can overcome fears and risk living your life as a follower of Christ, no matter what the cost.

Perseverance

Perseverance is the firm determination to follow your goal and live by your values. Perseverance flows from the virtues of courage and faith. Perseverance is the steadfast belief in your commitment to be a follower of Jesus Christ. It is having the courage, in spite of pressure or obstacles, to keep your eye on your ultimate goal—eternal life and happiness with God.

Wisdom

Wisdom is the virtue that helps you see the world through the eyes of faith. It helps you see the world as God sees it. Wisdom can help you recognize and practice two other

special virtues that will carry you into the future—the virtues of hope and love. These will help you truly live as children of God.

Future

It has been said that young people make up 50 percent of our population and 100 percent of our future. You are part of the Church now and part of the Church of the future. You make a difference in the life of the Church. So, believe and trust and hope in God, who dwells within you. Believe in yourself and your God-given gifts and strengths. Believe that you are a messenger of hope and love in the world.

faith decision

- In a small group discuss something each of you has learned about the history of the Church that will help you be a more active member of the Church today.

- Think about the virtues of faith, courage, perseverance, wisdom, hope, and love. Which of these virtues do you believe are already strong within you, and which do you need to strengthen?

As an important member of the Church of today and tomorrow, I believe I can make a difference. I will begin by

_____

_____

_____

_____ .

Faith Vocabulary

Define the term:

aggiornamento

People and Places and Events

Identify these people and events.

1. Vatican Council II

2. Pope John XXIII

3. Pope Paul VI

4. Pope John Paul II

Main Ideas

Choose either (a) or (b) from each set of items. Write a brief paragraph to answer each of your choices.

1. (a) Explain what Pope John XXIII hoped to accomplish by convening Vatican Council II.

   (b) Discuss the work that was accomplished at Vatican Council II.

2. (a) Explain how Pope Paul VI continued the work of Vatican Council II.

   (b) Discuss how Pope John Paul II continued the work of Vatican Council II.

3. (a) Explain how Pope John XXIII "opened the windows" of renewal in the Church.

   (b) Discuss the social teaching of the Catholic Church since Vatican Council II.

Critical Thinking

Using what you have learned in this chapter, briefly explain this statement:
"The joy and hope, the grief and anguish of the [people] of our time, especially of those who are poor or afflicted in any way, are the joy and hope, the grief and anguish of the followers of Christ as well" (*Church in the Modern World*, 1).

Family Discussion

In what ways can our family be a living sign of hope for the future?

Visit our
web site at
www.FaithFirst.com

THE LITURGICAL YEAR

The Church gathers throughout the year to remember and share in the the saving work of Christ. Each day of the year is made holy by the Church gathering together with Christ, the Head of the Church, to give praise, honor, and glory to the Father through the power of the Holy Spirit. Each week the Church, the new People of God, gathers on Sunday, or the Lord's Day, to celebrate and share in the Paschal mystery. In addition to Sunday celebrations, the liturgical year of the Church is made up of a cycle of seasons, solemnities, feasts, and memorials. The lessons in this unit focus on the seasons of the liturgical year of the Church. This page lists many of the solemnities, feasts, and memorials that are celebrated throughout the year.

JANUARY
Mary, the Mother of God
(January 1)
Elizabeth Ann Seton, Religious
(January 4)
John Neumann, Bishop (January 5)
Agnes, Virgin and Martyr
(January 21)
Conversion of Saint Paul, Apostle
(January 25)
Thomas Aquinas, Priest and
Doctor (January 28)

FEBRUARY
Presentation of the Lord
(February 2)
Blase, Bishop and Martyr
(February 3)
Agatha, Virgin and Martyr
(February 5)
Our Lady of Lourdes (February 11)
Chair of Saint Peter, Apostle
(February 22)

MARCH
Perpetua and Felicity, Martyrs
(March 7)
Patrick, Bishop, (March 17)
Joseph, Husband of Mary
(March 19)
Annunciation (March 25)

APRIL
Mark, Evangelist (April 25)
Catherine of Siena, Virgin and
Doctor (April 29)

MAY
Joseph the Worker (May 1)
Athanasius, Bishop and Doctor
(May 2)
Philip and James, Apostles (May 3)
Matthias, Apostle (May 14)
Isidore (May 15)
Visitation (May 31)
Holy Trinity
(First Sunday after Pentecost)

Body and Blood of Christ
(Sunday after Holy Trinity)
Sacred Heart (Friday following
Second Sunday after Pentecost)

JUNE
Charles Lwanga and Companions,
Martyrs (June 3)
Barnabas, Apostle (June 11)
Anthony of Padua, Priest and
Doctor (June 13)
Birth of John the Baptist (June 24)
Peter and Paul, Apostles (June 29)

JULY
Thomas, Apostle (July 3)
Blessed Kateri Tekakwitha, Virgin
(July 14)
Our Lady of Mount Carmel
(July 16)
Mary Magdalene (July 22)
James, Apostle (July 25)
Joachim and Ann, Parents of Mary
(July 26)
Martha (July 29)
Ignatius of Loyola, Priest (July 31)

AUGUST
Transfiguration (August 6)
Lawrence, Deacon and Martyr
(August 10)
Clare, Virgin (August 11)
Assumption (August 15)
Queenship of Mary (August 22)
Rose of Lima, Virgin (August 23)
Bartholomew, Apostle (August 24)
Monica (August 27)
Augustine of Hippo, Bishop and
Doctor (August 28)

SEPTEMBER
Birth of Mary (September 8)
Peter Claver, Priest (September 9)
Triumph of the Cross
(September 14)
Our Lady of Sorrows
(September 15)

Matthew, Apostle and Evangelist
(September 21)
Michael, Gabriel, and Raphael,
Archangels (September 29)

OCTOBER
Theresa of the Child Jesus, Virgin,
(October 1)
Francis of Assisi (October 4)
Our Lady of the Rosary
(October 7)
Teresa of Jesus, Virgin and Doctor
(October 15)
Luke, Evangelist (October 18)
Isaac Jogues and John de Brébeuf,
Priests and Martyrs, and
Companions (October 19)
Simon and Jude, Apostles
(October 28)

NOVEMBER
All Saints (November 1)
All Souls (November 2)
Martin de Porres, Religious
(November 3)
Frances Xavier Cabrini, Virgin
(November 13)
Elizabeth of Hungary
(November 17)
Presentation of Mary
(November 21)
Cecilia, Virgin and Martyr
(November 22)
Andrew, Apostle (November 30)
Christ the King
(Last Sunday in Ordinary Time)

DECEMBER
Immaculate Conception
(December 8)
Our Lady of Guadalupe
(December 12)
Christmas (December 25)
Stephen, First Martyr
(December 26)
John, Apostle and Evangelist
(December 27)
Holy Innocents (December 28)

Ordinary Time

From New Year's Day to the final day of the year we live our lives according to the traditional yearly calendar. But the Church and its members live out the days of the year in a different way, in a way that celebrates the liturgical year. The Church celebrates its liturgical year to help us remember the story of God's love for us.

The Liturgical Year

The liturgical year of the Church begins with the First Sunday of Advent. This is either the last Sunday in November or the first Sunday in December. The last Sunday of the liturgical year is the feast of Christ the King, which is the last Sunday in Ordinary Time.

Ordinary Time

The longest part of the Church's year is called Ordinary Time but the Church's liturgical year is far from ordinary! Its rituals, colors, and symbols are rich in tradition and meaning. The word *ordinary* comes from a Latin word meaning "number." We call this time of the Church's liturgical year Ordinary Time because the Sundays and weeks are named by the use of numbers.

During Ordinary Time we listen to and remember the works of Jesus. We take these stories of Jesus' life, look at our lives closely, and try to live as true followers of Jesus in our world today.

What is Ordinary Time?

Church Year. Stained glass.

Speak, Lord

The word of God proclaimed at Mass is God speaking to us today. We ask the Spirit to open our minds and hearts as we listen to God's own word to us.

> After John had been arrested,
>   Jesus came to Galilee
>   proclaiming the gospel
>   of God:
>   "This is the time of
>   fulfillment." . . .
> As he passed by the Sea of Galilee,
>   he saw Simon and his brother
>   Andrew casting their nets
>   into the sea;
>   they were fishermen.
> Jesus said to them,
>   "Come after me, and I will
>   make you fishers of men."
>   MARK 1:14–20

In this reading from the Third Sunday in Ordinary Time we too are called to follow Jesus. We ask the Spirit to open our minds and hearts to respond to this call throughout all the seasons of the year.

Describe how Ordinary Time helps us live as disciples of Jesus.

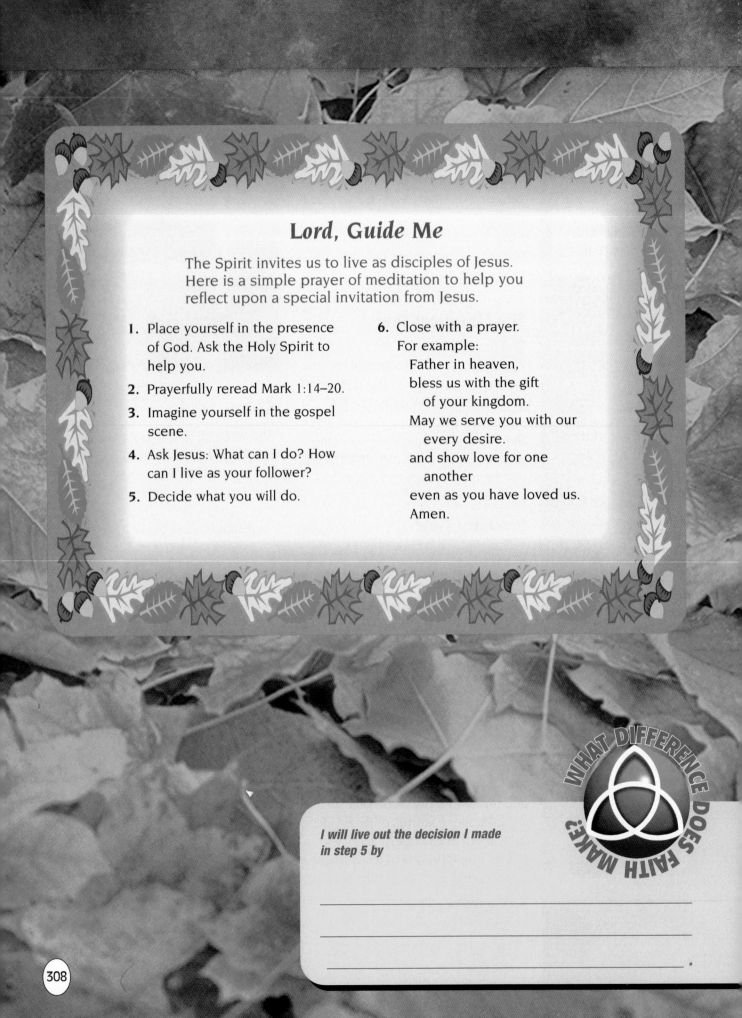

Lord, Guide Me

The Spirit invites us to live as disciples of Jesus. Here is a simple prayer of meditation to help you reflect upon a special invitation from Jesus.

1. Place yourself in the presence of God. Ask the Holy Spirit to help you.

2. Prayerfully reread Mark 1:14–20.

3. Imagine yourself in the gospel scene.

4. Ask Jesus: What can I do? How can I live as your follower?

5. Decide what you will do.

6. Close with a prayer.
   For example:
   Father in heaven,
   bless us with the gift
      of your kingdom.
   May we serve you with our
      every desire.
   and show love for one
      another
   even as you have loved us.
   Amen.

I will live out the decision I made in step 5 by

_____

_____

_____

WHAT DIFFERENCE DOES FAITH MAKE?

The First Week of Advent

FAITH FOCUS

What does keeping watch for Jesus mean during the season of Advent?

THE WORD OF THE LORD

Read and reflect on one of this year's Scripture readings the Church proclaims on the First Sunday of Advent.

YEAR A
1st Reading:
Isaiah 2:1–5
2nd Reading:
Romans 13:11–14
Gospel:
Matthew 24:37–44

YEAR B
1st Reading:
Isaiah 63:16b–17, 19b; 64:2–7
2nd Reading:
1 Corinthians 1:3–9
Gospel:
Mark 13:33–37

YEAR C
1st Reading:
Jeremiah 33:14–16
2nd Reading:
1 Thessalonians 3:12–4:2
Gospel:
Luke 21:25–28, 34–36

How wonderful it is to be welcomed somewhere! We enjoy it when people watch for and celebrate our arrival. When they welcome us into their homes, we feel good. They are prepared for us, greet us, and offer us something to eat and drink. How do you welcome someone into your home or group?

Joyful Hope

During Advent we prepare to welcome Jesus. We wait in joyful hope and expectation for his coming. We spend our days praying, preparing, and watching for his arrival.

During Advent the Church reminds us that the Son of God entered our history. Jesus' birth in Bethlehem and his life on earth are well documented. During Advent the

Church also reminds us that Christ will come again in majesty. We remember the past with great thanksgiving and look toward the future with great hope.

Why is Advent a season of joyful hope?

We listen to the word of God and remember we must prepare diligently and attentively for Christ's coming among us. Jesus said to his disciples:

"Therefore, stay awake!
For you do not know on which
    day your Lord will come.
Be sure of this: if the master of
    the house
    had known the hour of night
    when the thief was coming,
    he would have stayed awake
    and not let his house be
    broken into.
So too, you also must be prepared,
    for at an hour you do not
    expect, the Son of Man
    will come."   MATTHEW 24:42–44

Why is Advent a season of diligent preparation?

Welcome, Lord!

The Church helps us keep both of these comings of Christ in mind. To Christ who has already come in the past, we prepare to say, "Welcome!" To Christ who is here among us today in the present, we say, "Welcome!"

The four Sundays of Advent anchor our attention and focus our hearts on Christ. If we watch closely, we will be ready to welcome Christ in all the ways he comes to us.

*Jesus/Apocalypse.
Stained glass.*

An Advent Prayer

During Advent we remember the birth of Jesus, his coming into our lives each day, and the promise of his final coming at the end of time.

LEADER: Jesus promised that he would always be with us when we were gathered together in his name.

ALL: (Sing two verses of the hymn "O Come, O Come, Emmanuel.")

LEADER: Let us listen to Jesus who is present to us through his word.

READER: Lord, open my lips. And my mouth shall proclaim your praise. A reading from the First Letter of Paul to the Thessalonians.
(Read 1 Thessalonians 3:12–4:2.)
The word of the Lord.

ALL: Thanks be to God.

LEADER: Let us ask the Spirit to help us understand God's word to us.

ALL: (Reflect on the meaning of God's word.)
1. How does God the Father invite us to prepare for the coming of his Son among us?
2. How can the Spirit help us prepare for the coming of Jesus?

LEADER: Let us ask God to prepare our hearts and minds for his coming among us.

READER: Lord, we look forward to your coming in majesty.

ALL: Come, Lord Jesus.

READER: Lord, make us alert to your presence among us.

ALL: Come, Lord Jesus.

READER: Lord, help us prepare for Christmas.

ALL: Come, Lord Jesus.

LEADER: Lord our God,
help us to prepare
for the coming of Christ
your Son.
May he find us waiting
eager in joyful prayer.
Grant this through Christ
our Lord.

ALL: Amen.

FROM OPENING PRAYER,
FIRST WEEK OF ADVENT

This Advent, in what ways are you "staying awake" for the arrival of Christ?

WHAT DIFFERENCE DOES FAITH MAKE?

THE WORD OF THE LORD

Read and reflect on one of this year's Scripture readings the Church proclaims on the Second Sunday of Advent.

YEAR A
1st Reading:
   Isaiah 11:1–10
2nd Reading:
   Romans 15:4–9
Gospel:
   Matthew 3:1–12

YEAR B
1st Reading:
   Isaiah 40:1–5, 9–11
2nd Reading:
   2 Peter 3:8–14
Gospel:
   Mark 1:1–8

YEAR C
1st Reading:
   Baruch 5:1–9
2nd Reading:
   Philippians 1:4–6, 8–11
Gospel:
   Luke 3:1–6

Excitement. Anticipation. Hope. Your best friend is going to call. She has good news and wants to share it with you. You are anxious to know what it is. You want to call your friend right now—but you know that you have to wait. During Advent we learn from many wonderful people how to wait for and welcome Jesus into our lives.

Those Who Waited

On the Second, Third, and Fourth Sundays of Advent, the Church reminds us to be always ready to welcome the Lord. We meet people who longed for and waited in joyful hope for the coming of the Messiah.

THIS IS MY BELOVED SON

Baptism of Jesus.
Stained glass.

We learn about Elizabeth and Zechariah, about John the Baptist, their son, and about Mary and Joseph.

Elizabeth and Zechariah

Zechariah, the father of John the Baptizer, was a Jewish priest. The name Zechariah means "Yahweh has remembered." The Gospel tells us that Zechariah and his wife, Elizabeth (a Hebrew name that means "El [God] is fullness") were an elderly couple who had no children (see Luke 1:7, 36–38). You can imagine Zechariah's surprise and disbelief when he learned that he and his wife Elizabeth were to have a son. (See Luke 1:8–16.)

Who were Zechariah and Elizabeth?

John the Baptist

Elizabeth and Zechariah rejoiced in the birth of their child, John. He grew up to be the "voice in the desert" announced by Isaiah the Prophet. He would prepare the people of Israel to receive the Anointed One of God, the Messiah.

> As it is written in Isaiah the
>   prophet:
> Behold, I am sending my messenger
>   ahead of you;
>   he will prepare your way.
> A voice of one crying out in the desert:
>   "Prepare the way of the LORD,
>   make straight his paths."
> MARK 1:2–3

Describe the work of John the Baptist.

The Canticle of Zechariah

The angel Gabriel announced to Zechariah that his wife, Elizabeth, would give birth to their first child. After the birth of John, Zechariah lifted up his heart in prayer and blessed God. Zechariah's prayer is called the Benedictus. The Church prays the Benedictus every morning during Morning Prayer in the Liturgy of the Hours. Join with the Church and pray the Benedictus in the morning to bless God for his goodness to you.

Blessed be the Lord, the God of Israel;
he has come to his people and set
    them free.
He has raised up for us a mighty savior,
born of the house of his servant David.
Through his holy prophets he promised
    of old
    that he would save us from our
        enemies,
    from the hands of all who hate us.
He promised to show mercy to our
    fathers
and to remember his holy covenant.
This was the oath he swore to our father
    Abraham:
to set us free from the hands of our
    enemies,
free to worship him without fear,

holy and righteous in his sight
    all the days of our life.
You, my child, shall be called the
    prophet of the Most High;
for you will go before the Lord to
    prepare his way,
to give his people knowledge of
    salvation
by the forgiveness of their sins.
In the tender compassion of our God
the dawn from on high shall break
    upon us,
to shine on those who dwell in
    darkness and the shadow of
    death,
and to guide our feet into the way of
    peace.

FROM MORNING PRAYER, LITURGY OF THE HOURS

How can you be a messenger of Jesus during Advent?

_____

_____

_____

The Third Week of Advent

FAITH FOCUS

How does listening to the prophet Isaiah prepare us for the coming of Jesus Christ?

THE WORD OF THE LORD

Read and reflect on one of this year's Scripture readings the Church proclaims on the Third Sunday of Advent.

YEAR A
1st Reading:
   Isaiah 35:1–6a, 10
2nd Reading:
   James 5:7–10
Gospel:
   Matthew 11:2–11

YEAR B
1st Reading:
   Isaiah 61:1–2a, 10–11
2nd Reading:
   1 Thessalonians 5:16–24
Gospel:
   John 1:6–8, 19–28

YEAR C
1st Reading:
   Zephaniah 3:14–18a
2nd Reading:
   Philippians 4:4–7
Gospel:
   Luke 3:10–18

What is the first thing you think of when you hear the word *prophecy* or *prophet*? Most people think of the future. In the Bible a prophet is "a person who speaks words inspired by God and so expresses God's message." A prophecy is "a statement that reveals the divine will." A prophet's words have meaning for the present—not just for the future.

Isaiah the Prophet

During Advent we often listen to Isaiah the Prophet. Isaiah spoke to God's people about a holy and just one who would come from the family of Jesse, the father of David.

For over three hundred years the Jewish people had been looking for the holy and just one Isaiah spoke about. One day a group of Jews sent priests and Levites to John to find out if he was the one promised by the prophets.

John the Baptist's response to the priests and Levites pointed their search in the right direction. He was not the one the Jewish people were looking for. He, John, was the one sent to "[m]ake straight the way of the Lord" (John 1:23).

Describe the connection between Isaiah the Prophet and John the Baptist.

Make Straight the Way

"Make straight the way of the Lord" would have sent the imaginations and memories of the priests and Levites into high gear. That phrase used by John would have created multicolor pictures of vast crowds walking the road leading into the city ahead of a returning king or military leader.

The crowds would be brushing rocks off the road and smoothing it out so the hero's chariot would not, even by accident, tip over. They would be

313

Announce the Coming of the Lord

This week begin each day by filling your mind and heart with the expectation of the coming of the Lord. Join with the Church in praying this responsorial psalm sung at Mass on the Third Sunday of Advent.

LEADER: Cry out with joy and gladness, for among you is the great and Holy One of Israel.

RESPONSE: Cry out with joy and gladness, for among you is the great and Holy One of Israel.

LEADER: Give thanks to the LORD, acclaim his name; among the nations make known his deeds, proclaim how exalted is his name.

RESPONSE: Cry out with joy and gladness, for among you is the great and Holy One of Israel.

LEADER: Sing praise to the LORD for his glorious achievement; let this be known throughout all the earth. Shout with exultation, O city of Zion, for great in your midst is the Holy One of Israel.

RESPONSE: Cry out with joy and gladness, for among you is the great and Holy One of Israel.

FROM LECTIONARY, RESPONSORIAL PSALM, THIRD SUNDAY OF ADVENT, YEAR C

lining the dirty, dusty roads leading into the city with cloaks, blankets, and palm branches so the hero would not have dust blown in his face or his uniform dirtied. Making straight the way of the Lord, the returning ruler to his people was a magnificent dream of color and activity and sound.

The time of the Messiah's coming that Isaiah spoke about was near. John would give all his energies to prepare the way for the Holy One of Israel.

Explain the phrase "make straight the way of the Lord."

The Lord's Arrival Is Near

John's work is our work. We too prepare the way for the coming of the Lord. We work diligently to remove the rocks from our lives. We smooth out our decisions. We clear away the dust and dirt that prevents us from seeing what we need to do to live as faithful followers of the Lord.

How do we prepare for the Lord during Advent?

WHAT DIFFERENCE DOES FAITH MAKE?

What can you do during Advent to "make straight the way of the Lord"?

_____

_____

_____

The Fourth Week of Advent

FAITH FOCUS

How does exploring the history of Jesus' family help us celebrate the Advent season?

THE WORD OF THE LORD

Read and reflect on one of this year's Scripture readings the Church proclaims on the Fourth Sunday of Advent.

YEAR A
1st Reading:
Isaiah 7:10–14
2nd Reading:
Romans 1:1–7
Gospel:
Matthew 1:18–24

YEAR B
1st Reading:
2 Samuel 7:1–5, 8b–12, 14a, 16
2nd Reading:
Romans 16:25–27
Gospel:
Luke 1:26–38

YEAR C
1st Reading:
Micah 5:1–4a
2nd Reading:
Hebrews 10:5–10
Gospel:
Luke 1:39–45

Exploring one's family history and creating a family tree is very popular. So many are involved in this work that libraries have created separate genealogy sections. How far back can you trace your family history? What do you know about your ancestors?

The Family Roots of Jesus

Advent is a time that the People of God remember the past and look to the future. During Advent we recall the names and places that are part of the history of God's people. We especially recall the promises God made to his people. (See Isaiah 7:13–14, Micah 5:1.)

All God's promises point to Jesus, who descended from David and whose birth to the Virgin Mary took place in Bethlehem, the city of David. Jesus is at the center not only of the history of the Israelites but of all humankind. Jesus is the Savior of the world.

Describe the importance of David and Bethlehem in the ancestry of Jesus.

The Jesse Tree, the Family Tree of Jesus

The Gospel contains two family trees, or genealogies, of Jesus—one in Matthew's account of the Gospel and one in Luke's account. Matthew, writing to Jews who had become followers of Jesus, traces Jesus' roots back to Abraham with whom the history of the Israelites began (see Matthew 1:1–25). Written to Gentiles, non-Jews, Luke's genealogy goes

The Visitation. Stained glass.

back to Adam, the father of humankind (see Luke 3:23–38).

For centuries Christians have used the names in these genealogies of Jesus in the Gospel to create the Jesse tree. Jesse, the father of David, lived about one thousand years before Jesus was born. The Jesse tree contains the names of great men and women of faith. Reflecting on the lives of these ancestors of Jesus, we can come to know God's great love for us. We prepare for our celebration of Christmas and the fulfillment of God's promises to us.

How does the Jesse tree help us remember the story of God's people?

Mary's Prayer of Praise

Mary said yes to God's invitation to be the mother of his Son. May we prepare our hearts to receive Jesus, the Son of God, the son of Mary, born into the house of David. Join with Mary in blessing and praising God.

The Magnificat

My soul proclaims the greatness of the Lord,
my spirit rejoices in God my Savior
for he has looked with favor on his lowly servant.
From this day all generations will call me blessed:
the Almighty has done great things for me,
and holy is his Name.
He has mercy on those who fear him
in every generation.
He has shown the strength of his arm,
he has scattered the proud in their conceit.
He has cast down the mighty from their thrones,
and has lifted up the lowly.
He has filled the hungry with good things,
and the rich he has sent away empty.
He has come to the help of his servant Israel
for he has remembered his promise of mercy,
the promise he made to our fathers,
to Abraham and his children for ever.

FROM EVENING PRAYER, LITURGY OF THE HOURS

What can you do during Advent to remember that Jesus is at the center of all history?

_____

_____

_____

WHAT DIFFERENCE DOES FAITH MAKE?

The First Week of Christmas

FAITH FOCUS

Why do we call Jesus the Light of the World?

THE WORD OF THE LORD

Read and reflect on one of the Scripture readings the Church proclaims on Christmas Day.

YEARS A, B, and C
MASS AT MIDNIGHT
1st Reading:
   Isaiah 9:1–6
2nd Reading:
   Titus 2:11–14
Gospel:
   Luke 2:1–14

MASS AT DAWN
1st Reading:
   Isaiah 62:11–12
2nd Reading:
   Titus 3:4–7
Gospel:
   Luke 2:15–20

MASS DURING THE DAY
1st Reading:
   Isaiah 52:7–10
2nd Reading:
   Hebrews 1:1–6
Gospel:
   John 1:1–18 or
   John 1:1–5, 9–14

There is a Christmas bumper sticker that reads "Jesus Is the Reason for the Season." Why do you think people would put such a bumper sticker on their car? What other Christmas bumper stickers or billboards or posters have you seen and read? What messages about Christmas do they contain? How do they help you celebrate the Christmas season?

The Light of the World

Lights! More lights. If there is one decoration that helps us see what we are celebrating throughout the Christmas season, it is Christmas lights. Before and after Christmas Day, homes and neighborhoods and cities are lit up with gleaming, glittering, blinking white, blue, red, and green lights.

From the night of Jesus' birth, light has announced the birth of the Savior (see Luke 2:8–11). The gospel reading proclaimed at Mass on Christmas Day is from the prologue to the Gospel according to John.

In this prologue Jesus is identified as the "light of the human race" (John 1:4).

> In the beginning was the Word,
>   and the Word was with God,
>   and the Word was God. . . .
> What came to be
>   through him was life,
>   and this life was the
>   light of the human race;
>   the light shines in the
>   darkness,
>   and the darkness has not
>   overcome it.
>
> JOHN 1:1, 3–5

John used many signs and symbols in writing down the Gospel. These make us stop and think about the deeper meaning of the passage we are reading. The words *word*, *life*, *light*, and *darkness* run throughout the prologue of John's account of the Gospel. As we read the prologue this Christmas season, we profess our faith in Jesus. Jesus is the eternal Word of God who took on flesh and came into the world. Through him we are reborn as children of God and strive to live as lights of Christ in our world.

Describe the importance of the symbol of light in John's prologue.

The Angelus

For centuries the Church has proclaimed the gospel story of the birth of Jesus through the praying of the Angelus at dawn, at noon, and at dusk.

LEADER: The angel spoke God's message to Mary,

ALL: and she conceived of the Holy Spirit.
Hail, Mary. . . .

LEADER: "I am the lowly servant of the Lord:

ALL: let it be done to me according to your word."
Hail, Mary. . . .

LEADER: And the Word became flesh

ALL: and lived among us.
Hail, Mary. . . .

LEADER: Pray for us, holy Mother of God,

ALL: that we may become worthy of the promises of Christ.

LEADER: Let us pray.
Lord,
fill our hearts with your grace:
once, through the message of an angel
you revealed to us the incarnation of your Son;
now, through his suffering and death
lead us to the glory of his resurrection.
We ask this through Christ our Lord.

ALL: Amen.

In what way can Christians be lights of hope for their family, friends, and neighbors?

What happens when we really want something? We drop what we are doing and focus all our efforts on seeking it out. Think of a time you have done just that.

The Newborn King

Around the time of Jesus' birth some Jewish people were waiting and looking for a strong military leader who would lead them in overthrowing the Romans, who were occupying the land of Palestine. Jerusalem was the center of Jewish life and worship. The palace of King Herod located in Jerusalem was a constant reminder of this humiliating control by the Romans.

At that time astrologers, or magi, in the East saw a brilliantly shining star.

THE WORD OF THE LORD

Read and reflect on one of the Scripture readings the Church proclaims on Epiphany.

YEARS A, B, and C
1st Reading:
  Isaiah 60:1–6

2nd Reading:
  Ephesians 3:2–3a, 5–6

Gospel:
  Matthew 2:1–12

They interpreted the appearance of the star to mean that a great leader would soon be born. In the Gospel proclaimed on Epiphany, we hear about magi who saw this star at its rising and set out on a long, difficult journey to find the newborn king. Arriving in Jerusalem, the magi went to the palace of King Herod, asking about the newborn King of the Jews. King Herod became threatened at the inquiry and conviction of the magi and began asking questions himself. The chief priests and scribes explained to Herod what Micah the Prophet had written about 700 years before the birth of Jesus (see Matthew 2:6).

Micah also spoke about a future leader who would be a true leader, a leader faithful to God. Through Micah, God had announced that this leader, a messiah, would be born in Bethlehem.

Describe the promise of the prophet Micah.

Finding the Newborn King

The magi pressed on, following the star until it stopped and stood over the place "where the child was. On entering the house they saw the child with Mary his mother" (Matthew 2:11).

Jesus is the bright light of God's salvation for all people. He will rule the hearts of all people who seek him. God's salvation is for everyone.

How can the search and journey of the magi be an example for our journey as Christians?

Mary, the Mother of God

The magi found the child Jesus with Mary, his mother. Mary is truly the mother of the Word, the Son of God, made flesh. During the Christmas season, on January 1, the Church celebrates the solemnity of Mary, the Mother of God. We profess our faith in this belief of the Church about Mary.

> Father,
> source of light in every age,
> the virgin conceived and bore your Son
> who is called Wonderful God, Prince of Peace.
> May her prayer, the gift of a mother's love,
> be your people's joy through all ages.
> May her response, born of a humble heart,
> draw your Spirit to rest on your people.
> Grant this through Christ our Lord.
> Amen.

ALTERNATIVE OPENING PRAYER,
SOLEMNITY OF MARY, MOTHER OF GOD

WHAT DIFFERENCE DOES FAITH MAKE?

How will you seek out salvation this Christmas?

_____

_____

_____

The First Week of Lent

FAITH FOCUS

How are you a sign of new life during Lent?

THE WORD OF THE LORD

Read and reflect on one of this year's Scripture readings the Church proclaims on the First Sunday of Lent.

YEAR A
1st Reading:
   Genesis 2:7–9; 3:1–7
2nd Reading:
   Romans 5:12–19 or
   Romans 5:12, 17–19
Gospel:
   Matthew 4:1–11

YEAR B
1st Reading:
   Genesis 9:8–15
2nd Reading:
   1 Peter 3:18–22
Gospel:
   Mark 1:12–15

YEAR C
1st Reading:
   Deuteronomy
   26:4–10
2nd Reading:
   Romans
   10:8–13
Gospel:
   Luke 4:1–13

Signs of new life abound with the coming of springtime. Whether we live in the north or the south, springtime brings welcome changes. Snow melts, weather becomes consistently warmer, and dormant grass comes back to life. What signs of new life surround you as springtime approaches?

The Season of Lent

The season of Lent is the Church's sacred springtime. It begins on Ash Wednesday and ends at the beginning of the celebration of the Evening Mass of the Lord's Supper on Holy Thursday. On Ash Wednesday we are reminded of our Lenten task. Ashes are placed on our forehead with the words:

> Turn away from sin and be faithful to the gospel.
>
> FROM ROMAN MISSAL, ASH WEDNESDAY

Lent is a season of dedicated effort to eliminating from our lives everything that keeps us from turning our hearts to God. It is a season of rebirth and renewal. During this season the faithful reflect on their rebirth in Christ at Baptism. We renew our baptismal commitment. We do penance for our sins and strengthen our decision to be faithful to the Great Commandment to love God and to love our neighbor as ourselves with everything we have—our whole mind, heart, and soul.

Lent is also the season of the liturgical year during which catechumens dedicate themselves to their final preparations for initiation into the Church. At the Easter Vigil the Church celebrates the Sacraments of Initiation with them. They receive new life in Christ and become members of the Body of Christ, the Church.

Describe the Church's season of Lent.

Jesus Prepared for His Ministry

The Church proclaims the gospel account of the temptation of Jesus on the First Sunday of Lent. A temptation is a strong feeling to do or say something that we know is against God's will or not to do something good that we are able to do we know is right. During Lent we share in the work of identifying and overcoming temptations. We ask the Spirit to guide us, as he guided Jesus, in overcoming those obstacles that turn our hearts away from God.

How does the gospel account of Jesus being tempted in the desert help us during Lent?

The Work of Lent

Traditionally, the Church shows us three ways to grow in our love for God and others during Lent—to give alms, to fast, and to pray.

- **Almsgiving**—Almsgiving praises God as the source of all blessings. When we give alms, we share our time, talent, or treasures with other people in need, especially the poor.
- **Fasting**—Fasting is doing with less. When we fast, we acknowledge that God alone is the true source of our happiness. We combine our fasting with almsgiving and share with those in need what we have decided to do without.
- **Praying**—Praying helps us make God the true center of our life. We raise our minds and hearts to God. We focus our life on God and recognize his continuous presence with us. We strive to become people of prayer, who pray always.

How does the Church help us renew our love for God and others during Lent?

Prayer of Saint Columba

Saint Columba lived in the sixth century. He established a monastery on the island of Iona off the coast of Ireland. Pray this ancient prayer of Saint Columba. Ask Jesus to walk with you and lead you on your Lenten journey.

Be thou a bright flame for me,
Be thou a guiding star for me,
Be thou a smooth path for me,
Be thou kindly shepherd
    behind me.
Today—tonight—and forever.
Amen.

WHAT DIFFERENCE DOES FAITH MAKE?

How can your celebration of Lent help you keep your heart focused on God?

_____

_____

_____

The Second Week of Lent

THE WORD OF THE LORD

Read and reflect on one of this year's Scripture readings the Church proclaims on the Second Sunday of Lent.

YEAR A
1st Reading:
Genesis 12:1–4a
2nd Reading:
2 Timothy 1:8b–10
Gospel:
Matthew 17:1–9

YEAR B
1st Reading:
Genesis 22:1–2, 9a, 10–13, 15–18
2nd Reading:
Romans 8:31b–34
Gospel:
Mark 9:2–10

YEAR C
1st Reading:
Genesis 15:5–12, 17–18
2nd Reading:
Philippians 3:17–4:1 or Philippians 3:20–4:1
Gospel:
Luke 9:28b–36

Sometimes spring dances all around us while winter sits in our heart. This can happen when something that we have done makes us feel bad or ashamed or guilty. God can change our gray and gloomy winter moods into a life-giving and glorious spring.

A Change of Heart

During the season of Lent the Holy Spirit constantly calls us to leave our winter attitudes behind and to skip into spring. The Spirit calls us to conversion. To convert means to turn from one thing to another. During Lent the Spirit helps us turn to God and away from choices that weaken or interrupt our friendship with God.

In the Old Testament, God commanded his people to embrace conversion. God asked them to turn from injustice and immorality and to turn toward his mercy and salvation and unconditional love. The Spirit asks us to turn our back on old and sinful ways and to turn our face toward the good news of God's reign among us. In a word, the Spirit calls us to repent.

The season of Lent offers us many opportunities to take God's words seriously and to apply them to our own lives. During Lent we make a conscious effort to set time aside to examine our conscience and ask, How am I conducting myself as a follower of Christ? Is my mind too occupied with earthly things? We ask the Spirit to help us answer those questions honestly.

What does the Spirit call us to do during Lent?

Sacrament of Reconciliation

Catholics celebrate repentance and conversion in our lives in the sacrament of Reconciliation. In Reconciliation:

- we acknowledge the ways we have chosen to turn our hearts away from God's love.
- we confess our sins to a priest.
- we accept and do a penance as a sign of our decisions and willingness to cooperate with the Spirit to change our ways.
- we are forgiven our sins and receive the grace to faithfully live our life in Christ.

With God's help and the help of the church community, we travel the road of conversion during Lent, keeping our sight on the kingdom of God.

Why do we celebrate the sacrament of Reconciliation during Lent?

The Lord Is My Light

The Lord God is always with us. Pray this responsorial psalm often during Lent.

LEADER The LORD is my light and my salvation.

ALL The LORD is my light and my salvation.

LEADER Hear, O LORD, the sound of my call;
have pity on me, and answer me.
Of you my heart speaks; you my glance seeks.

ALL The LORD is my light and my salvation.

LEADER I believe that I shall see the bounty of the Lord
in the land of the living.
Wait for the LORD with courage; be stouthearted, and wait
for the LORD.

ALL The LORD is my light and my salvation.

BASED ON PSALM 27:1, 7–8, 13–14
FROM RESPONSORIAL PSALM,
SECOND SUNDAY OF LENT, YEAR C

How can you reflect during Lent on the choices you are making to live as a follower of Jesus?

_____

_____

_____

The Third Week of Lent

FAITH FOCUS

How does prayer help you grow in your relationship with God?

THE WORD OF THE LORD

Read and reflect on one of this year's Scripture readings the Church proclaims on the Third Sunday of Lent.

YEAR A
1st Reading:
   Exodus 17:3–7
2nd Reading:
   Romans 5:1–2, 5–8
Gospel:
   John 4:5–42 or
   John 4:5–15, 19b–26, 39a, 40–42

YEAR B
1st Reading:
   Exodus 20:1–17 or
   Exodus 20:1–3, 7–8, 12–17
2nd Reading:
   1 Corinthians 1:22–25
Gospel:
   John 2:13–25

YEAR C
1st Reading:
   Exodus 3:1–8a, 13–15
2nd Reading:
   1 Corinthians 10:1–6, 10–12
Gospel:
   Luke 13:1–9

Friends enjoy being with each other, talking with each other, and simply spending time together. Why is spending time with our friends so important?

Our Friendship with God

Spending time with God is a sign of our friendship with God. It is a sign that we want to be with God and acknowledge his presence with us. It strengthens our friendship with him.

We spend time with God in many ways. We share our thoughts and feelings with him. We listen to his word to us in the Scriptures. Walking or sitting outdoors, we are aware of his presence with us and within us. No matter how we choose to spend our time with God we are telling him that we cherish our friendship with him.

Another word for spending time with God is *prayer*. When we pray, we are with God. During Lent we work at developing the habit of prayer. We work at growing as people of prayer and strengthening our friendship with God.

How is spending time with God the same as prayer?

Finding God—Everywhere

The gospel account of Jesus and the Samaritan woman at the well reminds us that we often meet God in places we do not at first expect to meet him. God, you might say, makes his presence known to us in the ordinary things we do each day. That is what happened to Moses who was leading his flock across the desert. Off in the distance a fire flaming out of a bush caught Moses' attention. As Moses approached the fire, a voice cried out, "Moses. Moses." It was God revealing himself to Moses. (See Exodus 3:3–6.)

People of prayer are open to God's presence with them. In the gospel story of Jesus meeting the Samaritan woman at Jacob's well, the woman was simply doing her ordinary daily chores. She came to the well to fill her bucket with water. Her openness to Jesus enabled her life to be filled with living water. (See John 4:5–42.)

How does listening to God's word to us in the story of Moses and in the story of the Samaritan woman help us grow as people of prayer?

A Morning Prayer

During Lent we strive to grow in our awareness that we are a people of prayer. We do this when we begin each day with prayer. Pray this morning prayer with others or alone.

LEADER Praise to Jesus, our Savior; by his death he has opened for us the way of salvation. Let us ask him:

ALL *Lord, guide your people to walk in your ways.*

LEADER God of mercy, you gave us new life through baptism,

ALL make us grow day by day in your likeness.

LEADER May our generosity today bring joy to those in need,

ALL in helping them may we find you.

LEADER Help us to do what is good, right and true in your sight,

ALL and to seek you always with undivided hearts.

LEADER Forgive our sins against the unity of your family,

ALL make us one in heart and spirit.

Our Father . . .

LEADER God of mercy, free your Church from sin and protect it from evil. Guide us, for we cannot be saved without you. We ask this through our Lord Jesus Christ.

ALL Amen.

FROM LITURGY OF THE HOURS, MONDAY, THIRD WEEK OF LENT, MORNING PRAYER

How will you create personal time for prayer this Lenten season?

WHAT DIFFERENCE DOES FAITH MAKE?

The Fourth Week of Lent

THE WORD OF THE LORD

Read and reflect on one of this year's Scripture readings the Church proclaims on the Fourth Sunday of Lent.

YEAR A
1st Reading:
    1 Samuel 16:1b, 6–7, 10–13a
2nd Reading:
    Ephesians 5:8–14
Gospel:
    John 9:1–41, or John 9:1, 6–9, 13–17, 34–38

YEAR B
1st Reading:
    2 Chronicles 36:14–16, 19–23
2nd Reading:
    Ephesians 2:4–10
Gospel:
    John 3:14–21

YEAR C
1st Reading:
    Joshua 5:9a–12
2nd Reading:
    2 Corinthians 5:17–21
Gospel:
    Luke 15:1–3, 11–32

How do you feel about classmates or members of a team who are always telling you and others how great they are? What about those people who respond to your good news by turning attention to themselves by saying, "Well, I . . ."? Bragging is something that really turns us off. Why is that?

Bless the Lord

Jesus encourages us to be silent about our goodness, for our good works will speak for themselves. He tells us that only God needs to know that we fast and pray and give to others. (See Matthew 6:1–7, 16–18.)

Jesus spoke clearly. We should perform these good actions quietly and not draw attention to ourselves. We are to look bright and cheerful and not gloomy and sad when we give something up. In all that we do or say we bless and praise God and not ourselves.

Lent is a time for us to renew our focus. Will we be people who brag or people who bless? Will our words and actions extol, or lift up, God's name or our own?

What motivates followers of Christ to fast, pray, and give alms during Lent and all throughout the year?

The Greatest of Gifts

As we approach Holy Week we remember that Lent is a time to renew our efforts to extol God's name. It is a time to renew our attitude of gratitude to God for all his gifts to us. We especially thank God the Father for the gift of his Son, Jesus, in whom and through whom we have received the gift of eternal life.

All Jesus said and did drew attention to his Father and his Father's love for us. The only thing we have to boast about is God's great love for us and for all people. The celebration of Lent renews our efforts to live this great truth.

How does celebrating Lent help us renew our attitude of gratitude toward God?

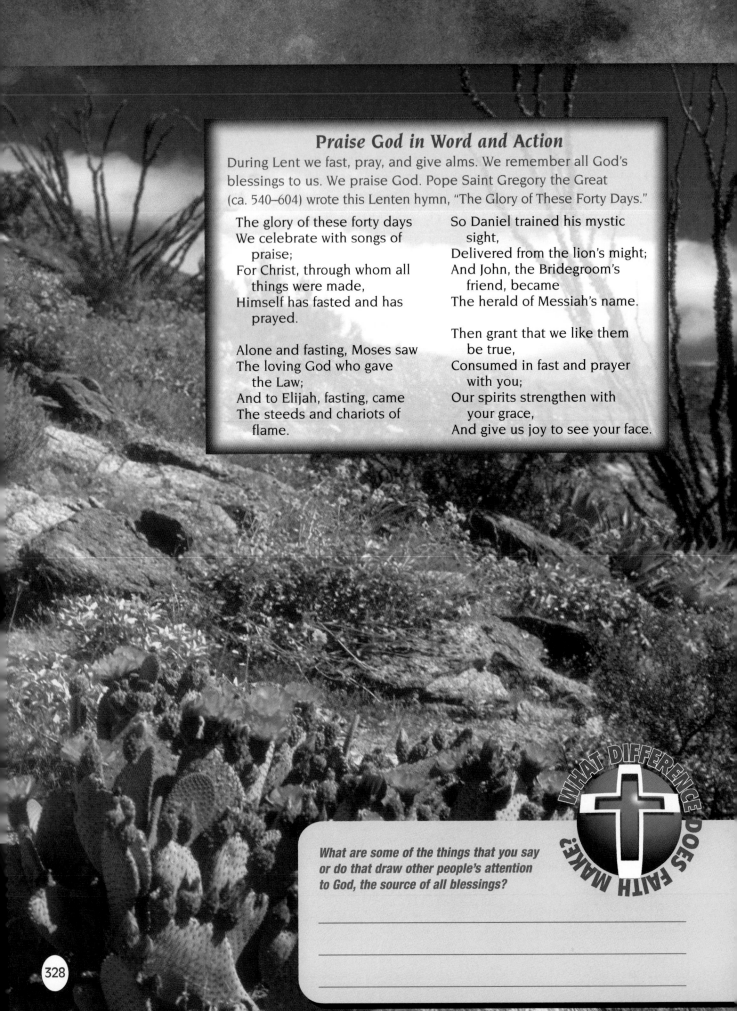

Praise God in Word and Action

During Lent we fast, pray, and give alms. We remember all God's blessings to us. We praise God. Pope Saint Gregory the Great (ca. 540–604) wrote this Lenten hymn, "The Glory of These Forty Days."

The glory of these forty days
We celebrate with songs of
    praise;
For Christ, through whom all
    things were made,
Himself has fasted and has
    prayed.

Alone and fasting, Moses saw
The loving God who gave
    the Law;
And to Elijah, fasting, came
The steeds and chariots of
    flame.

So Daniel trained his mystic
    sight,
Delivered from the lion's might;
And John, the Bridegroom's
    friend, became
The herald of Messiah's name.

Then grant that we like them
    be true,
Consumed in fast and prayer
    with you;
Our spirits strengthen with
    your grace,
And give us joy to see your face.

WHAT DIFFERENCE DOES FAITH MAKE?

What are some of the things that you say or do that draw other people's attention to God, the source of all blessings?

_____

_____

_____

The Fifth Week of Lent

FAITH FOCUS

How do we show mercy to one another?

THE WORD OF THE LORD

Read and reflect on one of this year's Scripture readings the Church proclaims on the Fifth Sunday of Lent.

YEAR A
1st Reading:
   Ezekiel 37:12–14
2nd Reading:
   Romans 8:8–11
Gospel:
   John 11:1–45 or
   John 11:3–7, 17, 20–27,
   33b–45

YEAR B
1st Reading:
   Jeremiah 31:31–34
2nd Reading:
   Hebrews 5:7–9
Gospel:
   John 12:20–33

YEAR C
1st Reading:
   Isaiah 43:16–21
2nd Reading:
   Philippians 3:8–14
Gospel:
   John 8:1–11

"Have mercy!" How often have characters in videos and movies begged for their life, using those words. When a person in that situation begs for mercy, what is he or she asking? When we pray at Mass, "Lord, have mercy," what are we praying for?

God of Mercy

On this fifth Sunday of Lent we profess our faith and trust in God's mercy for us. Mercy is an important attribute of God. It is an expression of God's love. It is God's love in action in our lives. We have come to know God's mercy as his will to do only good for us. It is revealed to us in his plan to create us and to forgive us and to save us. Mercy is at the heart of God's everlasting covenant with us. It is a sign of his unconditional loyalty and faithfulness to us.

During Lent as we prepare for the celebration of the death and resurrection of Jesus, we remember that God's mercy is most fully revealed to us in Jesus Christ. God's greatest act of love for us is his most generous act of forgiveness—the death and resurrection of his Son.

Describe what we mean by God's mercy.

Fellowship. Stained glass.

Blessed Are the Merciful

Mercy is also an important dimension of our Christian character. Our attitude toward all people is to be the same as the attitude of Jesus. We are to seek and do good for others. We must be ready to forgive as God forgives. This is not how the scribes and Pharisees wanted Jesus to act toward the woman they caught in adultery. They tested Jesus, seeing if he would agree with Jewish law that required the woman be stoned to death. (See John 8:1–11.)

During the Lenten season we not only ask God to be merciful to us, we also renew our efforts to be merciful toward other people. We do this by taking the time to reflect on ways we can live the Corporal Works of Mercy and the Spiritual Works of Mercy.

Lord, Have Mercy

The penitential rite at Mass is a prayer of mercy. We place our trust in the mercy of God.

PRIEST Coming together as God's family, with confidence let us ask the Father's forgiveness for he is full of gentleness and compassion.

PRIEST Lord Jesus, you healed the sick:

ALL Lord, have mercy.

PRIEST Lord Jesus, you forgave sinners:

ALL Christ, have mercy.

PRIEST Lord Jesus, you give us yourself to heal us and bring us strength:

ALL Lord, have mercy.

PRIEST May almighty God have mercy on us, forgive us our sins, and bring us to everlasting life.

ALL Amen.

The works of mercy are:

Corporal Works of Mercy
Feed people who are hungry.
Give drink to people who are thirsty.
Clothe people who need clothes.
Visit prisoners.
Shelter people who are homeless.
Visit people who are sick.
Bury people who have died.

Spiritual Works of Mercy
Help people who sin.
Teach people who are ignorant.
Give advice to people who have doubts.
Comfort people who suffer.
Be patient with other people.
Forgive people who hurt you.
Pray for people who are alive and for those who have died.

When we do these things, we show that we only wish good for other people. We treat them as we know God treats us.

Describe the actions of a merciful person.

WHAT DIFFERENCE DOES FAITH MAKE?

What can you do this Lent to grow as a person of mercy?

_____

_____

_____

FAITH FOCUS

How do our actions and attitudes on Palm Sunday of the Lord's Passion reflect Jesus' journey into Jerusalem?

THE WORD OF THE LORD

Read and reflect on one of this year's Scripture readings the Church proclaims on Palm Sunday of the Lord's Passion.

YEAR A
Procession:
  Matthew 21: 1–11
1st Reading:
  Isaiah 50:4–7
2nd Reading:
  Philippians 2:6–11
Gospel:
  Matthew 26:14–27:66 or
  Matthew 27:11–54

YEAR B
Procession:
  Mark 11:1–10 or
  John 12:12–16
1st Reading:
  Isaiah 50:4–7
2nd Reading:
  Philippians 2:6–11
Gospel:
  Mark 14:1–15:47 or
  Mark 15:1–39

YEAR C
Procession:
  Luke 19:28–40
1st Reading:
  Isaiah 50:4–7
2nd Reading:
  Philippians 2:6–11
Gospel:
  Luke 22:14–23:56
  or Luke 23:1–49

Sharing in the memories of our ancestors makes us one with them. A grandparent tells us about our great-great-grandparents who sailed past the Statue of Liberty on their way to America. We find their names are recorded in the ledgers at Ellis Island in New York Bay. We wonder what it would be like to visit Ellis Island and walk through the same rooms our ancestors did. What are your favorite family stories?

All year long we listen to the Gospel proclaimed at Mass. We listen and learn about Jesus and how to live as his disciples. During Holy Week we listen to the climax, or heart, of Jesus' life and work on earth. We listen to the events of his last days on earth, the events of his Paschal mystery.

Passion Sunday/Palm Sunday

Palm Sunday of the Lord's Passion is the first day of Holy Week. This Sunday previously was called Passion Sunday or Palm Sunday. Christians use both of these names for this Sunday because:

1. palm branches are blessed and distributed on this day when we remember Jesus' entrance into Jerusalem.
2. the Passion of the Lord is proclaimed for the first time during Holy Week at the Liturgy of the Word on this day.

Jesus' Entrance into Jerusalem

During Holy Week we remember and take part in Jesus' last days on earth. Our celebration of Holy Week begins with Jesus' final journey into Jerusalem. There he would celebrate his final Passover with his disciples.

The first part of our celebration is called the Commemoration of the Lord's Entrance into Jerusalem. We begin by gathering outside our parish church. The priest welcomes us and focuses our attention on why we have gathered:

Dear friends in Christ, for five weeks of Lent we have been preparing, by works of charity and self-sacrifice, for the celebration of our Lord's paschal mystery. Today we come together to begin this solemn celebration in union with the whole Church throughout the world. Christ entered in triumph into his own city, to complete his work as our Messiah: to suffer, to die, and to rise again. Let us remember with devotion this entry which began his saving work and follow him with a lively faith. United with him in his suffering on the cross, may we share his resurrection and new life.

FROM ROMAN MISSAL
PALM SUNDAY OF THE
LORD'S PASSION

After palm branches are blessed and the Gospel proclaimed, we process into our parish church. Carrying palm branches, we proclaim Jesus to be the Messiah as the crowd did when they heard Jesus was coming to Jerusalem. We sing, "Hosanna in the highest."

The Passion of the Lord

The singing soon quiets down. The tone and focus of the celebration changes. We move from Jesus riding in triumph into Jerusalem to meeting Jesus whose true glory is in his suffering and death. (See Philippians 2:6–11.)

Holding our palm branches in our hands, we stand and listen to the proclamation of Jesus' passion and death. We take our place among Jesus' first disciples and make his final journey from the Passover room through the Garden of Gethsemane to the courtyard of Pilate's palace, and finally to Calvary, the place of his death.

Describe the focus of the Liturgy of the Word on Palm Sunday of the Lord's Passion.

Give Praise to the Lord

In many churches the hymn "All Glory, Laud, and Honor" is sung at the celebration of the liturgy on Palm Sunday of the Lord's Passion. The original hymn was written by Theophilus of Orleans (ca.760–821) and translated in the nineteenth century by John Neale (1818–1866).

Refrain:
All glory, laud, and honor
To you, Redeemer, King!
To whom the lips of children
Made sweet hosannas ring.

Verses:
You are the King of Israel,
And David's royal Son.
Now in the Lord's Name
    coming,
Our King and Blessed One. . . .

The people of the Hebrews
With palms before you went:

Our praise and prayers and
    anthems
Before you we present.

To you before your passion
They sang their hymns of
    praise:
To you, now high exalted,
Our melody we raise.

Their praises you accepted,
Accept the prayers we bring,
Great source of love and
    goodness,
Our Savior and our King.

WHAT DIFFERENCE DOES FAITH MAKE?

What are some ways that you can walk with Jesus on Palm Sunday of the Lord's Passion?

Triduum/Holy Thursday

FAITH FOCUS

How does Holy Thursday celebrate God's love for us and our love for God and others?

THE WORD OF THE LORD

Read and reflect on one of the Scripture readings the Church proclaims at the Evening Mass of the Lord's Supper on Holy Thursday.

YEARS A, B, AND C
1st Reading:
   Exodus 12:1–8, 11–14
2nd Reading
   1 Corinthians 11:23–26
Gospel:
   John 13:1–15

Think of your life up to now. Remember the people, the events, the happiness, the sorrow, the stumbling blocks, the triumphs. Now pick the one event that means the most to you. What makes it important and meaningful to you?

The Easter Triduum

The Paschal mystery of Jesus is the central event of his life. It is his Passover from life through death to new life for the salvation of the world. Christians celebrate this Paschal mystery in the three-day celebration of the Easter triduum. The word *triduum*, which means "three days," identifies the duration of the celebration.

> Christ redeemed us all and gave perfect glory to God principally through his Paschal mystery: dying he destroyed our death and rising he restored our life. Therefore the Easter triduum of the passion and resurrection of Christ is the culmination of the entire liturgical year. . . . The Easter triduum begins with the evening Mass of the Lord's Supper, reaches its high point in the Easter Vigil, and closes with evening prayer on Easter Sunday.

FROM ROMAN MISSAL
GENERAL NORMS FOR THE
LITURGICAL YEAR AND CALENDAR

During this high point of the Church's liturgical year we celebrate and remember the Paschal mystery. We also celebrate our own dying and rising to new life in Christ through Baptism.

Last Supper. Stained glass.

The Lord's Supper

The Easter triduum begins with the evening Mass of the Lord's Supper on Holy Thursday. The liturgy of Holy Thursday focuses on the events of the Last Supper, the last Passover meal which Jesus celebrated with his disciples before his arrest, trial, death, and burial.

At the Last Supper Jesus gave his disciples the command to love one another (see John 15:12–13). Jesus rose from the table, put an apron around his waist, knelt down, and washed the feet of his disciples. When he was finished, Jesus made sure they understood what he really was doing—showing them how to love another as he loves them. (See John 13:1–15.)

Returning to the table, Jesus continued the celebration of the Passover meal with his disciples. He changed the bread and wine they were to share into his own Body and Blood.

Celebrating this new Passover meal was not a one-time event. Jesus commanded his disciples, "[D]o this in memory of me" (Luke 22:19). He gave us the Eucharist. Each celebration of the Eucharist recalls and makes present the sacrifice of Jesus. We join with Christ in offering ourselves to the Father. We are sent forth to serve others as Jesus served us.

What are the similarities among the Passover meal, the Last Supper, and the Eucharist today?

Pange Lingua

At the conclusion of Mass on Holy Thursday, the Blessed Sacrament is carried in procession. It is brought to a place where it will be reserved. In many parish churches people watch in prayer before the Blessed Sacrament throughout the night. During the procession the hymn "Pange Lingua" is sung. Praying this prayer helps us remember the sacrifice Jesus freely made for all people.

Hail our Savior's glorious Body,
Which his Virgin Mother bore;
Hail the Blood which, shed for sinners,
Did a broken world restore;
Hail the sacrament most holy,
Flesh and Blood of Christ adore!

Come, adore this wondrous presence;
Bow to Christ, the source of grace!
Here is kept the ancient promise
Of God's earthly dwelling-place!
Sight is blind before God's glory,
Faith alone may see his face!

Glory be to God the Father,
Praise to his coequal Son,
Adoration to the Spirit,
Bond of love, in Godhead one!
Blest be God by all creation
Joyously while ages run!

FROM *CATHOLIC HOUSEHOLD BLESSINGS & PRAYERS*

How can you serve others as Jesus did?

WHAT DIFFERENCE DOES FAITH MAKE?

Triduum/Good Friday

FAITH FOCUS

Why does the Church gather to celebrate the liturgy on Good Friday?

THE WORD OF THE LORD

Read and reflect on one of the Scripture readings the Church proclaims at the celebration of the Lord's Passion on Good Friday.

YEARS A, B, AND C
1st Reading:
   Isaiah 52:13–53:12

2nd Reading:
   Hebrews 4:14–16; 5:7–9

Gospel:
   John 18:1–19:42

The death of a family member, of a friend, of anyone we love often causes great sorrow and grief, a feeling of bereavement, or great loss. Imagine the grief of Mary, the mother of Jesus, standing at the foot of the cross watching, listening to the ridicule and mockery of the crowd as her son died on the cross.

A Time of Grief

For Mary and the first followers of Jesus, the death of Jesus was a tremendous loss that, at first, resulted in an overpowering experience of grief for them. On Good Friday Christians share in that grief. We listen as the gospel account of Jesus' passion and death is proclaimed.

Sharing that grief in this part of our celebration of the Easter triduum prepares us to share in the overwhelming joy that filled the lives of Mary and the disciples at the news and sight of the Risen Lord.

On Good Friday our churches are empty of the signs of joy and life. We are struck by the sight of the bare altar and the empty tabernacle with its open door. In silence the worshiping assembly sits awaiting the entrance of the ministers. Dressed in red, they enter. Quietly they lie face down before the altar for a moment, rise, and stand for the opening prayer. They then sit for the first reading from Scripture in which God speaks to us through the prophet Isaiah.

> Yet it was our infirmities that he bore,
>   our sufferings that he endured.
>
> ISAIAH 53:4

We now realize that God is speaking about his own Son, Jesus the Nazorean. We realize that Jesus has borne the guilt of us all and through his suffering and death he has reconciled us with God.

Describe what the Scripture readings on Good Friday tell us about Jesus and about ourselves.

Second Fall. Stained-glass Stations of the Cross.

Veneration of the Cross

During the Good Friday liturgy we take time to venerate the cross of Christ. As the choir sings, "My people, what have I done to you? How have I offended you? Answer me!" we express our sorrow for the sins the Lord bore for us. We show our love for Jesus whose love for us was so great that he gave his life so we might have life and live in God's love forever.

Expressing Our Love

Christians in every age and in every culture have recorded their reflections on the death of Christ. This African-American spiritual, "Were You There," captures for us the feelings of grief and sorrow we experience on this day.

Were you there when they crucified
   my Lord?
Were you there when they crucified
   my Lord?
Oh! Sometimes it causes me to
   tremble, tremble, tremble,
Were you there when they crucified
   my Lord?

Were you there when they nailed him
   to the tree?
Were you there when they nailed him
   to the tree?

Oh! Sometimes it causes me to
   tremble, tremble, tremble,
Were you there when they nailed him
   to the tree?

Were you there when they pierced
   him in the side?
Were you there when they pierced
   him in the side?
Oh! Sometimes it causes me to
   tremble, tremble, tremble,
Were you there when they pierced
   him in the side?

WHAT DIFFERENCE DOES FAITH MAKE?

How can you show your love for Jesus who gave us life that we may live for ever in God's love?

_____

_____

_____

Triduum/Easter

FAITH FOCUS

Why is the celebration of Easter a time of great hope and joy?

THE WORD OF THE LORD

Read and reflect on one of the Scripture readings the Church proclaims at the Easter Vigil.

YEARS A, B, and C
1st Reading:
   Genesis 1:1–2:2 or
   Genesis 1:1, 26–31a

2nd Reading:
   Genesis 22:1–18 or
   Genesis 22:1–2, 9a,
   10–13, 15–18

3rd Reading:
   Exodus 14:15–15:1

4th Reading:
   Isaiah 54: 5–14

5th Reading:
   Isaiah 55:1–11

6th Reading:
   Baruch 3:9–15, 32–4:4

7th Reading:
   Ezekiel 36:16–17a, 18–28

Epistle:
   Romans 6:3–11

Gospel:
   Matthew 28:1–10
   (YEAR A)
   Mark 16:1–7 (YEAR B)
   Luke 24:1–12 (YEAR C)

What do you remember about the great days of your life? Choose a day that has been especially wonderful. Relive it in your mind. Sing "Alleluia!" in your heart. Feel your heart fill with joy and gratitude and great thanksgiving. What a blessed day that was!

The Light of Christ

For the Church the most wonderful day of our life in Christ is Easter. On that day we begin our fifty-day celebration of Jesus' resurrection from death to new life. We sing Alleluia over and over again and renew our joy in our own rising to new life in Baptism. We renew our hope in the promise of our own rising to eternal life with God forever.

In the darkness of the Easter Vigil night, the light of the Easter candle shines forth as both a reminder and a promise of that new life. The deacon or priest proclaims, "The Light of Christ." The worshiping assembly responds in praise and thanksgiving, "Thanks be to God." We watch as the lighted candles are carried in procession to the ambo. The flame of the Easter candle, the light of Christ, is shared with every member of the assembly. The darkness is slowly dispelled as the candles held by the assembly are lighted one by one.

Standing next to the Easter candle, the lone voice of the deacon jubilantly proclaims the "Exultet," or Easter Proclamation. Holding their lighted candles in their hands, the assembly listens. We next turn our attention to the Scriptures as God reminds us of his loving plan of creation and salvation—the never-ending story of God's goodness to us.

Describe how using the Easter candle helps us celebrate our life in Christ.

Celebrating New Life in Christ

After the story of God's plan of creation and salvation in Christ has been retold, the Church now initiates the catechumens into the new life of Christ. Through the waters of Baptism, they are joined to Christ. They die to sin and rise to new life. They receive the gift of the Holy Spirit and in the sacrament of Confirmation, they celebrate the fullness of the Spirit's presence in their lives.

The Liturgy of the Eucharist follows. The newly baptized and confirmed now join the assembly of the faithful in giving praise and thanks to the Father. They approach the Table of the Lord, sharing in the Body and Blood of Christ for the first time. In the splendor of the light of the Risen Christ, the assembly, nourished by the Easter sacraments, departs. We go forth to love and serve the Lord, messengers of the good news that "Christ raised from the dead, dies no more" (Romans 6:9).

Describe the initiation of new members into the life of Christ at the Easter Vigil.

The Easter Proclamation

Rejoice, heavenly powers! Sing, choirs of angels!
  Exult, all creation around God's throne!
  Jesus Christ, our King, is risen!
  Sound the trumpet of salvation!

Rejoice, O earth, in shining splendor,
  radiant in the brightness of your King!
  Christ has conquered! Glory fills you!
  Darkness vanishes for ever!

Rejoice, O Mother Church! Exult in glory!
  The risen Savior shines upon you!
  Let this place resound with joy,
  echoing the mighty song of all God's people!

It is truly right
that with full hearts and minds and voices
we should praise the unseen God, the all-powerful Father,
and his only Son, our Lord Jesus Christ.

For Christ has ransomed us with his blood,
  and paid for us the price of Adam's sin
  to our eternal Father!

This is our passover feast,
  when Christ, the true Lamb, is slain,
  whose blood consecrates the homes of all believers.

This is the night when first you saved our fathers:
  you freed the people of Israel from their slavery
  and led them dry-shod through the sea. . . .

This is the night when Christians everywhere,
  washed clean of sin
  and freed from all defilement,
  are restored to grace and grow together in holiness.

This is the night when Jesus Christ
  broke the chains of death
  and rose triumphant from the grave. . . .

Father, how wonderful your care for us!
  How boundless your merciful love!
  To ransom a slave
  you gave away your Son.

O happy fault, O necessary sin of Adam,
  which gained for us so great a Redeemer! . . .

The power of this holy night
  dispels all evil, washes guilt away,
  restores lost innocence, brings mourners joy. . . .

Night truly blessed when heaven is wedded to earth
  and man is reconciled with God!

Therefore, heavenly Father, in the joy of this night,
  receive our evening sacrifice of praise,
  your Church's solemn offering.

Accept this Easter candle. . . .
  [May it always] dispel the darkness of this night!

FROM ROMAN MISSAL, THE EASTER VIGIL

WHAT DIFFERENCE DOES FAITH MAKE?

How can you share your belief in Jesus' resurrection this Easter?

_____

_____

_____

The Second Week of Easter

THE WORD OF THE LORD

Read and reflect on one of this year's Scripture readings the Church proclaims on the Second Sunday of Easter.

YEAR A
1st Reading:
    Acts 2:42–47
2nd Reading:
    1 Peter 1:3–9
Gospel:
    John 20:19–31

YEAR B
1st Reading:
    Acts 4:32–35
2nd Reading:
    1 John 5:1–6
Gospel:
    John 20:19–31

YEAR C
1st Reading:
    Acts 5:12–16
2nd Reading:
    Revelation 1:9–11a, 12–13, 17–19
Gospel:
    John 20:19–31

Important family celebrations usually take place in stages. First, we plan and prepare for the celebration. Second, we celebrate the event. Third, we move into the post-celebration period in which family members share their memories of the celebration— sometimes over and over again for a long period of time. What celebrations of this kind have you taken part in?

The Celebration of Celebrations

Our celebration and sharing in the Paschal mystery of Christ is central to our life as Christians. In Christ, with Christ, and through Christ, God's loving plan of creation and salvation is fulfilled.

The lighted Easter candle standing in the midst of the worshiping assembly throughout Easter is a constant visible reminder of our faith and hope in Christ and his Paschal mystery. On the candle we see the alpha and omega, the first and last letters of the Greek alphabet that Christians use as symbols for Christ.

Christ yesterday and today
the beginning and the end
Alpha
and Omega
all time belongs to him
and all the ages
to him be glory and power
through every age for ever.
Amen.

FROM ROMAN MISSAL, EASTER VIGIL, PREPARATION OF THE EASTER CANDLE

For the Church the three-day celebration of the Easter triduum is the high point of the liturgical year. Lent prepares us for celebrating the Easter triduum. We celebrate it for three days. For fifty days we extend its celebration. We joyfully share our memories and understanding of this great mystery of our faith.

We need time to ponder this great mystery of salvation. We need time to reflect on the reality of our new life in Christ. We need time to consider the many ways we can meet God in our daily life.

How do we show that Easter is the greatest celebration of the Church?

Risen Christ. Stained glass.

Living Our New Life in Christ

During the weeks of the Easter season, we think about the meaning of Christ's resurrection for our lives. We recall the words of the Risen Lord to Thomas the Apostle: "Blessed are those who have not seen and have believed" (John 20:29).

We have not seen the Risen Lord. He has not appeared to us as he did to the disciples. Yet we believe.

We believe that the Risen Jesus lives. We believe that the Spirit whom Jesus promised the Father would send in his name dwells with us. We believe that Christ will come again in glory at the end of time. Because we believe we give witness to the resurrection of Jesus as the apostles did (see Acts of the Apostles 4:32–35). This will make a difference for all those with whom we share our faith.

Describe the difference our belief in the Resurrection makes in our lives.

Rejoice, Alleluia!

Rejoice with Mary

Join now with Mary in her Easter joy. Jesus is truly risen!

Queen of heaven, be joyful, alleluia,
For he whom you have humbly borne for us, alleluia,
Has arisen, as he promised, alleluia,
Offer now our prayer to God, alleluia.

"REGINA CAELI LAETARE,"
TWELFTH-CENTURY LATIN HYMN

Alleluia!

How can you make every day of your life a celebration of Easter?

WHAT DIFFERENCE DOES FAITH MAKE?

_____

_____

_____

The Third Week of Easter

FAITH FOCUS

What does the story of Emmaus tell us about the meaning of Easter?

THE WORD OF THE LORD

Read and reflect on one of this year's Scripture readings the Church proclaims on the Third Sunday of Easter.

YEAR A
1st Reading:
   Acts 2:14, 22–23
2nd Reading:
   1 Peter 1:17–21
Gospel:
   Luke 24:13–35

YEAR B
1st Reading:
   Acts 3:13–15, 17–19
2nd Reading:
   1 John 2:1–5a
Gospel:
   Luke 24:35–48

YEAR C
1st Reading:
   Acts 5:27–32, 40b–41
2nd Reading:
   Revelation 5:11–14
Gospel:
   John 21:1–19, or
   John 21:1–14

When have you felt sad because you felt someone disappointed you? When have you believed someone would do something and you had some evidence the person didn't? Everyone experiences situations similar to these. Sometimes, however, we jump to conclusions about a person without seeking out all the evidence. When all the evidence is in, we discover our conclusions were false. How much better we feel when this happens!

The Stranger on the Road

The disciples walking to Emmaus from Jerusalem had such an experience. They were disappointed. They were saddened but their disappointment and sadness soon disappeared.

On the day of the Resurrection two disciples were returning to Emmaus from Jerusalem. It was a journey of about seven miles. As they were walking along the disciples were discussing the report that Jesus had been raised from the dead. A stranger came up alongside the disciples and joined them for the journey. They began telling the stranger about "Jesus the Nazarene, who was a prophet mighty in deed and word before God and all the people" (Luke 24:19) whom they hoped "would be the one to redeem Israel" (Luke 24:21). They said he had been crucified, although others claimed he had been raised to life.

The stranger began explaining the writings of the Scriptures to them. His knowledge amazed them. As the day was ending, the two disciples invited the stranger to stay with them. While they were at table, Jesus took bread, blessed and broke it, and gave it to them. "With that their eyes were opened and they recognized him, but he vanished from their sight" (Luke 24:31).

Describe what happened to the disciples of Jesus while they were traveling from Jerusalem to Emmaus.

On the Way to Emmaus. Adrian Kupman (1910–), Austrian painter.

The Presence of Jesus

In the breaking of the bread, the two disciples realized that their traveling companion was truly Jesus. We too recognize the presence of the Risen Christ in the blessing, breaking, and sharing of bread in the Eucharist.

The Risen Christ is really present with us under the appearances of bread and wine. The consecrated bread is truly the Body of Christ. The consecrated wine is truly the Blood of Christ.

Overjoyed, the two disciples ran all the way back to Jerusalem to tell the others the good news. We too leave our celebration of the Eucharist as messengers of the Resurrection. We do this by living our faith in Jesus and by keeping his commandments (see 1 John 2:3–5).

How do we profess our faith in the Risen Jesus in our celebration of the Eucharist?

Speak, Lord Jesus

The risen Jesus is present with us in the Scriptures, God's own word to us. Before you begin reading the Scriptures or listening to them being read, pray:

Lord Jesus, open the Scriptures to us;
make our hearts burn while you speak to us.
Alleluia!

FROM LECTIONARY, THIRD SUNDAY
OF EASTER, YEAR B, ALLELUIA VERSE,

Where in your community do you "see" the Risen Christ? How do you react when you encounter him?

_____

_____

_____

THE WORD OF THE LORD

Read and reflect on one of this year's Scripture readings the Church proclaims on the Fourth Sunday of Easter.

YEAR A
1st Reading:
   Acts 2:14a, 36–41
2nd Reading:
   1 Peter 2:20b–25
Gospel:
   John 10:1–10

YEAR B
1st Reading:
   Acts 4:8–12
2nd Reading:
   1 John 3:1–2
Gospel:
   John 10:11–18

YEAR C
1st Reading:
   Acts 13:14, 43–52
2nd Reading:
   Revelation 7:9, 14b–17
Gospel:
   John 10:27–30

When we trust people, we believe what they tell us. Our belief is founded on the goodness and the trustworthiness of the person. What is something that you believe because someone you trust shared it with you?

Founded on the Apostles

Through the Spirit many came to believe in Jesus because of their trust in the apostles. The faith of Christians rests on the foundation of the apostles. They witnessed the new life of the Risen Lord, and they proclaimed this good news to the world.

Proclaim the Good News

Just as Peter and the apostles dared to proclaim Jesus so, too, must we. We are to proclaim the good news of his death and resurrection. We are to invite, especially by the example of our lives, all people of good will to change their ways and to follow the way of Jesus, the Good Shepherd. (See John 10:1–10.)

At the Easter Vigil many newcomers were initiated into new life in Christ. They became members of the Church committed to living the way of Christ, the Good Shepherd.

The Good Shepherd. James J. Tissot (1836–1902), French painter.

During the Easter season, we join with the neophytes, or the newly initiated, in a special period of reflection and prayer. We ask the Spirit to guide us in living as trusted followers of Christ, the Good Shepherd.

Discuss why a person would become a Christian today.

We Belong to the Lord

We follow the Good Shepherd. In him we place all our trust. On the Fourth Sunday of Easter, the Church around the world prays:

LEADER   We are his people, the sheep of his flock. Alleluia.

ALL   We are his people, the sheep of his flock. Alleluia.

LEADER   Sing joyfully to the LORD, all you lands;
     serve the LORD with gladness;
     come before him with joyful song.

ALL   We are his people, the sheep of his flock. Alleluia.

LEADER   The LORD is good:
His kindness endures forever,
and his faithfulness, to all generations.

ALL   We are his people, the sheep of his flock. Alleluia.

BASED ON PSALM 100:1–2, 5,
FROM RESPONSORIAL PSALM,
FOURTH SUNDAY OF EASTER, YEAR C

Whom do you trust to lead you in living as a faithful follower of the Good Shepherd?

_____

_____

_____

FAITH FOCUS

How do we live Jesus' call to love one another?

THE WORD
OF THE LORD

Read and reflect on one of this year's Scripture readings the Church proclaims on the Fifth Sunday of Easter.

YEAR A
1st Reading:
    Acts 6:1–7
2nd Reading:
    1 Peter 2:4–9
Gospel:
    John 14:1–12

YEAR B
1st Reading:
    Acts 9:26–31
2nd Reading:
    1 John 3:18–24
Gospel:
    John 15:1–8

YEAR C
1st Reading:
    Acts 14:21–27
2nd Reading:
    Revelation 21:1–5a
Gospel:
    John 13:31–33a, 34–35

Think of the many ways you learn how to do something. Sometimes people simply give you instructions. Other times they might give you directions several times—and you still don't get it. Other people not only tell you what to do but also show you. When a coach, a teacher, an instructor demonstrates what to do, we seem to "get it" more quickly. The learning seems clearer—not always easier, but clearer.

Do As I Have Done!

Jesus not only told people what to do; he also showed them. For example, Jesus did not simply say, "Love one another"; he demonstrated to his disciples how they were to love one another. This helped them understand what Jesus meant when he told them:

> "I give you a new commandment:
>   love one another.
> As I have loved you, so you also
>   should love one another."
> JOHN 13:34

The First Christians

Jesus' disciples took his command to love one another very seriously. Like Jesus, they showed their love for one another not simply "in word and speech but in deed and truth" (1 John 3:18). When the number of Christians began to grow, the disciples experienced tension between preaching and ministering to those in need. Facing this tension, they did not resolve the problem by favoring one ministry over the other. They came up with

Jesus and Apostles. Stained glass.

a solution that supported both ministries.

> Brothers, select from among you
>   seven reputable men,
>   filled with the Spirit and
>   wisdom,
>   whom we shall appoint to this
>   task,
>   whereas we shall devote
>   ourselves to prayer
>   and to the ministry of the
>   word."
> ACTS OF THE APOSTLES 6:3–4

The Church has come to understand this passage as pointing to the ministry of deacons.

How did the Twelve solve the conflict between the ministry of the word and the ministry to those in need?

Living the Command to Love

There is no conflict between loving God and loving neighbor. Joined to Christ and to one another in Christ through Baptism, loving God and our neighbor is the only way to live our lives. We listen to Jesus and learn from him. When we do, we are able to live his command to show our love for God and neighbor in ways we never would have thought possible. (See John 14:12.)

How do we receive the strength to live Jesus' command to love?

Doing the Work of Jesus

In a prayer of meditation we use our imagination, mind, and desire to live the new life in Christ we have received in Baptism.

1. Sit quietly. Close your eyes and breathe slowly.
2. Place yourself in the presence of God the Father, Son, and Holy Spirit. Invite the Spirit to teach you to pray.
3. Imagine you are with the disciples. You are listening to Jesus. Open your eyes. Prayerfully read John 13:31–35 from your Bible. What might Jesus be saying to you?
4. Ask Jesus, "How can I do the works you want me to do?"
5. Decide how you can keep Jesus' command to love others as he loves you.
6. Pray a short prayer.

What can you do to bring new life to someone in need?

WHAT DIFFERENCE DOES FAITH MAKE?

_____

_____

_____

The Sixth Week of Easter

FAITH FOCUS

Why do we characterize Christians as Easter people?

THE WORD OF THE LORD

Read and reflect on one of this year's Scripture readings the Church proclaims on the Sixth Sunday of Easter.

YEAR A
1st Reading:
  Acts 8:5–8, 14–17
2nd Reading:
  1 Peter 3:15–18
Gospel:
  John 14:15–21

YEAR B
1st Reading:
  Acts 10:25–26, 34–35, 44–48
2nd Reading:
  1 John 4:7–10
Gospel:
  John 15:9–17

YEAR C
1st Reading:
  Acts 15:1–2, 22–29
2nd Reading:
  Revelation 21:10–14, 22–23
Gospel:
  John 14:23–29

How do you identify yourself? As a son or daughter? Sister or brother? Athlete? Artist? Computer whiz? Budding scientist? If you were to choose one characteristic of yourself that you would like other people to use to identify you, what would that characteristic be?

Easter People

In the fourth century Saint Augustine, bishop of Hippo, chose the one characteristic he thought best identifies Christians. He said, "We are Easter people. Alleluia is our song."

What does it mean to say Christians are Easter people? It means that we see with the eyes of faith. We believe that Jesus lives: he was raised from the dead, returned to his Father in glory, and is preparing a place for his faithful followers to be with him forever. Our faith has helped us understand the meaning of his promise to his disciples:

> "I will not leave you orphans;
>   I will come to you.
> In a little while the world will no
>   longer see me,
>   but you will see me, because
>   I live and you will live.
> On that day you will realize that
>   I am in my Father
>   and you are in me and I in you."
> JOHN 14:18–20

In the waters of Baptism you were washed clean of all sin. You rose to new life in Christ. You are loved by the Father. You received the gift of the Spirit, the Advocate, whom Jesus promised "remains with you and will be in you" (John 14:17). You have received this gift of life in Christ because of the love of God, who "sent his only Son into the world so that we might have life through him" (1 John 4:9).

Living Signs of God's Love

In the early Church, nonbelievers were amazed by the love Christians showed one another. So amazed were people that they questioned why the followers of Jesus lived the way they did. This opened the hearts of nonbelievers to the invitation of the Spirit to change their ways. Many nonbelievers became believers.

We have the same work to do today. Joined to Christ in Baptism, we too are to be living signs of the love of God. Jesus said to his disciples:

> "As the Father loves me, so I also love you.

Remain in my love.
If you keep my commandments,
    you will remain in my love,
    just as I have kept my Father's
        commandments
    and remain in his love."

                                    John 15:9–10

John the Evangelist thought about those words he first heard Jesus speak during the final moments together at the Last Supper. John came to realize what Jesus truly revealed to the world, especially through his death-resurrection: God is love.

Beloved, let us love one
        another,
    because love is of God;
    everyone who loves is
        begotten by God
    and knows God.

Whoever is without love does not
        know God,
    for God is love.
In this way the love of God was
        revealed to us:
    God sent his only Son into the
        world
    so that we might have life
        through him.
In this is love:
    not that we have loved God,
        but that he loved us
    and sent his Son as expiation
        for our sins.   1 John 4:7–10

The Church is the community of Easter people. We are filled with the Spirit of the Risen Lord Jesus. Our words and deeds announce: God is love. We strive to be living signs of hope in the world.

Describe the source of our hope and joy as Christians.

Alleluia Is Our Song

We are Easter people. Alleluia is our song. Confident that God is faithful to his word, we raise our voices filled with praise and hope.

Leader	Alleluia, alleluia.
All	Alleluia, alleluia.
Leader	Whoever loves me will keep my word, says the Lord, and my Father will love him and we will come to him.
All	Alleluia, alleluia.

Alleluia Verse
Sixth Sunday of Easter, Year A, B, C

In what ways do you show that you belong to the community of Easter people, the Church?

_____

_____

_____

WHAT DIFFERENCE DOES FAITH MAKE?

The Seventh Week of Easter

FAITH FOCUS

How does the Easter season give direction to our lives each day?

THE WORD OF THE LORD

Read and reflect on one of this year's Scripture readings the Church proclaims on the Seventh Sunday of Easter.

YEAR A
1st Reading:
   Acts 1:12–14
2nd Reading:
   1 Peter 4:13–16
Gospel:
   John 17:1–11a

YEAR B
1st Reading:
   Acts 1:15–17, 20a,
   20c–26
2nd Reading:
   1 John 4:11–16
Gospel:
   John 17:11b–19

YEAR C
1st Reading:
   Acts 7:55–60
2nd Reading:
   Revelation 22:12–14,
   16–17, 20
Gospel:
   John 17:20–26

Think of the many good things you have done for people. How did they respond? How many thanked you? How many just took the good you did for granted?

A Eucharistic People

Throughout the year, Christians celebrate God's goodness to us. Catholics around the world gather for the celebration of the Eucharist. We praise and give thanks to the Father. We share in the Paschal mystery of Jesus and celebrate our life in Christ. We proclaim:

> Lord, by your cross
>   and resurrection
> you have set us free.
> You are the Savior of the world.
> FROM ROMAN MISSAL,
MEMORIAL ACCLAMATION D

Eternal Life in Christ

The celebration of the Eucharist is central to our life in Christ. Joined to Christ in Baptism, we believe that we too will live forever. "We look for the resurrection of the dead, and the life of the world to come" (from Nicene Creed).

On this Seventh Sunday of Easter, God's own word strengthens our hope in this promise of Jesus.

> "Father, they are your gift to me. I wish that where I am they also may be with me, that they may see my glory that you gave me, because you loved me before the foundation of the world."
> JOHN 17:24

The Eucharist is our pledge of future glory. It is the promise of and the nourishment for attaining eternal life.

349

Give Thanks to the Father

We have new life in Christ. Let us give thanks to God the Father for this great act of goodness toward us.

Father, all-powerful and ever-living God,
we do well always and everywhere to give you thanks
through Jesus Christ our Lord.

We praise you with greater joy than ever in this Easter season,
when Christ became our paschal sacrifice.

He has made us children of the light, rising to new and everlasting life.
He has opened the gates of heaven to receive his faithful people.
His death is our ransom from death; his resurrection is our rising to life.

The joy of the resurrection renews the whole world,
while the choirs of heaven sing for ever to your glory:

Holy, holy, holy Lord, God of power and might,
heaven and earth are full of your glory.
  Hosanna in the highest.
Blessed is he who comes in the name of the Lord.
  Hosanna in the highest.

FROM ROMAN MISSAL,
PREFACE, EASTER II

Hosanna!

Hosanna!

WHAT DIFFERENCE DOES FAITH MAKE?

How do you see yourself being strengthened through the Eucharist?

_____

_____

_____

Pentecost

FAITH FOCUS

How does celebrating Pentecost help us live out our baptism?

What or who gives you the power to live your life? To share your deepest thoughts with friends? To willingly drench yourself in laughter? To weep when moved by something touching? To give to others solely out of love? Who or what is the power in your life that helps you live generously and wholly?

The Promised Spirit

For Christians, that power is the Holy Spirit. After his resurrection, Jesus promised his followers the Advocate, who would help them.

The feast of the Ascension celebrates the mystery of Jesus' return to the Father. This marks the end of Jesus' life on earth. As Jesus commanded them, the disciples returned to Jerusalem after Jesus' ascension. There, they awaited the Holy Spirit.

Gifts of the Spirit

The outpouring of the Spirit occurred on the Jewish harvest feast of Pentecost. The Church celebrates this day of the great outpouring of the Holy Spirit through signs of wind and fire.

On the fiftieth day of Easter— Pentecost—the Church celebrates its birth in the hearts of all who repent and receive Jesus as Lord and Messiah. The Church celebrates the sevenfold gifts of the Holy Spirit: wisdom, understanding, right judgment, courage, knowledge, reverence, and wonder. Because of the gifts of the Spirit, we can carry forward the saving work of the Risen Lord in our world today. By the power of the Holy Spirit, the work of Jesus continues in those of us who follow him.

How do the symbols of wind and fire help us understand the Holy Spirit?

The Gift of the Spirit

On the day of Pentecost the apostles received the Holy Spirit as Jesus promised. We receive the gift of the Spirit at Baptism. The Spirit guides us and gives us strength to be witnesses to Christ before all the world.

Let us bow our heads and pray for God's blessing.

*This day the Father of light
has enlightened the minds of the disciples
by the outpouring of the Holy Spirit.
May he bless us
and give us the gifts of the Spirit for ever.*

*May that fire which hovered over the disciples
as tongues of flame
burn out all evil from our hearts
and make them glow with pure light.*

*God inspired speech in different tongues
to proclaim one faith.
May he strengthen our faith
and fulfill our hope to see him face to face.*

Amen.

BASED ON SOLEMN BLESSING OVER THE PEOPLE
PENTECOST SUNDAY

**What signs of the Holy Spirit
do you see at work in your own life?**

_____

_____

_____

Sign of the Cross

In the name of the Father,
and of the Son,
and of the Holy Spirit. Amen.

Glory Prayer

Glory to the Father,
    and to the Son,
    and to the Holy Spirit:
as it was in the beginning, is now,
    and will be for ever. Amen.

Prayer to the Holy Spirit

Come, Holy Spirit, fill the hearts
    of your faithful.
And kindle in them the
    fire of your love.
Send forth your Spirit and
    they shall be created.
And you will renew the
    face of the earth.

Lord's Prayer

Our Father, who art in heaven,
hallowed be thy name;
Thy kingdom come;
Thy will be done on earth
    as it is in heaven.
Give us this day our daily bread;
and forgive us our trespasses
as we forgive those who trespass
    against us;
and lead us not into temptation,
but deliver us from evil.
Amen.

Benedictus

Blessed be the Lord, the God of Israel;
he has come to his people and set them free.

He has raised up for us a mighty savior,
born of the house of his servant David.

Through his holy prophets he promised of old
    that he would save us from our enemies,
    from the hands of all who hate us.

He promised to show mercy to our fathers
and to remember his holy covenant.

This was the oath he swore to our father Abraham:
to set us free from the hands of our enemies,
free to worship him without fear,
holy and righteous in his sight
    all the days of our life.

You, my child, shall be called the prophet of the
    Most High;
for you will go before the Lord to prepare his way,
to give his people knowledge of salvation
by the forgiveness of their sins.

In the tender compassion of our God
the dawn from on high shall break upon us,
to shine on those who dwell in darkness and the
    shadow of death,
and to guide our feet into the way of peace.

Nicene Creed

We believe in one God,
the Father, the Almighty,
maker of heaven and earth,
of all that is seen and unseen.

We believe in one Lord, Jesus Christ,
the only Son of God,
eternally begotten of the Father,
God from God, Light from Light,
true God from true God,
begotten, not made, one in Being
with the Father.
Through him all things were made.
For us men and for our salvation
he came down from heaven:

by the power of the Holy Spirit
he was born of the Virgin Mary, and
became man.

For our sake he was crucified under
Pontius Pilate;
he suffered, died, and was buried.
On the third day he rose again
in fulfillment of the Scriptures;
he ascended into heaven
and is seated at the right hand
of the Father.
He will come again in glory to judge
the living and the dead,
and his kingdom will have no end.

We believe in the Holy Spirit, the Lord,
the giver of life,
who proceeds from the Father
and the Son.
With the Father and the Son he is
worshiped and glorified.

He has spoken through the Prophets.
We believe in one holy catholic and
apostolic Church.
We acknowledge one baptism for the
forgiveness of sins.
We look for the resurrection of the dead,
and the life of the world to come.
Amen.

Apostles' Creed

I believe in God,
the Father almighty,
creator of heaven and earth.

I believe in Jesus Christ,
his only Son, our Lord.
He was conceived by the power
of the Holy Spirit
and born of the Virgin Mary.
He suffered under Pontius Pilate,
was crucified, died, and was buried.
He descended to the dead.
On the third day he rose again.
He ascended into heaven,
and is seated at the right hand
of the Father.
He will come again to judge
the living and the dead.

I believe in the Holy Spirit,
the holy catholic Church,
the communion of saints,
the forgiveness of sins,
the resurrection of the body,
and the life everlasting. Amen.

Act of Contrition

My God,
I am sorry for my sins
with all my heart.
In choosing to do wrong
and failing to do good,
I have sinned against you
whom I should love above all things.
I firmly intend, with your help,
to do penance,
to sin no more,
and to avoid whatever leads me to sin.
Our Savior Jesus Christ
suffered and died for us.
In his name, my God, have mercy.

Rosary

Catholics pray the rosary to honor Mary and remember the important events in the life of Jesus and Mary. There are fifteen mysteries of the rosary. The word *mystery* means "the wonderful things God has done for us."

We begin praying the rosary by praying the Apostles' Creed, the Lord's Prayer, and three Hail Marys. Each mystery of the rosary is prayed by praying the Lord's Prayer once, the Hail Mary ten times, and the Glory Prayer once. When we have finished the last mystery, we pray the Hail, Holy Queen.

Joyful Mysteries

1. The Annunciation
2. The Visitation
3. The Nativity
4. The Presentation
5. The Finding of Jesus in the Temple

Sorrowful Mysteries

6. The Agony in the Garden
7. The Scourging at the Pillar
8. The Crowning with Thorns
9. The Carrying of the Cross
10. The Crucifixion

Glorious Mysteries

11. The Resurrection
12. The Ascension
13. The Coming of the Holy Spirit
14. The Assumption of Mary
15. The Coronation of Mary

Hail Mary

Hail Mary, full of grace,
the Lord is with you!
Blessed are you among women,
and blessed is the fruit
    of your womb, Jesus.
Holy Mary, Mother of God,
pray for us sinners,
now and at the hour of our death. Amen.

Hail, Holy Queen

Hail, holy Queen, mother of mercy,
hail, our life, our sweetness,
    and our hope.
To you we cry, the children of Eve;
to you we send up our sighs,
mourning and weeping
    in this land of exile.
Turn, then, most gracious advocate,
your eyes of mercy toward us;
lead us home at last
and show us the blessed fruit
    of your womb, Jesus:
O clement, O loving, O sweet
    Virgin Mary.

CATHOLIC PRAYERS AND PRACTICES

Magnificat

My soul proclaims the greatness of the Lord,
my spirit rejoices in God my Savior
for he has looked with favor on his lowly servant.

From this day all generations will call me blessed:
the Almighty has done great things for me,
and holy is his Name.

He has mercy on those who fear him
in every generation.

He has shown the strength of his arm,
he has scattered the proud in their conceit.

He has cast down the mighty from their thrones,
and has lifted up the lowly.

He has filled the hungry with good things,
and the rich he has sent away empty.

He has come to the help of his servant Israel
for he has remembered his promise of mercy,
the promise he made to our fathers,
to Abraham and his children for ever.

A Vocation Prayer

God, I know you will call me
for special work in my life.
Help me follow Jesus each day
and be ready to answer your call.

The Divine Praises

Blessed be God.
Blessed be his holy name.
Blessed be Jesus Christ, true God and true
    man.
Blessed be the name of Jesus.
Blessed be his most sacred heart.
Blessed be his most precious blood.
Blessed be Jesus in the most holy sacrament
    of the altar.
Blessed be the Holy Spirit, the Paraclete.
Blessed be the great mother of God, Mary
    most holy.
Blessed be her holy and immaculate
    conception.
Blessed be her glorious assumption.
Blessed be the name of Mary, virgin and
    mother.
Blessed be Saint Joseph, her most chaste
    spouse.
Blessed be God in his angels and in his saints.

Grace before Meals

Bless us, O Lord,
    and these your gifts
which we are about to receive
    from your goodness.
Through Christ our Lord.
Amen.

Grace after Meals

We give you thanks for all your gifts,
    almighty God,
living and reigning now and for ever.
Amen.

The Great Commandment

"You shall love the Lord,
your God, with all your
heart, with all your soul,
and with all your mind. . . .
You shall love your neighbor as yourself."

MATTHEW 22:37, 39

Precepts of the Church

1. Participate in Mass on Sundays and holy days of obligation.

2. Confess sins at least once a year.

3. Receive Holy Communion at least during the Easter season.

4. Keep holy Sunday and the holy days of obligation.

5. Observe the prescribed days of fasting and abstinence.

6. Provide for the material needs of the Church, according to one's abilities.

The Beatitudes

"Blessed are the poor in spirit,
   for theirs is the kingdom of heaven.
Blessed are they who mourn,
   for they will be comforted.
Blessed are the meek,
   for they will inherit the land.
Blessed are they who hunger
      and thirst for righteousness,
   for they will be satisfied.
Blessed are the merciful,
   for they will be shown mercy.
Blessed are the clean of heart,
   for they will see God.
Blessed are the peacemakers,
   for they will be called children of God.
Blessed are they who are persecuted for the
      sake of righteousness,
   for theirs is the kingdom of heaven.
Blessed are you when they insult
      you and persecute you and utter every
      kind of evil against you [falsely]
      because of me.
   Rejoice and be glad, for your reward
      will be great in heaven." MATTHEW 5:3–12

The Ten Commandments

1. I am the LORD your God: you shall not have strange gods before me.
2. You shall not take the name of the LORD your God in vain.
3. Remember to keep holy the LORD's Day.
4. Honor your father and your mother.
5. You shall not kill.
6. You shall not commit adultery.
7. You shall not steal.
8. You shall not bear false witness against your neighbor.
9. You shall not covet your neighbor's wife.
10. You shall not covet your neighbor's goods.

The Seven Sacraments

Sacraments of Initiation
 Baptism
 Confirmation
 Eucharist

Sacraments of Healing
 Reconciliation
 Anointing of the Sick

**Sacraments at the Service
 of Communion**
 Holy Orders
 Matrimony

Corporal Works of Mercy

Feed people who are hungry.
Give drink to people who are thirsty.
Clothe people who need clothes.
Visit prisoners.
Shelter people who are homeless.
Visit people who are sick.
Bury people who have died.

Spiritual Works of Mercy

Help people who sin.
Teach people who are ignorant.
Give advice to people who have doubts.
Comfort people who suffer.
Be patient with other people.
Forgive people who hurt you.
Pray for people who are alive and for those
 who have died.

Stations of the Cross

1. Jesus is condemned to death.
2. Jesus accepts his cross.
3. Jesus falls the first time.
4. Jesus meets his mother.
5. Simon helps Jesus carry the cross.
6. Veronica wipes the face of Jesus.
7. Jesus falls the second time.
8. Jesus meets the women.
9. Jesus falls the third time.
10. Jesus is stripped of his clothes.
11. Jesus is nailed to the cross.
12. Jesus dies on the cross.
13. Jesus is taken down from the cross.
14. Jesus is buried in the tomb.
15. Jesus is raised from the dead.

Gifts of the Holy Spirit

Wisdom
Understanding
Right judgment (Counsel)
Courage (Fortitude)
Knowledge
Reverence (Piety)
Wonder and awe (Fear of the Lord)

Moral Virtues

Prudence
Justice
Fortitude
Temperance

Celebrating Reconciliation

Individual Rite of Reconciliation

Greeting

Scripture Reading

Confession of Sins

Act of Contrition

Absolution

Closing Prayer

Communal Rite of Reconciliation

Greeting

Scripture Reading

Homily

Examination of Conscience with Litany of
    Contrition and the Lord's Prayer

Individual Confession and Absolution

Closing Prayer

Celebrating Mass

Introductory Rites

Gathering

Entrance Procession and Hymn

Greeting

Penitential Rite

Gloria

Opening Prayer

Liturgy of the Word

First Reading
    (Usually from the Old
    Testament)

Responsorial Psalm

Second Reading
    (Usually from New
    Testament Letters)

Gospel Acclamation

Gospel

Homily

Creed (Profession of Faith)

General Intercessions

Liturgy of the Eucharist

Preparation of the Altar and Gifts

Prayer Over the Gifts

Eucharistic Prayer

Communion Rite

    Lord's Prayer

    Sign of Peace

    Breaking of Bread

    Communion

Prayer After Communion

Concluding Rite

Greeting

Blessing

Dismissal

The Books of the Bible

The Old Testament

Law (Torah) or Pentateuch

Genesis	(Gn)
Exodus	(Ex)
Leviticus	(Lv)
Numbers	(Nm)
Deuteronomy	(Dt)

Historical Books

Joshua	(Jos)
Judges	(Jgs)
Ruth	(Ru)
First Book of Samuel	(1 Sm)
Second Book of Samuel	(2 Sm)
First Book of Kings	(1 Kgs)
Second Book of Kings	(2 Kgs)
First Book of Chronicles	(1 Chr)
Second Book of Chronicles	(2 Chr)
Ezra	(Ezr)
Nehemiah	(Neh)
Tobit	(Tb)
Judith	(Jdt)
Esther	(Est)
First Book of Maccabees	(1 Mc)
Second Book of Maccabees	(2 Mc)

The Poetry and Wisdom Books

Job	(Jb)
Psalms	(Ps)
Proverbs	(Prv)
Ecclesiastes	(Eccl)
Song of Songs	(Sg)
Wisdom	(Wis)
Sirach/Ecclesiasticus	(Sir)

Prophets

Isaiah	(Is)
Jeremiah	(Jer)
Lamentations	(Lam)
Baruch	(Bar)
Ezekiel	(Ez)
Daniel	(Dn)
Hosea	(Hos)
Joel	(Jl)
Amos	(Am)
Obadiah	(Ob)
Jonah	(Jon)
Micah	(Mi)
Naham	(Na)
Habakkuk	(Hb)
Zephaniah	(Zep)
Haggai	(Hg)
Zechariah	(Zec)
Malachi	(Mal)

The New Testament

The Gospels

Matthew	(Mt)
Mark	(Mk)
Luke	(Lk)
John	(Jn)

Early Church

Acts of the Apostles	(Acts)

Letters of Paul and Other Letters

Romans	(Rom)
First Letter to the Corinthians	(1 Cor)
Second Letter to the Corinthians	(2 Cor)
Galatians	(Gal)
Ephesians	(Eph)
Philippians	(Phil)
Colossians	(Col)
First Letter to the Thessalonians	(1 Thes)
Second Letter to the Thessalonians	(2 Thes)
First Letter to Timothy	(1 Tm)
Second Letter to Timothy	(2 Tm)
Titus	(Ti)
Philemon	(Phlm)
Hebrews	(Heb)
James	(Jas)
First Letter of Peter	(1 Pt)
Second Letter of Peter	(2 Pt)
First Letter of John	(1 Jn)
Second Letter of John	(2 Jn)
Third Letter of John	(3 Jn)
Jude	(Jude)

Revelation

Revelation	(Rv)

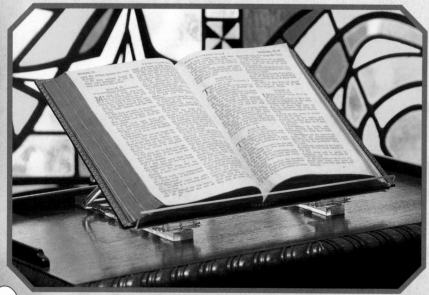

A

abbot
A monk who is the head of a monastery. (page 273)

Advocate
One who stands by a person's side, speaking for them, and standing up for them. (page 149)

aggiornamento
The Italian word Pope John XXIII used to describe the work of the Second Vatican Council. The word means "bringing up to date." (page 298)

analogy
Comparing two things, for the purpose of understanding or explaining, that are similar in some respects but are otherwise unlike. (page 46)

Annunciation
The announcement by the angel Gabriel to Mary that she was chosen by God to become the Mother of Jesus by the power of the Holy Spirit. (page 148)

apostolic succession
The connection popes and bishops have with the original apostles. The bishops are the successors of the apostles. (pages 174–175)

Ascension of Christ
The return of the Risen Christ to his Father, to the world of the divine. (page 122)

attribute
Qualities or characteristics that belong to a person or thing. (page 48)

B

beatific vision
Seeing God face-to-face in heavenly glory. (page 198)

Bible (Sacred Scripture)
The collection of all the writings God has inspired authors to write in his name. (page 22)

blasphemy
The act of claiming to be God. (page 59)

Body of Christ
We, the Church, along with Jesus as our head, are the Body of Christ. (page 171)

Book of Signs
The second part of the Gospel according to John is called this because it includes many stories of miracles, or signs, in the life of Jesus. (page 35)

C

canon of Sacred Scripture
The list of books that the Catholic Church teaches to be the inspired word of God. (page 23)

catacombs
An underground cemetery consisting of chambers or tunnels with recesses used as graves. (page 39)

charisms
Gifts or graces freely given to individual Christians by the Holy Spirit for the benefit of building up the Church. (page 151)

Christendom
The time when the pope exercises authority in the West that surpasses that of the Emperor in the West, and eventually the kings. (page 270)

Church
The word *church* means "convocation, those called together." Church is the sacrament of salvation—the sign and instrument of our reconciliation and communion with God and one another. The Body of Christ; the people God the Father has called together in Jesus Christ through the power of the Holy Spirit. (page 159)

collegiality
Fostering the active relationship between the bishops and the pope. (page 297)

communion of saints
All the faithful followers of Jesus, both the living and the dead. The communion of holy things and holy people that make up the Church. (page 194)

covenant
A testament; the faithful, loving commitment God made with the People of God and was renewed in Christ, the New Covenant. (page 24)

create
To make something out of nothing. (pages 46–47)

GLOSSARY

D

deposit of faith
The source of faith that is drawn from to pass on God's revelation to us; it is the unity of Scripture and Tradition. (page 27)

divine missions
The particular works of God in each of the three Persons of the Holy Trinity. The work of creation is attributed to the Father, the work of salvation is attributed to the Son, and the work of sanctification, or our holiness, is attributed to the Holy Spirit. (page 62)

divine nature
The heart of God's revelation of himself; that which makes God God. (page 48)

divine providence
God's caring love for us. The attribute of God that his almighty power and caring love is always with us. (page 49)

dogma
A truth taught by the Church as revealed by God. (page 61)

doxology
Prayers that conclude many of the liturgical prayers of the Church which are addressed primarily to God the Father. The word *doxology* means "praise-words." (page 237)

E-F

eternal
Having no end; timeless; everlasting. The attribute that states that God always was and always will be. (page 48)

evangelist
Teller of the good news, or the Gospel. Matthew, Mark, Luke, and John, writers of the accounts of the Gospel in the New Testament. (page 34)

everlasting
The attribute that states that God always was and always will be. (page 48)

expiation
An act that takes away guilt or makes amends for a wrongdoing. (page 111)

faith
The gift of God's invitation to us to believe and trust in him; it is also the power God gives us to respond to his invitation. (page 14)

Fourth Gospel
Another name for the Gospel according to John. (page 34)

G-J

Holy Spirit
The third Person of the Holy Trinity sent to us by the Father in the name of his Son, Jesus. (page 146)

Holy Trinity
The mystery of one God in three Persons—God the Father, God the Son, God the Holy Spirit. (page 58)

Immaculate Conception
Mary was totally preserved from the stain of original sin from the very first moment of her existence, or conception, in her mother's womb. Mary did not commit any personal sin throughout her entire life. (page 85)

Incarnation
A word meaning "take on flesh." It is the term the Church uses to name our belief that the Son of God truly became human while remaining truly God. Jesus is true God and true man. (page 87)

infallibility
The charism of the Spirit given to the Church that guarantees that the official teaching of the pope, or pope and bishops, on matters of faith and morals is without error. (page 175)

inspiration of the Bible
Our belief that the Bible is the inspired word of God written by human authors with the help of the Holy Spirit. (page 22)

K-L

kingdom of God
The image used in the Bible to describe all people and creation living in communion with God. The kingdom will be fully realized when Christ comes again in glory at the end of time. (page 89)

lament
A prayer of trust and hope in God during a time of suffering or great trial. (page 209)

Last Judgment
The judgment at which all the humans will appear in their own bodies, give an account of their deeds, and Christ will show his identity with the least of his brothers and sisters. (page 125)

lectio divina
The prayerful reading of Scripture that leads to thoughtful consideration of the meaning of God's word and its application to our lives. (page 234)

literary genres
Styles of writing. (page 23)

Lord
A title expressing our belief that Jesus is truly divine, or God. The word means "master, ruler, a person of authority." It is used in the Old Testament to name God. (page 86)

Lord's Prayer
The Our Father; the prayer Jesus taught us to pray. (page 244)

M-O

Magisterium
The teaching authority of the Church. (page 175)

marks of the Church
One, holy, catholic, and apostolic; the four essential characteristics of the Church. (page 172)

meditation
A silent prayer that allows us to express what is in our minds and hearts. We use our mind, heart, and imagination and seek to understand and follow what the Lord is asking us. (page 234)

messiah
A Hebrew term meaning "anointed one"; the Anointed One God promised to send his people. We believe Jesus is the Messiah promised by God. (page 74)

miracle
A wonderful sign of God working among people, inviting us to believe and trust in him. The word means "wonder, something marvelous." Jesus performed miracles to reveal God's love for people. (page 38)

missionary
One who carries out Christ's mission to preach the Gospel to all nations. (page 183)

monasticism
A way of living the Gospel. Men or women live in community and devote themselves to prayer, work, and learning. (page 271)

moral evil
The harm we willingly inflict on one another and on God's good creation. (page 110)

mystery
The word we use to describe the fact that we can never fully comprehend or fully grasp God. God is, and his loving plan for us is, a mystery. We only know who God is and what his plan for us is because he has revealed it. (page 58)

omnipresence
The attribute of God that he is always present to all of his creation. (page 49)

oral tradition
The passing on of God's revelation by word of mouth. (page 23)

original sin
Adam and Eve's choice of evil over obedience to God. The sin Adam and Eve committed by turning away from God by freely choosing to do what they knew God did not want them to do. (page 109)

P-Q

particular judgement
The assignment given to our souls at death to their final destiny by Jesus based on what we have done in our lives. (page 125)

Patristic Era
The period of brilliant learning and theological development led by writers known as the Fathers of the Church. (page 270)

philosophers
People who use logical reasoning to study and discover truths about nature, life, morals, and God. (page 12)

physical death
The separation of our immortal soul from our mortal body. (page 196)

prayer
Talking and listening to God. (page 220)

prayers of blessing and adoration
Prayers that declare that God is our almighty Creator. (page 212)

prayers of intercession
A form of a prayer of petition that flows out of love for all others. We pray for all people. (page 213)

prayers of petition
Prayers that express our faith and trust in God to help us with our true needs. (page 213)

Glossary

prayers of praise
Prayers that give glory to God simply because he is God. (page 213)

prayers of thanksgiving
Prayers that express our gratitude to God for his unlimited blessings. (page 213)

prophet
A Greek word meaning "one who speaks before others." One who is chosen by God to speak in his name. (page 96)

psalms
Prayer-songs in the Bible that express the feelings of the people of God. There are 150 psalms found in the Old Testament Book of Psalms. (page 208)

Psalter
Another name for the Book of Psalms. (page 208)

R

redemption
Christ delivering us from sin and death through his Paschal mystery. (page 111)

Resurrection of Christ
Jesus being raised from the dead to a new glorified life. (page 120)

resurrection stories
Accounts in the Gospel that give testimony of the Church to the fact of Jesus' resurrection. (page 132)

revelation
God's free gift of making himself known to us and giving himself to us by gradually communicating his own mystery in deeds and words. (page 14)

rosary
A form of both vocal prayer and meditation that invites us to ponder the mysteries of Christ's life while simultaneously reciting a repetitive pattern of prayers whether in the silence of our hearts or aloud with others. (pages 234–235)

S

Sacred Scripture (the Bible)
The collection of all the writings God has inspired authors to write in his name that are collected in the Bible. (page 22)

Sacred Tradition
The passing on of our faith in Christ by the Church through the power and guidance of the Holy Spirit. (page 27)

salvation
Humanity's deliverance from the power of sin and death through Jesus Christ who died for our sins in accordance with the Scriptures. (page 24)

Satan
The serpent-tempter that enticed the first humans to test the limits of their freedom. (page 108)

soul
The spiritual part of who we are that is immortal, or never dies. Our innermost being; that which bears the imprint of the image of God. (page 50)

suffering Servant
An idealization, or perfect image, of the faithful Jew suffering in exile. This was to help the world acknowledge Yahweh as the one true God once the Jewish people were freed from exile. We believe that Jesus Christ is the suffering Servant described in the Book of the Prophet Isaiah. (page 97)

T

Temple of the Holy Spirit
The image used to describe the indwelling of the Spirit in the Church and within the hearts of the faithful. (page 171)

temptation
The desire or attraction to do or say something wrong or not to do what we know we have the responsibility to do. (page 249)

theologians
People who study and deepen their understanding of the truths known by faith. (page 12)

theophany
A word meaning "an appearance of God." (page 76)

U-Z

vocal prayer
The spoken prayer, either aloud or within the quiet of our hearts. (page 234)

YHWH
The Hebrew letters for the name God revealed to Moses. (page 86)

INDEX